Please remember that this is a library book,
and that it belongs only temporarily to each
person who uses it. Be considerate. Do
not write in this, or any, library book.

Mass
Media
&
Environmental
Conflict

To our kids:

Elena Kay Neuzil
Nicholas and Benjamin Kovarik

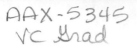
Mark Neuzil

Mass Media & Environmental Conflict

America's Green Crusades

SAGE Publications
International Educational and Professional Publisher
Thousand Oaks   London   New Delhi

For information address:

 SAGE Publications, Inc.
2455 Teller Road
Thousand Oaks, California 91320
E-mail: order@sagepub.com

SAGE Publications Ltd.
6 Bonhill Street
London EC2A 4PU
United Kingdom

SAGE Publications India Pvt. Ltd.
M-32 Market
Greater Kailash I
New Delhi 110 048 India

Printed in the United States of America

Library of Congress Cataloging-in-Publication Data

Neuzil Mark.
    Mass media and environmental conflict: America's green crusades/
Mark Neuzil, William Kovarik.
        p. cm.
    Includes bibliographical references and index.
    ISBN 0-7619-0332-1 (cloth).—ISBN 0-7619-0333-X (pbk.)
    1. Mass media and the environment—United States. 2. Mass media-
Social aspects—United States. 3. United States—Environmental
conditions. 4. United States—Social conditions—1800s
I. Kovarik, William. II. Title.
P96.E572U66   1996
363.7'00973—dc20   96-10051

This book is printed on acid-free paper.

        98 99 10 9 8 7 6 5 4 3 2

Sage Production Editor: Astrid Virding
Sage Typesetter: Janelle LeMaster
Cover Designer: Candice Harman
Cover Photograph: © 1991 Mark Neuzil

CONTENTS

WITHDRAWN

INTRODUCTION

o matter how it is measured, the environmental movement exists as one of the most important social movements of the 20th century. Earth Day 1990 saw millions of people mobilized around the world in an event designed to focus attention on environmental issues. In the West, hundreds of thousands of people belong to organizations such as the National Wildlife Federation, Sierra Club, Audubon Society, and Wilderness Society. One estimate suggested that roughly 7 million people were involved in some kind of national environmental organization in 1988 (Udall, 1988). The largest group, the National Wildlife Federation, numbered 3 million members and had an $85.6 million annual budget in 1990 (Weisskopf, 1990). In 1959, the Sierra Club listed 20,000 members; by 1991, its rolls had swelled to 650,000 (Sale, 1993).[1] Groups ranging from the Acid Rain Foundation to Zero Population Growth experienced similar success in recruiting members.

In addition to joining national organizations, individual and family lifestyles have changed, including simple behaviors such as recycling aluminum cans, increasing visits to national parks, and purchasing environmentally friendly products. Manufacturers have responded by featuring "green themes" in advertising campaigns— including some ads that have been called misleading by state attorneys general and termed "green-collar" fraud (Associated Press, 1991). More biodegradable, compostable, and recyclable materials are incorporated in packaging to meet consumer demand. Neighborhood cleanup programs enjoy wide participation in all sizes of communities. In many states, blue signs mark stretches of road where volunteers pick up litter regularly in Adopt-A-Highway programs (Ferguson, 1989). In Missouri, groups collect roadside trash while planting millions of daffodils.

The environmental movement is represented at many levels in the political arena as well. In 1992, environmentalists helped elect one of their own, Al Gore, to the vice presidency of the United States. Every state but Delaware has acres in the national park system, and the parks had collected $5 million per day in user fees by 1996 ("Cost of Gridlock," 1996). Government involvement means most changes in the landscape require the approval of one (or more) agencies and often involve public hearings and other forms of participation before a decision is reached. The legal system, bound by numerous air, water, land, and noise pollution regulations, recognizes environmental claims in the courtroom. Citizens in many states can apply to the courts for relief from what they view as harmful environmental policies of the government or others, and courts have generally upheld this right, even in cases in which the litigant cannot demonstrate personal financial loss or injury (Findley & Farber, 1988). Religious groups continue to recognize the importance of environmental thought. Pope John Paul II, in a 12-page document titled "Peace with God the Creator, Peace with All of Creation," wrote, "the ecological crisis has assumed such proportions as to be everyone's responsibility" (as quoted in Shabecoff, 1993, p. 127).[2]

How did the movement come to have this impact? One answer, and the focus of this book, is the mass media. Perhaps nowhere is the significance of the environmental movement more noticeable than in the mass media—and not just in green advertising campaigns. In 10 newspaper studies conducted by American Opinion Research in 1992, readers identified environmental news as the fastest growing topic of news interest (American Opinion Research, Inc., 1993). As a sign of the public's demand for environmental news, newspapers, magazines, and broadcast stations have assigned reporters to environmental beats since the 1970s. By 1993, more than two thirds of the nation's medium and large newspapers had reporters specializing in covering the environment (American Opinion Research, Inc., 1993).[3] Specialty magazines, such as *E Magazine* and *Whole Earth Review,* cater to a green audience. Eco-novels, such as *The Monkey Wrench Gang,* and nonfiction works, such as *The End of Nature,* enjoy continued popularity as booksellers add environmental sections to their shops. Two cable television channels focusing on environmental issues went on air in 1994. Recognizing the importance of mass communication, environmental groups responded with media-savvy tactics: A spokesperson for the Environmental Defense Fund in the Bush years stated, "Rather than go to court we lobby, write reports, court the media" (Sale, 1993, p. 88).

Conventional wisdom has the environmental movement as a product of the 1960s. Many mistake Rachel Carson's 1962 book, *Silent Spring,* as the beginning of environmental awareness in America (Smith & Theberge, 1983; see Efron, 1984). Some promote the view that environmental concerns are a fad concocted in the 1960s with the help of a pliant liberal media (Rothman & Lichter, 1986). Of course, environmental controversies existed long before Carson's book, the National Environmental Protection Act of 1969, the first Earth Day in 1970, or any number of other 1960s and 1970s events. One of the differences in the 1960s compared to earlier decades was the influence and popularity of television. Jon Cracknell (1993) has suggested that environmental stories are "mediagenic" with stories that provide good pictures and easy-to-understand symbols, such as seabirds stuck in an oil slick or the menacing shape of a nuclear power plant. Photogenic natural disasters, such as the Yellowstone Park fire of 1988 or the eruption of Mount St. Helens in 1980, may also be framed as environmental stories. The growth of television and the greening of America is a topic waiting to be explored.

Mass Media and Environmental Conflict: America's Green Crusades is a book about environmental conflict and the mass media in American history before the 1960s. What was the role of the mass media in the history of environmental conflict before television? How did the two interact in a historical setting to influence social change in the United States? *Green Crusades* takes the position that the mass media function to help control the direction of change in society. Social change is defined as the difference between the current and antecedent conditions in a social structure. Although concern about the physical environment has existed in American society since colonial times, social change (in this instance measured as a shift toward the environmental movement's goals) resulted most often when the environmental movement, the power structure, and the mass media were working in accord with the values of the social system. When the support of the power structure or the mass media wavered, the goal of social change became problematic for environmentalists. There are many antecedents to the post-1960s environmental explosion, some with significant social changes and others with little effect, and the mass media had a role in each issue.

As the frontier opened and industry expanded in the late 19th century, hardly a year went by when some form of green crusade was not under way somewhere. Concerns about conservation of wild or unusual lands, preservation of animals and fish, industrial use of waterways, and abatement of smoke were not the sudden and spontaneous products of the 1960s. Pickets with signs protesting air pollution were as likely to show up outside an offending power plant or incinerator in 1900 or during the 1940s as they are during the 1990s. Public outrage over deaths from air pollution in New York in 1924 and in Pennsylvania in 1948 can hardly be called less important than public protest in a later period. Garbage, sewage, and oil pollution closed beaches in the 1920s and 1940s and generated public health debates and regulatory skirmishes with industry, as it did after 1962. One key difference was that many green crusades of the past were likely to be local instead of national in scope, although similarities existed in the conflicts—the protesters often were middle- and upper-middle class reformers, sometimes working in harmony with power groups in the community, and the conflicts were covered in the news media and well-known to informed citizens. Other clashes were ignored by the mainstream media or covered only by alternative media or both for reasons discussed in this book.

Denis McQuail (1994) has suggested that there is a continuum of theoretical positions on the idea of socialization and social control.

At one end of the continuum is the view that media act nonpurpo-
sively to support dominant values in a community through a mixture
of individual and institutional choices and audience pressures. A
stronger version of this view sees the mass media as supportive of
the status quo because of a combination of market forces, journalis-
tic standards, and work requirements. At the far end, critical theorists assumed what is essentially a Marxist position of the media as
a tool of suppression used by the ruling class. Some critical theorists
resist the idea that the mass media are capable of producing meaningful social change (see Altschull, 1994; Chomsky & Herman, 1988;
other important critical studies on social control include Avery
& Eason, 1991; Baker, 1994; Downing, Mohammadi, & Sreberny-
Mohammadi, 1990; Ewin, 1976; Hardt, 1992; Kellner, 1990;
McManus, 1994; Murdoch & Golding, 1977).[4] The argument is
made that the media serve as a front for the ruling class and its
institutions, with little or no capacity to present alternative ideas or
challenging points of view. When social change occurs, some critical
theorists identify it as an anomaly or a change with only minor or
short-term impact. The critical model may underplay the role newspapers and other media have performed historically as agents of
change. This is not to claim that the environmental movement's
victories or defeats may be attributed solely to the mass media. The
mass media, however, have become an important ingredient in
almost all social movements' activities. In addition to the changes in
American society affected by the media-environmental movement
relationship, many goals of other social movements have been
reached with the help of the media, including civil rights and
women's rights.

THE IDEATIONAL MODEL
AND SOCIAL MOVEMENTS

In environmental debates, social change may be affected by several factors—the support of the movement, the policies of the power
structure, the activities of mass media, and so on. All are part of the
social system of American society, which created and reflected many

notions about the environment and conservation over several generations. This is called an ideational model in which a fourth factor —a combination of ideas, values, and ideologies—also may affect social change. An ideational model simplifies reality to explain it in small parts—the normal and the typical, the patterns and processes that make up the shared attributes of social circumstances. The German scholar Max Weber devised the concept, and he is often presented as someone who promoted the independent role of ideas in social life.[5] Beliefs are effective, Weber stated, only if held within a circumscribed range of other social forces—in this case, the power structure, the mass media, and the environmental movement. In Weber's studies, ideas and values in Calvinism and various religions had an important, independent effect on history—more so than elementary representations of underlying interests (Weber, 1958; see also Weber, 1947; for analysis of Weber with regard to this area, see Gerth & Mills, 1946; Schroeder, 1992). Weber noted how the concept of how salvation was to be achieved shaped the activities of early Protestants.

Weber (1958) argued that certain value systems in Western society, combined with material causes, produced the development of industrialism. One of the many reactions against industrialism was a form of collective behavior that we have come to call the environmental movement.[6] Formal and informal organizations coalesced from segments of the population that became aware and aroused by perceived threats to their interests. Turner and Killian (1957) stated that people began "to supplement their informal discussion with some organization to promote their convictions effectively and insure more sustained activity" (p. 307). Societies are filled with groups of people who plan strategy and tactics to promote or prevent social change; such collectives are called social movements (Harper, 1989).

The American response to industrialism and other 19th-century factors is in line with two social conditions recognized by the sociologist Neil Smelser (1963) as necessary for the emergence and development of a social movement: structural conduciveness and structural strains. In the United States, structural conduciveness existed in the form of a vast frontier, rich deposits of natural resources, and the forces of industrialization, immigration, and urbanization.

Structural strains occurred in relation to the way that the conducive structures were recognized. The idea that there is a "public outcry" about such issues is misleading. "Public opinion" may be measured through elections or polls, but, as Elliott King and Michael Schudson (1995) noted, "it must be coaxed into existence by leadership of various kinds—articulated by parties and interest groups, mobilized by social movements, sounded by reporters and Congressional aides talking to cab drivers or irate constituents" (p. 148). The actions of institutions and individuals (and changes in social conditions) are important in the creation of a zeitgeist (social climate) that may contribute to social change.

The social construction of reality, as advanced by Peter Berger and Thomas Luckmann (1967), theorizes that there is no such thing as a single "objective" definition of truth; instead, there are various and often competing realities, each held by different groups or cultures. Because the same set of facts has varying meanings to different groups at different times, each group holds its own consensual reality. Of particular importance in this work is the emergence of environmentalism as a social problem dependent on societal recognition— and therefore mass media performance. A "public" comes into existence, according to American philosopher John Dewey (1927), because it becomes concerned about a perceived threat to the community. One could say that without a social problem there is no public, and without a public there is no social problem. Dewey's student, the sociologist Robert Park (1941), said that a public will disappear should the mass media ignore a social problem, and that the media's ability to define problems is their true power. Therefore, media access is sought by groups concerned with advancing their causes. Park (1941) stated, "The power of the press is the influence that news- papers exercise in the formation of public opinion and in mobilizing the community for political action" (p. 1). Park stressed that there could be no public opinion regarding any political action unless the public is informed.

This does not mean the media always promote social change. Numerous examples can be cited in which mass media have limited or prevented such change. Real change in values toward the environment and environmental policy has occurred, however, and the media have played an important role in this process.

MASS MEDIA AND
SOCIAL SYSTEM THEORY

One component of most definitions of news is the coverage of conflict. John Chancellor, a senior correspondent and anchor for NBC-TV News, said that news is a chronicle of conflict and change (as cited in Hough, 1995, p. 2). Thinkers from the days of Heraclitus of Ephesus in Ancient Greece have focused on social conflict; St. Thomas Aquinas addressed the justness of war (the most severe form of conflict) in Question 40 of his *Summa Theologia*. Early sociologists linked social changes to conflicts in the system. Scholars from Karl Marx and Georg Simmel in the 19th century to Ralf Dahrendorf and Lewis Coser nearly a century later commented on conflict functions, both positive and negative. Conflict theory assumes inequality is the inherent source of strain in the social system. Coser (1956), in *The Functions of Social Conflict,* noted that conflict establishes and maintains the balance of power. Social conflict can also generate new norms, stimulate thought, fuel the economy, or provide changes in technology, as in the weapons of war.

Something of a continuum of how the mass media function in history has emerged from the literature of journalism and mass communication scholars. At one end, scholars have seen the mass media and their members—mostly editors and reporters—as functioning as a progressive agent of social change. An example of this perception is found in Lewis Filler's (1976) classic work, *The Muckrakers,* in which he saw the turn-of-the-century journalists as riding the crest of the Progressive era, giving voice to the people and their reformers. In Filler's view, first published in 1939, muckrakers were a major threat to private interests by fulfilling the "watchdog" function often assigned to journalists. Historian Walter Brasch (1990) said the Progressive era gave freedom to the muckrakers, encouraged them, took their results, and tried to improve America. In this view of the media, journalists are seen as crusading forces, leading society to a better place, fulfilling First Amendment responsibilities while banishing evil and corruption. Here, the role of the media is sometimes called the "Fourth Estate." [7]

Near the other end of the continuum of how the mass media function throughout history is the idea of media as an agent of social control. In the variations of these views, as mentioned previously, the media are objects of and instruments of social control by the power structure in the community. Media deference to powerful groups in society on some level is well documented. For example, by writing stories on a particular topic and ignoring others, the media help define what is acceptable behavior in society and what is not. Schudson (1978; see also Leonard, 1986; Schiller, 1981), in his classic book *Discovering the News,* argued that news crusades in the 19th century legitimated the status quo in society.

In this work and others, several themes emerge about the behavior of the mass media as a form of social control. All communication processes have a control function in them; the key assumption underlying this idea is that knowledge is the basis of social power (Coser, 1971; Galbraith, 1978). In addition, mass media scholars George A. Donohue, Phillip J. Tichenor, and Clarice Olien (1973) noted that the control of knowledge is central to the development and maintenance of social power, which is where the mass media enter the picture. Media, they said, are a subsystem that at times control and may be controlled by other subsystems. They defined a social system as "a series of interrelated subsystems with primary functions including the generation, dissemination and assimilation of information to effect further control as a means to an end or an end in itself" (Donohue et al., 1973, p. 652).

Donohue et al. (1973) believe the maintenance function of the mass media may be fulfilled by two sets of processes: feedback control and distribution control. Feedback control means the media execute a regulatory function for other subsystems. The information provided is used to make decisions that perform to keep the system at equilibrium. Distribution control serves a maintenance function by selectively disseminating or censoring information; it can occur with feedback control or independently. News stories about conflict can play a role in system maintenance—although the media produce stories about alternative or challenging ideas, those reports may allow institutions or subsystems to adapt and survive. The mass media sometimes serve as a safety value in conflict situations. For example, the reporting of information could speed the resolution process.

Mass media tend to promote interests of elite or powerful groups. These groups also tend to attempt to control the media for their own uses. Herbert Gans (1979) noted that dominant values and system norms also shape media content, which in turn reinforces them. Reporters and editors are structurally dependent on dominant power groups as sources of information, partly because they offer a regular supply of news. One only need note the number of stories originating in Washington, DC, and New York City—the political and economic centers of power in the United States—to see this in action. In addition, bureaucratic agencies and procedures serve as legitimizing agents for the mass media. Lacking these formal structures for news generation, some environmental problems may go unnoticed. In addition, the nature of the reporting of events such as a congressional hearing invariably favors those holding the hearing at the expense of the protesting group. Alternative special interest groups may lack resources or organizational skills or both. Lower-status collectives are often unable to gain access to the mass media by themselves. Without access, their definition of a social problem may be marginalized or ignored altogether.

Under some conditions, the mass media may promote social change. For example, as a social system becomes more pluralistic, a greater diversity of groups tends to fight over a fixed amount of resources, and media coverage reflects those battles. There is no guarantee that these stories will generate change, but they are a necessary condition for change. Also, in larger, more pluralistic areas, the mainstream media tend to be established power structures themselves and thus have more autonomy from other powerful groups. News stories may be dysfunctional for some in power. The liberal nature of journalists sometimes is a factor. Although journalists tend to support the dominant value system (Gans, 1979), other research shows that they tend to be slightly more liberal than either the general public or the elite groups (Weaver & Wilhoit, 1986). This also suggests that media at times have the capacity to produce stories critical of the status quo. Finally, the competitive nature of the press—which may reflect business pressures—drives the media to pursue a big story, such as the Three Mile Island disaster, whether the story fits the power structure's agenda or not. The history of journalism is filled with persons such as publisher William Randolph Hearst, who delighted in tweaking the Republican establishment in the early 1900s, whereas his papers supported many causes of the working class.

The increasingly pluralistic nature of American society means many forms of mass media exist. Media types that often challenge basic institutions and values of the system are called different names—for example, advocacy, alternative, counterculture, or the specialized press (see Dennis & Rivers, 1974; Kessler, 1984).[8] Sometimes, deviant groups create their own media to disseminate information; other times, they are successful in attracting attention from alternative media forms, which may be independent of any group but support a particular anti-status quo ideology, such as the socialist publication *The Milwaukee Leader* in the early 20th century. In one example of how the specialized media function, a study revealed that the most prominent clustering of federal environmental policy decisions occurred between 1968 and 1972. Before these agencies were developed, there was increasing environmental content in specialty magazines. An increase in environmental content in general interest magazines, however, did not occur until after the new environmental agencies were in place. Therefore, environmental issues were initiated not by the general interest media but by professional interest groups, specialized publications, and the government bureaucracy, roughly in that order. Only then did the mainstream media become interested (Strodthoff, Hawkins, & Schoenfeld, 1985). One doubts whether this model would hold fast in every news story.

Legitimacy is granted and denied by the mass media—one person's terrorist is another's freedom fighter. A primary goal of the environmental movement has been to gain the attention of the wider public; as a result, activists have used the mass media, which may contribute to their success or failure in given situations. In some cases, the movement started its own media outlets. More often, leaders of successful movements became skilled at interacting with mainstream media outlets, or dramatic events thrust groups and issues into the media arena (for more information on the role of dramatic events, see Hilgartner & Bosk, 1988). For example, the Wilderness Society reported an increase of 28,000 members in the 2 months after the dramatic Exxon *Valdez* oil spill—three times its average gain—after the media helped link the group to the story (Weisskopf, 1990).

There is one more set of media functions discussed in this book that needs to be mentioned. These functions are known by different names, but in performance they accelerate or decelerate social problems or, in some cases, the movements themselves. When the media cover a story, a certain public legitimacy is added to the collective, event, or issue. If the nature of the issue and the groups involved are in line with the values of the social system, the issue could be accelerated in various public arenas. Schudson (1995) stated that the media "bring it into a common public forum where it can be discussed by a general audience. They not only distribute the report of an event or an announcement to a large group, they amplify it" (p. 19). With that amplification comes increased attention in the marketplace of ideas and acceleration or deceleration of the issue. When three children under age 6 were poisoned by carbon monoxide from a faulty furnace in Minnesota and two died, news reports of the tragedy spurred sales of carbon monoxide detectors to the point of selling out stores across the state (Estrada, 1996). An example of issue deceleration occurred with the negative reaction to power line protesters in Minnesota smearing themselves with animal feces in front of television cameras in an attempt to halt a power company from building new lines (Tichenor, Donohue, & Olien, 1980). In Todd Gitlin's (1980) study of the media and in Students for a Democratic Society (SDS), both media functions can be seen. In the early days of the SDS, the *New York Times* coverage of the movement contributed to the rapid membership growth of the organization; Gitlin, however, saw media coverage as decelerating to the SDS when coverage trivialized or marginalized its efforts. At the same time the media were contributing to the deceleration of the SDS, they accelerated many of its issues, particularly the Vietnam War, when the issues were adopted by other, more mainstream groups (Gitlin, 1980).

Journalists have been made conscious of local and regional environmental controversies from the early 18th century to the 1950s, when a national dialogue about air and water pollution emerged. Long before the 1960s, serious concerns about environmental issues were closely and hotly debated, with the media involved. From the muckrakers' work in the public health reform movements to scientific and political fights to conserve western lands and resources, journalists participated in many environmental controversies of their era. It was not their nature to believe that, as a Standard Oil spokesman pleaded with reporters during the leaded gasoline controversy of 1924, "nothing ought to be said about this matter in the public interest" ("Odd Gas Kills One," 1924, p. 1). Such a position would be antithetical to the long-standing role of the press. Acceleration of an issue by the media places the conflict on some public agenda—whether it be in the courts, legislatures, schools, big business, or elsewhere. How the issue is defined may reflect the protest group's goals, its opposition, or some combination of the two.

ENVIRONMENTAL HISTORY

Since the establishment of the historical field of American environmental history in the 1950s and 1960s, the discipline has been dominated by a few forms of analysis. The great person theory, or its related notion, the "rational actor" theory, is the interpretive framework historians adopt in many fields, including many biographies in environmental history. Great person history equates the behavior of groups, such as the environmental movement, with the actions of individuals, such as Aldo Leopold or Rachel Carson. Rationality and high success-low cost motivations are among the important assumptions of this theory. Change is in the hands of a few individual leaders making well-defined choices. Its weaknesses include the ideas that rationality cannot explain all human behavior, ideology and culture are subjective, and all options are not always recognized by the people involved. Environmental historians employing the great person theory often highlighted the careers of government officials in the first half of this century, men such as Leopold, Robert Marshall, Arthur Carhart, Stephen Mather, and Ding Darling, as being critical to the origin of the movement. Research on activists such as Horace Albright, Howard Zahniser, David Brower, and their patron saint, John Muir, may also fall into the great person category (see Baldwin, 1972; Cohen, 1984; Flader, 1974; Fox, 1981; Lendt, 1979; Reiger, 1975; Roth, 1988; Swain, 1970). Women are conspicuous by their absence from these and other types of environmental histories, with the notable exception of the scholarship done by Carolyn Merchant (1980, 1984), particularly *The Death of Nature: Women, Ecology and the Scientific Revolution,* and literary historian Annette Kolodny (1984), *The Landscape Before Her,* a study of women's perceptions of the American West (see also LaBastille, 1980).

Another dominant theme in the development of American environmental history is intellectual history and its component, the history of ideas. The idea of wilderness in American thought, for example, was thoroughly discussed in Roderick Nash's (1967) *Wilderness and the American Mind* in three editions. Samuel Hays (1959), in *Conservation and the Gospel of Efficiency,* examined the notion of conservation in the Progressive era. As Richard White (1985) pointed out in his review of the field, Nash and Hays used wilderness and conservation as the means to a larger end: Nash examining American thought and Hays interpreting the Progressives and their political and social actions. White deduced that the success of Nash and Hays ferreting out the intellectual history of the environmental movement added depth to the field at the expense of breadth. With the exception of some historical geographers, the "reciprocal influences of environmental and social change temporarily disappeared" (White, 1985, p. 300): Historians defined environment in frontier terms, neglecting urban areas and their concerns. It was not until the work of Martin Melosi and others nearly two decades after Nash that urban environmental themes began to receive significant attention. Melosi drew several ideas together, including concerns with public health and the aesthetics of everyday life as far back as the late 1800s. He blurred the line between the history of public health and environmental history, if such a line was ever necessary (Melosi, 1980, 1981; for a summary of the neglect of urban concerns in environmental history, see Melosi, 1979).

The prevalence of the great person biographies and the intellectual histories opened up roads in environmental thought but left others lightly traveled. As more scholars entered the field, and with the success of journals such as *Environmental History Journal,* the subject broadened to more theoretical interpretations, historical models, and methodologies. In the early 1970s, the American Society for Environmental History was organized to help institutionalize the field. By 1993, Donald Worster (1993) noted the important connections that environmental history had established with the natural sciences (such as ecology) and social sciences (such as anthropology and geography). Many distinguished scholars emerged from the field, including but not limited to Worster, William Cronon (1992), Susan Flader (1974), and Alfred Crosby (1986). Global themes, by such authors as Richard H. Grove (1995), have enriched the subject.

At least one path is still largely unexplored: The role of the mass media in the history of environmentalism in the United States. The role of the media as a social institution is conspicuous by its absence in many of the earlier histories; in other cases, the media are dismissed as unimportant. For example, one historian wrote that the debate over the Malthusian population predictions of the 1960s meant "the media had to present ecological issues seriously. The mass media had never done so before" (Bramwell, 1989, p. 212). One exception is the work of journalism historian Stephen Ponder, who has examined the role of newspapering and public relations in conservation issues during the Progressive era (Ponder, 1986a, 1986b, 1994; see also Kates, 1995). The history of environmental conflict and the performance and contribution of mass media, such as newspapers, magazines, and (in some cases) books, interlock because the mass media of nearly every historical era contained reports of environmental conflict.

One way this book differs from others is its emphasis on the continuation of the expansion of what constitutes a "green crusade." Although the traditional debate has focused on topics such as the national park system and the politics of conservation, the idea of including workplace hazards, lead in gasoline, air pollution, and other health risks is more recent. Furthermore, the two schools of historical thought—environment and public health—seldom acknowledge each other. A notable exception is Robert Gottlieb's (1993) *Forcing the Spring,* which makes the case for a connection between public health issues and environmental awareness. Gottlieb resurrects the ideas of Robert Marshall, who in the 1930s proposed a common thread for an environmental movement split between the control of nature and those who defined environment as the experience of daily life in its urban and industrial setting—the liberation of society was a condition for the liberation of nature (Gottlieb, 1993).

Gottlieb includes urban and rural themes in his analysis, spending much of his time on issues rising since the publication of Carson's *Silent Spring* in 1962. *Green Crusades* expands the argument into specific historical areas of conflict in the pre-*Silent Spring* era, including both the frontier environment and urban public health concerns.

ORGANIZATION OF THE BOOK

Environmental conflicts by their nature are multidisciplinary, and so is the audience for *Green Crusades:* the mass communication history student; the environmental studies student; students in sociology, ecology, or social history; and the interested general reader. The theoretical notions mentioned here are not our original constructs, but marrying the mass media to the environmental movement in American history is relatively rare. We do not aim to tell the story of every environmental conflict in American history, nor do we seek to describe blow-by-blow detail on any one event. The environmental conflicts told in *Green Crusades* are a representative sample of the interaction of the mass media, environmental groups, other social institutions, and commonly held values.

Green Crusades examines the mass media and environmental conflicts in three areas: the type and timing of media involvement, circumstances in which environmentalists' goals were met in some fashion, and circumstances in which those goals were not realized. The examples conclude before the publication of Carson's *Silent Spring* in 1962 because Carson's book has been well documented as a mobilization point in the history of the environmental movement. As Alan Schnaiberg (1980) wrote, the 1960s and 1970s environmental movement differed from early movements because it became a mass movement with a greater number of groups involved on a higher level of participation. Mass communication was, again, a key: The environmental concerns of the 1960s entered the mass consciousness through the mass media, "frequently at the prompting of mass demonstration of dissent over threats to the environment" (Pepper, 1984, p. 16).

The first section of this book consists of two chapters, set in a comparative format. The first chapter is a story of specialized media —*Forest and Stream* magazine and the role of sportsmen in the creation of game laws in the 1870s and 1880s. Chapter 2 is an example of mainstream media involvement in an environmental controversy, in the case of the Radium Girls, the Consumers League, and newspaper editor Walter Lippmann. Chapters 3 and 4—examinations of national parks and the Alaskan land grab of the early 1900s—represent the type of social change that occurred when the media, environmental groups, and the power structure functioned in a loose coalition. Chapter 5 shows what happened when the coalition came apart at Hetch Hetchy dam in Yosemite National Park. Chapter 6, dealing with the leaded gasoline controversy of the 1920s, highlights the conflict management function of the media during a brief but intense issue. Chapter 7 consists of the accelerating impact of media coverage of a dramatic event in the form of sudden, deadly air pollution at Donora, Pennsylvania, in 1948.

In the history of the environmental movement—from the mid-19th century to Rachel Carson in the 1960s—the mass media, the environmentalists, the government, and various power groups have interacted on many levels to affect social change. The role of books, magazines, and newspaper articles was important in the creation of a community—a regional or national community—with environmental awareness and understanding. At the same time, the mass media also played a significant role in the formation of powerful groups, as environmentalists used the help of others to accomplish their goals. Mobilization of any protest movement relies on the mass media to communicate goals, recruit new believers, and sustain current members. As Park (1941) stated, "there is and there can be no such thing as news, in so far as concerns politics, except in a community in which there is a body of tradition and common understanding in terms of which events are ordinarily interpreted" (p. 11). The mass media helped shape the limits of the debate while maintaining cohesion among group members and enlarging the base of support (see Kielbowicz & Scherer, 1986). It is significant that the environmental movement grew at roughly the same time that newspapers and magazines assumed a mature form as agents of social control and change.

Some conflicts in *Green Crusades* have not been examined by historians in detail. Other stories have been told before but without the emphasis on the mass media and the interaction with other groups in society. The participation (or nonparticipation) of the mass media is highlighted in each of the areas of conflict. The reader should be left with the idea that when environmentalists acted in concert with the prevailing values of the social system, various power groups, and the media, change often occurred. Sometimes, contrary to simplistic notions about the media only being lapdogs to the powerful, the press promoted change that ran counter to the interests of the elites.

NOTES

1. Sale (1993) estimates about a 30% overlap in environmental movement group membership. In the 1950s, no one could join the Sierra Club without being recommended by two sponsors.

2. The document was dated December 5, 1989.

3. Partially to meet the demand for reporters and editors, the University of Colorado in 1992 established a Center for Environmental Journalism.

4. Much of the foundation of the critical model comes from what is called the Frankfurt School, which has played an important role in the shaping of theories of ideology in the 20th century. Proponents of this school include Theodore Adorno, Max Horkheimer, Antonio Gramsci, Herbert Marcuse, and Stuart Hall, among others.

5. In Weber's writings on politics and bureaucracy, however, it is clear that the notion of ideas affecting the social structure by themselves is not well developed.

6. In a broader sense, the 19th- and 20th-century American regard for nature, public health, the well-being of children, and the safety of workers transcends mere reaction to industrialism. Other cultural and social factors were at work as well. The 19th century saw the rise of the temperance movement, prison and insane asylum reform, feminism, utopian groups, public schools, and so on.

7. Criticisms of this approach include Carey (1974), Dicken-Garcia and Stevens (1980), and McKerns (1977).

8. David Paul Nord (1986) called the work done by William Lloyd Garrison in the abolitionist paper *The Liberator* associational or participatory journalism.

ACKNOWLEDGMENTS

nsofar as this book succeeds, it is in large part attributable to family, friends, and fellow scholars without whose support this project could never have been undertaken. On the list of people deserving thanks are Hazel Dicken-Garcia, Phil Tichenor, Bill Babcock, Don Geesaman, Nancy Roberts, Tom Connery, Dave Nimmer, Gene McGivern, Dave Pyle, Gary Parker, Tom Levandowski, Steve Laumakis, Mary Thomas, Sally Kohlstedt, David Pearce Demers, David Abrahamson, K. Vishwanath, James Grunig, Larissa Grunig, Maurine Beasley, Reese Cleghorn, Jon Franklin, Sam Riley, Ken Rystrom, Clayland Waite, Richard Worringham, David Dobkins, Carey Brown, William Haskett, Hal Bernton, Scott Sklar, Richard Scharschburg, and John J. McDonough. Our wives, Amy Kuebelbeck and Linda Burton, deserve a special word of thanks for tolerance and understanding of their Czech mates.

—Mark Neuzil

—Bill Kovarik

1

SPECIALIZED MEDIA

Forest and Stream Magazine and
the Redefinition of Hunting

he noted observer of American life in the 1830s, Alexis
de Tocqueville, saw Americans as joiners. Associations of
all types, including those involving workers, churches,
and education, were filled with citizens who voluntarily
showed up and pitched in. Although these groups served
a social function, Tocqueville (1969) stated, "if they want to proclaim
a truth or propagate some feeling by the encouragement of a great
example, they form an association" (p. 518; see also Nord, 1986). One
way social groups communicate ("proclaim a truth or propagate some
feeling") is through the production of their own media. The United

1

States has a long history of specialized media representing groups such as abolitionists, feminists, immigrants, radicals, various religious organizations, and so on (see Kessler, 1984). Such groups often are shut out from the mainstream press and resort to their own newspapers, newsletters, and magazines to promote their views. These publications also serve a socialization role by letting the organization's members know of activities, events, and gossip. Often, the issues raised by these specialty publications move to the mainstream media, as was the case with some women's issues in the 1960s advocated by magazines such as *Ms*. Sometimes, the alternative media themselves become more mainstream, as happened with *Rolling Stone,* the rock magazine founded on a shoestring in 1967 only to become a multimillion dollar publishing enterprise within a decade.

Some attention in journalism history has been focused on the alternative press, specifically abolitionist, feminist, labor, immigrant, and pacifist media. Although the alternative press has often been thought of as representing the underclass, society's elites sometimes needed mass communication vehicles to promote their views as well. The conservation movement of the 19th century, which was dominated by wealthy easterners, achieved many of its goals, defeated its opponents, and mobilized and expanded the movement with the help of advocate publications. Prominent among them were the hunting and fishing magazines, which grew with great strength in the years following the Civil War. Perhaps the most influential was *Forest and Stream,* guided by its first two publishers, Charles Hallock and George Bird Grinnell.

CLASS TENSIONS

At first glance, the town of Hallock, Minnesota, appears an unlikely place to begin a story about the post-Civil War conservation movement in the United States. The small farming community sits a mere 20-minute drive from the Canadian border in the far northwest corner of Minnesota, near the rich and fertile valley of the Red River. Surrounded by fields of sunflowers and sugar beets, Hallock is home to about 1,300 people, many of whom fish in the summer and hunt white-tailed deer, ducks, geese, and grouse in the fall.

The town is significant in the history of the relationship between mass media and environmental conflict because of its founder and namesake, Charles Hallock (Figure 1.1), who was among the first Americans to recognize the significance of game management and mobilize hunters to achieve that goal. Hallock preached the importance of a new kind of relationship to wildlife in the 1870s through the pages of a magazine he founded, financed, edited, and eventually lost. The publication was called *Forest and Stream*. The magazine no longer exists, but the conservation groups organized around the wildlife management idea—the Audubon Society, the Boone & Crockett Club, and the American Ornithological Union—still influenced the environmental movement 100 years later.

Forest and Stream forcefully and sometimes eloquently participated in the development of a national hunting ethic in the post-Civil War era on behalf of one influential segment of the emerging conservation movement. The magazine and the groups it nourished focused on defining a new kind of hunting ethic at the expense of other types of relationships with wildlife, particularly market hunting (the taking of wild game for economic reasons). The drama included several cultural factors: (a) the fledgling conservation movement, (b) advancements in weapons technology, (c) declining wildlife populations, and (d) cultural changes in land use patterns.

The hunting controversy was fueled by a larger societal debate about industry, urbanization, and a sense of loss in the last half of the 19th century. Historian Richard Hofstadter (1925) saw the basis of the major social upheaval of the 1890s, the Progressive movement, as acts of the old family, colleged, well educated to return to their previous high status, which was slipping, whereas the moralities of those they detested were ascending. As the United States transformed from an agricultural to an industrial nation, market hunting in particular elicited a negative response from *Forest and Stream,* partly because it was an occupation staffed by "lower" classes (many of the hunters were immigrants of Eastern European lineage) in the emerging mass production-based society. The focus of the hunting debate lowered the status of the market gunners and helped restore deference to the elite view. The transformation of culture from the upper classes to the general public has as a key structural element the "effort to find, characterize, and adapt to an American way of life

Figure 1.1. *Forest and Stream* founder.
Charles Hallock, one of the journalists who began the crusade for wildlife laws in the United States, founded the sporting journal *Forest and Stream* in 1873. Hallock also developed a town named after him in northwestern Minnesota, partly to cater to elite hunters from the East. Reproduced from the Minnesota Historical Society (No. C.H. 1).

as distinguished from the material achievements (and failures) of an American industrial civilization" (Susman, 1984, p. 156). Conflicts about hunting assumed symbolic properties: Many divisions and contradictions within the 20th-century environmental movement can be traced to the debate over wildlife and hunting ethics in the 19th-century United States.

Throughout the pages of the specialty magazine, Hallock and the activist editors who followed built a case for a new, distinctly American hunting ethic that had lasting political and cultural effects. The magazine helped define a particular way of relating to wildlife; participation was based on class and status distinctions.

The implied belief that culture was the province of the elite and the elite's desire to see it spread to the masses created class tension. The same idea was a common criticism of the environmental movement in the 1960s and 1970s. In the late 20th century, the environmental movement was sometimes viewed as a moral, elitist crusade because the major groups supporting its goals were middle and upper-middle class. The alliance was unstable. "The ecological movement was never a singular nor a stable entity, but involved rather different social components" (Schnaiberg, 1980, p. 378), including but not limited to conservation versus preservation forces in the 1890s (Hays, 1959).[1] Hunters and anglers from blue-collar communities supported environmental causes in the 20th century because of the incursion of industry "destroying many of the habitats for game and fish" (Schnaiberg, 1980, p. 381). An ironic source of conflict came when animal rights activists included themselves in the same environmental movement umbrella that covered groups such as Ducks Unlimited, whose members shot waterfowl for sport. This extends from the conflict over wildlife preservation in the 1800s, which had sport hunting and nature appreciation as two parts of its thrust (Dunlap, 1988).

CULTURAL FACTORS:
TECHNIQUES AND TECHNOLOGY

In ancient times, evidence exists that culture rules and norms encouraged conservation, particularly regarding wildlife. J. Donald

Hughes (1994) mentioned the protection from hunting of mother birds and their offspring in ancient Greece and Rome by common rule. William Cronon (1983) described the hunt and its relationship to European property systems in colonial New England, noting that the natives were more efficient hunters who also stopped when they were satisfied with the size of their kill. One view is that ideas about conservation in the United States came from writers, philosophers, and painters, such as James Fenimore Cooper, Ralph Waldo Emerson, and John James Audubon (Nash, 1982). An important link among many early conservationists was that they belonged to an elite group of eastern society. Many, notably Audubon, were hunters.

Conservationists had a difficult beginning. The biases against conservation in the 19th century were many: a seemingly abundant land, a survival ethic that included besting nature, individualism, and a Judeo-Christian tradition of humans dominating nature (Nash, 1974, p. 3). Sportsmen began as a small group and grew in numbers after the Civil War as the amount of leisure time in American society increased. A sportsman typically was "a gentleman hunter or fisherman who believed that wildlife had a value other than as food. With his finely tooled shotgun and light bamboo flyrod, he elevated hunting and fishing to the level of a sport" (Nash, 1974, p. 4). Many sportsmen practiced hunting ethics imported from England by killing game for sport (rather than food or profit), hunting during daylight hours, shooting birds on the wing (rather than sitting), and respecting breeding seasons by staying home. It was the animals' "unfettered existence, rather than their food value, which made them valuable to [English] sportsmen" (Munsche, 1981, p. 20). Recognizing a market, sporting journals such as *Forest and Stream* sought sportsmen as subscribers and advertisers. "It was clear that the upper-class Easterners who constituted the mainstay of the [New York Game Protective Association] had a very different relationship toward the land than did frontiersmen" (Nash, 1974, p. 4).

All hunters kill game; differences arise in ideology and technique. Although sportsmen shot game as part of an act of nature appreciation or to recreate the pioneer experience, market hunters usually killed as a way of life. Market hunters (Figure 1.2) often worked for the railroads (Buffalo Bill Cody is an example) and lumber companies, which needed to feed large crews as cheaply as possible

Figure 1.2. Minnesota market hunters.
Three market hunters, who worked to provide lumberjacks in northern Minnesota and Wisconsin with food, pose with the camp butcher and a day's kill, including a moose and a white-tailed deer. By the time this picture was taken in 1905, most of the market hunters were legislated out of a job by fish and game laws. Reproduced from the Minnesota Historical Society (No. 31684).

(Kimball & Kimball, 1969). Market hunting in the United States was important economically only for the last half of the 19th century. Such hunters needed a primitive wilderness with an abundance of game and a growing market to sell their product. In the middle of the century, market hunting was a regional business, but with the expansion of the railroads and advances in refrigeration, markets spread to the East Coast. Another trade, millinery, also had an effect on game populations as milliners kept up with shifting fashions by buying feathers and skins. Mostly Eastern European farmers, frontiersmen, rural youth, and Southern European immigrants, the market hunters' vagabond nature made it difficult for them to affect social change, although they did have friends in the railroad and timber industries and in Congress.[2]

Market hunting was a respected profession in the early days of the United States: "From the colonial days, the hunter who took game to sell had been respected and held a position about equivalent to that of the village butcher or the city meatpacker today" (Borland,

1975, p. 116). Even the stridently anti-game for sale *Forest and Stream* damned with faint praise when it stated, "Successful market hunting requires ability and pluck, which, if properly directed, would insure success in a more honorable pursuit" ("Our Candid Advice," 1883, p. 281). One market hunter, H. Clay Merritt, claimed his profession was the stimulus for the development of modern refrigerated rail cars. Livestock could be transported on the hoof without need for refrigeration, but wild game carcasses would spoil in a 3- or 4-day train trip (Kimball & Kimball, 1969, p. 78).

While the numbers of sportsmen grew, hunting technology was changing, making the killing of game easier for any hunter. Many important developments in firearms technology occurred in the era, including

- The replacement of the flintlock firing mechanism with percussion caps
- The replacement of the muzzleloader gun with the breechloader
- The development, in England, of double-barreled guns that automatically ejected spent cartridges
- The invention of the repeating rifle by American Henry Winchester in 1873
- The popularization of the revolving cylinder with the magazine in the center shaft by 1879
- The invention of smokeless nitrocellulose powder in 1886, which allowed for a smaller caliber of bullets that could be coated with metals harder than lead, resulting in cartridges of higher ballistic values (Habusch, 1980)[3]

The breechloader gun skyrocketed in popularity in the United States in the 1870s, at about the same time the hunting magazines experienced a boom. In 1873, the breechloader represented about one fourth of the gun sales in the United States; by 1883, three of every four guns sold were breechloaders ("The Property," 1883, p. 1). All these technological changes increased the efficiency of a hunt.

As the number of hunters increased and their weapons changed, some wildlife populations plunged. Fewer than 40 wild bison (American buffalo) existed by the turn of the century (Table 1.1); the passenger pigeon, heath hen, and Carolina parakeet vanished completely. The grizzly bear numbered approximately 100,000 in the

Table 1.1   Bison Populations in the Wild in the United States by Year

Year or Era	Number of Bison
Pre-white settlers	60 million[a]
1830	40 million[a]
1889	541
1891	300
1900	39
1978	30,000

SOURCE: Stewart (1978).
a. Estimate.

United States in the 1850s; in 1848, five hunters in Oregon brought 700 grizzly bear pelts back after a year-long hunt (Grainger, 1978). By the 1970s, the bears' range in the continental United States was limited to small areas of the northern Rocky Mountains, and best estimates figured that less than 1,000 grizzly bears remained in the lower 48 states (Chapman, 1982).

SPORTSMEN'S GROUPS MOBILIZE

In the post-Civil War era, sportsmen's groups concerned with the conservation of wildlife mobilized with increased frequency across the country (Table 1.2). *Forest and Stream*'s second publisher, George Bird Grinnell, who reported killing 100 antelope or more in a single day using the new Winchester repeaters in 1874, founded a forerunner of the Audubon Society in 1886, and its charter members included such distinguished citizens as Oliver Wendell Holmes, John Greenleaf Whittier, and the Reverend Henry Ward Beecher (Reiger, 1972, p. 91; for a detailed review of Grinnell's involvement, see Reiger, 1975). Grinnell, along with Teddy Roosevelt, was a cofounder of the Boone & Crockett Club in 1887, a big-game hunting organization originally limited to 100 members, including men such as Elihu Root, Madison Grant, J. P. Morgan, and Henry Cabot Lodge. Such men emerged from the "sophisticated Eastern background that produces some of the most ardent conservationists" (Nash, 1974, p. 9; Figure 1.3).

Table 1.2. Inception Dates of Groups Concerned With Conservation

Group	Year
New York Sporting Association[a]	1844
National Rifle Association	1871
Appalachian Mountain Club	1876
American Ornithological Union	1883
Audubon Society	1886
Boone & Crockett Club	1887
National Geographic Society	1888
Sierra Club	1892
Mazamas (Mountaineering) Club	1894
American Scenic and Historic Preservation Society	1895
Campfire Club of America	1897

SOURCE: Neuzil (1991).
a. Name changed to New York Association for the Protection of Game in 1874.

There is little doubt that the majority of these clubs served a social function, but when the time came to influence public opinion in a meaningful way, the groups had an advantage in terms of numbers, resources, and organization. The Boone & Crockett Club "exercised great influence over a long period of time primarily by using the individual contacts and personal alliances that its well-placed members were able to make" (Tober, 1981, p. 190). In particular, Grinnell campaigned against the market hunters: "Nothing angered him more than the market gunners, who blanketed the nation's fields and woodlands with their deadly barrage" (Graham, 1971, p. 40).

The groups organized independently, but gradually became mobilized with the help of the sporting journals. Most groups were local; attempts to organize nationally usually failed until the 20th century and often ran into criticism from the mainstream media. The New York Sportsmen's Association, in an attempt to expand to a national membership, changed its name to the New York Association for the Protection of Game in 1874 and sponsored a "national" conference that failed to attract much media attention. The *New York Times* suggested that arms manufacturers called the meeting to stage a "grand pigeon shoot" ("Association for the Protection," 1874, p. 5).

Table 1.3   Changes in Improved Farmlands in Selected States as a
                 Percentage of Total Acreage, 1850-1900

| | % Total Acreage | | |
State	1850	1880	1900
Pennsylvania	29.8	46.3	45.6
Ohio	37.3	68.5	73.0
Illinois	14.0	72.3	76.7
Minnesota	a	13.5	34.3
Iowa	2.3	29.8	69.5
Texas	a	7.4	11.4
Total United States	5.8	14.7	21.4

SOURCE: U.S. Census Office (1902).
a. Acreage given but percentage less than 1%.

Specialized publications thus served the bulk of the groups' communication needs.

Each side, the sportsmen and the market hunters, blamed the other for the drop in wildlife populations, whereas greater cultural concerns, specifically changing land use patterns associated with farming, logging, mining, transportation, and building, went unchallenged. Farming patterns were one important change, but the data do not reflect the additional changes brought on by urbanization, mining, logging, and other activities (Table 1.3).

For example, consider the cases of two of the more well-known American wildlife stories, bison and passenger pigeons. Both species required large, unbroken expanses of land to exist. As property was divided by cities, railroads, and roads, bison and pigeons were driven to smaller, easily hunted areas. Government wildlife policy in response to the dwindling animal populations was relatively slow to develop, sporadically enforced, and marginally effective: Wildlife regulations prior to 1850 were rare. Some of the statutes restricted hunting (by designating protected animals during breeding seasons), whereas others encouraged it (by bounties on those creatures considered pests). In Massachusetts, for example, an 1848 law set a $10 fine for persons frightening away pigeons from hunters' nets (Kimball & Kimball, 1969, p. 88). None of the political responses considered land use patterns or restrictions on private property.

GOVERNMENT ACTIONS

Early state laws were infrequently enforced, if at all, and sometimes revoked. For example, New York banned the use of "batteries" (a set of mounted guns) on boats hunting waterfowl in 1834, but the law was repealed.[4] Rhode Island passed a law in 1846 outlawing the shooting of wood ducks, black ducks, woodcocks, and snipe in the spring, but the law also was repealed (Borland, 1975, p. 89). Many of Massachusetts' laws protecting fisheries were rewritten in the 1830s as industries developed the waterways. In New England, declining fish populations, particularly table fare such as salmon and shad, led to competing demands on the environment in the 1860s (Cumbler, 1991). Although many statutes did not remain on the books, public debate about wildlife management had begun, and it established precedents for legal restrictions on both hunting and technology.

Any wildlife management ran counter to American ideology. The United States had a history of nondiscriminatory access to wildlife, which partly stemmed from lower-class colonists' frustrations with English game laws. In England, game laws date back several centuries. By one count, two dozen acts designed to regulate hunting passed Parliament between 1671 and 1831 (Munsche, 1981, p. 8).[5] There was no mistaking the purpose of the laws: to "ensure that the hunting of game—particularly hares, partridges and pheasants— was the exclusive privilege of the landed gentry" (Munsche, 1981, p. 8). Simply put, English game laws were class legislation. By the late 16th century, English game laws included a ban on night hunting, when some wildlife, particularly birds, were most vulnerable. Such legislation assumed those hunting at night were not interested in sport as much as food and profit.

Colonists saw English game laws as a contribution to their troubled lives in Europe—a form of social control used by the ruling class. Vermont judge Laforest H. Thompson, in an 1895 ruling, wrote, "Among instrumentalities used to bring about the undesirable condition of life, were the iniquitous fish and game laws of England, enacted by a ruling class for their own enjoyment" (Tober, 1981, p. 19). Americans responded with almost unrestricted access to wildlife in the era of post-Revolution Anglophobia and the myth of inexhaustible natural resources. "American wildlife policy from the colonial period through the late 19th century established freetaking as its principal goal," stated historian Thomas Lund (1980, p. 57). Early Americans rejected the English system of lords and landed gentry.

After the Civil War, many American sportsmen, members of the eastern elite, favored the aristocratic English view. The English tradition included hunting on horseback with hounds, hawking, having servants load and reload weapons and literally "beat the bushes" to scare up wildlife.[6] American easterners generally followed the same methods. Those easterners were generally wealthy, well educated, and lived in an urban area—characteristics not shared with market hunters. Gradually, the eastern sportsmen's numbers and influence increased to the point where public policy was affected by their attitudes at the expense of other groups, particularly market hunters.

THE MAGAZINE AND ITS EDITORS[7]

Many historians have detailed the history of American magazines, including the development of the so-called sporting journals in the Reconstruction era and later (see Betts, 1953; Mott, 1938a, 1938b). By 1885, 20 journals devoted themselves to "the sporting life" in the United States (Mott, 1938a, p. 210); four years later, at least 56 such journals existed (Mott, 1938b, p. 68). With urbanization and industrialization, structural specialization began to increase in American society, and media, especially magazines, reflected that reality. Specialization was becoming a primary characteristic of the magazine industry by the last quarter of the 19th century. Among the earliest popular sporting journals of the day and their date of inception were *Fur, Fin and Feather* (1868), *Game Fanciers' Journal* (1870), *American Sportsman* (1872), *Forest and Stream* (1873), *Chicago Field* (1874), *Appalachia* (1876), *Field and River* (1877), *Forest, Forge and Farm* (1880), *American Angler* (1881), and *Outing* (1882) (Mott, 1938a, pp. 210-211; see Estes, 1985).

Technological developments in presses, stereotyping, and engraving contributed to the magazines' development, as did a national dis-

Figure 1.3. A young Teddy.
Future president Theodore Roosevelt poses in hunting garb and gun in 1885. As a young man, Roosevelt bagged eight big-game trophy heads and was a founder of the influential Boone & Crockett Club. As president, he set aside thousands of acres of public land. From Library of Congress Presidential file. Reproduced from the Collections of the Library of Congress (No. 23232).

tribution system helped by more favorable postal rates, the rise of public libraries, and the growth of education. "The magazine industry became a mirror, reflecting all these changes, from the grandiose to the minute" (Tebbel & Zuckerman, 1991, p. 57). The total number of magazines published in the United States grew from 700 in 1865 to 1,200 in 1870 to 2,400 in 1880 and to 3,300 in 1885 (Tebbel & Zuckerman, 1991, p. 57). Of course, there was a high mortality rate.

Forest and Stream, a weekly based in New York City, was called "high class" and a "leader" by journalism historian Frank Luther Mott, who noted that the magazine was "active in founding the Audubon Society and wielded an important influence in game conservation reforms" (Mott, 1938a, p. 210). Mott's analysis was accurate but may have been somewhat understated.[8] Economic historian James Tober (1981) wrote that the "sportsman's ideology and public image were simultaneously created and reinforced" (p. 46) by the growing number of sporting journals, foremost of which was *Forest and Stream.*

Publishers and editors (especially when the same person filled those roles) sometimes leave their distinct worldview on their publications by force of personality. Such was the case with *Forest and Stream.* First published on August 14, 1873, Hallock founded *Forest and Stream* to produce a weekly journal on hunting, fishing, horse racing, shooting, and other outdoor activities.[9] Hallock (1834-1917) was the son of a well-known journalist, Gerard Hallock, and a descendant of Peter Hallock, one of the English pilgrims of 1640. Gerard Hallock joined the *Journal of Commerce* in 1828, copurchasing the paper from the Tappan family in 1831 (McKerns, 1989).[10] Gerard Hallock, a leader in operating harbor and overland expresses to speed news gathering, served as the first president of the New York Associated Press from its beginnings in the 1840s until his retirement in 1861. After his retirement, he managed extensive real estate holdings in the New Haven, Connecticut, area.

Charles Hallock attended Yale (1850-1851) and Amherst (1851-1852, 1870-1871), receiving an AB degree from the latter institution in 1871 (Johnson & Malone, 1946). His journalism career began in New Haven, where he served as an assistant editor for the *New Haven Register* from 1955 to 1956. He then joined his father at the *Journal of Commerce,* where he worked until his father's retirement in 1861. During the Civil War, Charles Hallock moved to Canada, where he worked as a broker in St. John, New Brunswick, and Halifax, Nova Scotia, also serving on the staff of the St. John *Telegraph and Courier.* After the war, Hallock returned to the United States to become financial editor of *Harper's Weekly* for 1 year.

Charles Hallock's involvement in the conservation movement preceded his establishing *Forest and Stream.* Hallock was one of the founders of the Blooming Grove Park Association of Pennsylvania, and he served as its first secretary for 2 years. Memberships sold for $450 per year, indicating a wealthy clientele. Blooming Grove, the first game preserve in the United States, was a pet project of members of high society in New York, including newspaper publisher Horace Greeley. Founded in 1871—a year before the establishment of the first national public park, Yellowstone—the private park contained 30,000 acres in Pike County divided into regions for the protection of breeding populations of certain species, including whitetailed deer (Foss, 1971, p. 8).

Blooming Grove struggled, however, and accusations of mismanagement appeared in sporting journals.[11] Whether Charles Hallock had anything to do with the alleged mismanagement of Blooming Grove is unclear, but similar claims were linked to him by the purchaser of his magazine when he sold *Forest and Stream* to George Bird Grinnell in 1879 (Reiger, 1972). After the sale, Hallock continued in the magazine business, serving as an editor of *Wildwood's Magazine, Nature's Realm,* and *Western Field and Stream.* In the meantime, he promoted a community in northwest Minnesota (advertised as a "Farm Colony for Sportsmen") that became the town of Hallock in 1880.[12]

Grinnell (1849-1938) (Figure 1.4) came from a wealthy and influential family in upper Manhattan. (There were five governors in the genealogical lines of his father, George Blake Grinnell, and mother, Helen Alvord Lansing Grinnell.) George Blake Grinnell was the head of a New York textile firm that suffered when the flow of raw materials from southern plantations ceased during the Civil War. The elder Grinnell, who worked in partnership with Cornelius Vanderbilt, dug his company out of debt, however, and was able to retire in 1873 at the age of 50 (Reiger, 1972).

Figure 1.4. Conservation crusader.
George Bird Grinnell, founder of the original Audubon clubs through the pages of *Forest and Stream* magazine, was a big-game hunter, friend of presidents, and held a PhD from Yale. Grinnell organized many of the first conservation groups and promoted them in his magazine. Reproduced from the Collection of the Library of Congress (No. 72116).

The Grinnell family grew up on 30 acres in Audubon Park, the former estate of the famous naturalist. The younger Grinnell shot muskrats on the Harlem River with Jack Audubon, grandson of John

James Audubon, and Lucy Bakewell Audubon, John's widow, tutored him in math. When George Bird Grinnell founded an early version of the Audubon Society, he named it for her as much as for her husband (Reiger, 1972, p. 22).

Educated under the famed scientist Othniel C. Marsh at Yale, where he received his BA in 1870 and his PhD in paleontology in 1880, the younger Grinnell was an explorer, big-game hunter, rancher, editor, author, ethnologist, naturalist, and conservationist. He made several trips West to collect fossils and to hunt elk and other animals in the early 1870s. He was a member of the Marsh expedition in 1870, General Philip Sheridan's 1874 trip, and the William Ludlow mission to survey Yellowstone National Park in 1875. George Custer invited Grinnell on his ill-fated Little Big Horn expedition, but the New Yorker declined because Custer would not allow time for Grinnell to collect fossils, and he continued his studies at Yale under Marsh (Reiger, 1972, pp. 124-125).[13] One of Grinnell's closest friends was Lonesome Charley Reynolds, Custer's chief scout, who was killed at Little Big Horn.

THE HALLOCK-GRINNELL SHIFT

An 1875 letter sent home illustrated the class-based view of the market hunters in the West George Bird Grinnell was developing. After seeing buffalo killed for their hides in Yellowstone, he wrote, "The general feeling of the better class of frontiersman, guides, hunters, and settlers, is strongly against those who are engaged in the work of butchery" (Reiger, 1972, p. 118).

At about the same time, back at the New York offices of *Forest and Stream,* Charles Hallock fired Ernest Ingersoll, the editor of *Forest and Stream's* natural history column, and asked Grinnell to take the job. Grinnell had been writing short hunting stories under the pen name of "Ornis" since 1873. Hallock emphasized to Grinnell that the magazine was an important "vehicle of information" and that its contributors and subscribers "are among the leading men of this country and parts of Europe" (as quoted in Reiger, 1972, p. 126). The editor-publisher agreed to let Grinnell finish his doctorate at Yale while working at the magazine for a salary of $10 per week.

Meanwhile, Grinnell's wealthy father had been buying up the magazine's stock for a few years and owned more than one third of its shares by 1879 (Reiger, 1972, pp. 126-127, 143).[14] When the younger Grinnell returned from a western trip in mid-1879, he found *Forest and Stream*'s offices nearing a boiling point. Hallock, Grinnell said, "had become more eccentric, drinking heavily, and neglecting his duties to the paper" (as quoted in Reiger, 1972, p. 126). The magazine's part-time treasurer and an important stockholder, E. R. Wilbur, disgusted with Hallock, forced him to resign. Meanwhile, Grinnell's doctors told the young man, suffering from headaches and insomnia while working for Marsh, to change occupations. Wilbur urged him to come to New York.

The sale of the magazine to the Grinnells was completed in a short time, with Hallock grudgingly selling all of his stock. At about the time of the sale, *Forest and Stream*'s subscription list contained approximately 10,000 names.[15] George Bird Grinnell said later, "We printed a good paper, had a large circulation, and began almost at once to make plenty of money. . . . But it took some little time to pay off the debts incurred in previous years" (as quoted in Diettert, 1992, p. 15). To help with the financial end of things, Grinnell appointed Wilbur as the firm's full-time treasurer and business manager.

After buying *Forest and Stream,* the 29-year-old Grinnell assumed control of the editorial side of the business. He published and edited *Forest and Stream* for 38 years. Four years after Grinnell left the magazine, it became a monthly. *Forest and Stream* merged with *Western Field and Stream* to form *Field & Stream* in 1930. Although perhaps best remembered as an author of several books on the life of American Indians, Grinnell had an important impact on conservation, primarily through his magazine, his cofounding of several sporting clubs, and his friendship with Teddy Roosevelt, with whom he coauthored three books. Grinnell's obituary in the *New York Times* called him the father of American conservation ("Dr. G. B. Grinnell," 1938). Biographer John Reiger wrote that Grinnell "consolidated the inchoate dissatisfaction among sportsmen with the rapid destruction of wildlife and habitat, and channeled it into a crusade to husband natural resources" (Reiger, 1972, p. 3).

Did Grinnell see a market for his purchase, or was he simply looking for something to do between western trips? The number of outdoor magazines established at the same time would seem to indicate a spot existed in the marketplace for such work. His investment was enhanced by the Postal Act of 1879, which gave second-class (and less expensive) mailing privileges to magazines. By 1890, publishing was a lucrative business because advertising dollars poured in from all sorts of businesses, particularly patent medicines (Tebbel & Zuckerman, 1991, p. 118). Making money may not have been Grinnell's primary motivation, however. His interest in what became called the conservation movement may have spurred his actions more than any possible financial gain.

THE MAGAZINE'S POSITION:
A SPOKESMAN FOR SPORTSMEN

Whether under Hallock and Grinnell, *Forest and Stream* continually echoed an elite view, promoting the English hunting ethic of restricted access to wild game at the expense of the traditional egalitarian American approach. The magazine targeted an elite audience and reinforced the notion that eastern, upper-class sportsmen knew what was best. The argument reflected the larger debate in society over the rapid growth of the industrial sector, the urbanization of the cities, and what to do with waves of immigrants. Economic conflict and political corruption marked a period when the middle class was growing in power. The old, aristocratic ways were being swept aside. That is, unless Hallock and Grinnell could prevent it.

English game laws written between the 14th century and the mid-1800s stated that only prominent citizens were allowed to possess certain weapons, to take game, and ultimately to eat certain animals (Lund, 1980, pp. 13-18). In 1874, *Forest and Stream* cited "the highest English authority" related to the "known fact that all the best measures for protection of game . . . must always emanate from those who shoot and fish for pleasure" ("Co-Operative Game," 1874, p. 74).

In sales appeals to advertisers, *Forest and Stream* emphasized its elite audience: "They are men who can afford to buy luxuries" ("Advertise," 1876, p. 345). The pitch to advertisers went on to say that the magazines' readers "are not a miscellaneous class" nor a part of the larger part of society that is "occupied with their avocation in their daily struggle for subsistence, and have no time or money for outdoor recreations and the gratification of natural tastes" ("Advertise," 1876, p. 345). As market hunters and game dealers were ascribed to lower classes of society, one way for them to escape to the middle class was to select another profession.

The magazines' rates reflected an elite audience appeal. At a time when the average nonfarm annual income was $450, *Forest and Stream* charged $5 for an annual subscription (or 10¢ per copy). Its advertising rates in 1873 were 25¢ per line (40¢ on an outside page). The first edition stated that the "object of this journal [is] to cultivate refined taste for natural objects" ("Announcement," 1873, p. 8). Surely the magazine numbered market hunters among its readers, who were looking for any information about wildlife. Market hunters also were advertisers, and their primary market was the eastern restaurants that served exotic wild game to an elite clientele.[16] Many market hunters sold their kill to middle managers called game dealers, who distributed the meat to restaurants and butcher shops.

Elite sportsmen, aided by the sporting journals, were much better at organizing than market hunters or game dealers. The pricing structure of the magazine encouraged mobilization. Sporting clubs received the magazine at a reduced subscription rate: three copies for $10 per year or five copies for $16 annually. A social use was apparent in the editor's notes and other editorial material. The first issue, for example, urged secretaries of clubs and associations to send in "brief notes of movements" or to purchase ads for announcements ("Announcement," 1873, p. 8). Each issue usually listed a calendar of events for the week for clubs in New York, Massachusetts, Pennsylvania, and other states.

The magazine contained responses to letters from readers almost every week but did not carry the letters themselves, so it is difficult to determine the exact view of the letter writers. The magazine often carried information on club meetings and organizational news in response to readers. For example, one such answer was given to a writer named David, who asked for more information on a rifle club in his area. He was directed to the secretary of the National Rifle Association in New York City ("Announcement," 1873, p. 9).

Outside the pages of the magazine, there were other indications of the social use of the journal. Many of the early rod and gun clubs were named in tribute to early wildlife enthusiasts like Audubon and Izaak Walton. At least one club was called the Forest and Stream club and another was named after Hallock (Tober, 1981, p. 50). The editor did his own mobilizing as well. In 1874, Hallock organized the International Association for Preservation of Game; the following year, he formulated a series of uniform game laws to be adopted by clubs (Johnson & Malone, 1946, p. 157). In 1878, Hallock published the first of two directories to aid communication between groups— *Hallock's American Club List and Sportsman's Glossary*. The author followed that book with *Hallock's Dog Fancier's Directory and Medical Guide* in 1880 (Johnson & Malone, 1946, p. 156).

Grinnell, in particular, was an organization man: He had his hand in the origination or the promotion of the most influential conservation groups of the day, including the Boone & Crockett Club, the American Ornithologists Union, and the forerunner of the Audubon Society. Within 2 years of Grinnell's founding of an early version of the Audubon Society, boosted by continuous mentions in the columns of his magazine, membership reached 50,000 (Graham, 1971, p. 32). The Society, however, lacked a strong centralized organization and resources. Grinnell and his staff found the club difficult to control. In 1888, Grinnell stopped mentioning the Society in the magazine in "self-defense" (Graham, 1971, p. 41). The group lost focus by 1889 but regrouped at the turn of the century in opposition to the feather trade.

Although it was consistently against market hunting in some of its editorial pages, *Forest and Stream* published weekly prices from New York game dealers from 1874 to 1876 and occasionally in other years. The magazine also carried advertisements from game dealers. Although *Forest and Stream*'s editors published game dealers' ads and quoted the weekly market rate for game, they continued to castigate the market hunters, printing long lists of huge kills and ridiculing or lamenting the results.

The weaponsmakers avoided mentioning killing in their advertisements and only mentioned the new technology occasionally. A Remington firearms advertisement typically emphasized the performance of Remington rifles in shooting matches and did not men-

tion wildlife at all. Barton, Alexander & Waller advertisements highlighted the new technology of the breechloaded double-barreled guns
in illustrations, but did not mention shooting, hunting, or wildlife.

One might assume that weapons manufacturers worried about
legislation of technology, and partly as a result de-emphasized killing of wild game and technology in their ads. There is some evidence
of limits placed on technology prior to 1873 and thus reason for the
weaponsmakers to fear such legislation.[17] An 1872 Maryland law
prohibiting vessels within one-half mile of shore in the waterfowl-
rich Chesapeake Bay also banned the use of swivel guns; users of
sink boxes had to pay a $20 annual fee; and sneakboats cost $5 per
year (Tober, 1981, p. 141).[18] Two years earlier, North Carolina had
prohibited the use of any gun "other than can be fired from the
shoulder" as well as construction of blinds, boxes, or batteries in any
waters away from shore.[19] Some market hunters experimented with
self-regulation; by common agreement on Chesapeake Bay, hunting
was limited to Mondays, Wednesdays, and Fridays "to keep huge
flocks from leaving the bay" (Kimball & Kimball, 1969, p. 8).

The weapons manufacturers knew their position was tenuous.
Armsmakers, such as Winchester, Remington, Smith and Wesson,
and U.S. Arms, recognized that,

> By their own technology they might eventually wipe out the wildlife
> on which their livelihood depended. Increasingly, their representa-
> tives could be heard among those calling for shorter gunning seasons
> and lower bag limits; but in no case would they assent to restrictions
> on "inventive genius." (Graham, 1971, pp. 183-184)

State fish commissions, established in the middle of the century,
served as a model for control of wildlife. *Forest and Stream,* however, began its crusade for regulations by insisting that states be
left out of the equation. Noting the prejudice that existed toward
English game laws in the United States, the journal "doubt[ed] very
much the efficacy in having state officials tend to these duties" ("A
Word," 1873, p. 88). Instead, the magazine asked for private citizens
to be paid from state funds (from a licensing plan) to guard private
property. When that idea failed to gain legitimacy, the magazine's
position changed and the editors supported state intervention. By
1875, the journal had a column titled "Game Protection," which

called for chief game commissioners appointed by the governor of each state ("Game Protection," 1875, p. 312).

Throughout the last quarter of the 19th century, *Forest and Stream* continued to lecture hunters on the "proper" way to kill game, which meant English methods. When one man shot several deer in July for food, the magazine criticized him for "killing game out of season" (though there were no government regulations on seasons) and "violating the laws of nature" ("Game in Season for September," 1873, p. 24).[20] The editors described the hunter as "one of the many who have helped within a few years to almost annihilate the game of the forest and stream of our northern wilderness" ("Game in Season for September," 1873, p. 24). The same edition urged other cultural changes on its readers, including asking hunters to "kill no bird unless it has a chance for its life on the wing and no four-footed game except in its season of health, and possessed of all the advantages which God has given it for escape" ("Game in Season for September," 1873, p. 24). The magazine concluded, "Against this waste we shall wage a constant war" ("Game in Season for September," 1873, p. 24). Faultfinding extended to politicians. When the governor of Missouri crossed into Kansas to shoot grouse "out of season," a writer asked, "Is there no grain of principle left in men?" ("Game in Season for September," 1873, p. 24). Hunting techniques were criticized as well. The common practice of killing deer after herding them into water by dogs upset the editors: "We hear of several deer being killed last week on Long Island . . . by members of the Southside Club . . . we regret that the animals were run into water by dogs" ("Game in Season for October," 1873, p. 170). In this way, the emotional and dramatic qualities of the magazine stories sought to reform their own readers (Figure 1.5).

Like other reform movements of the era, the goals of the sportsmen, if met, would not require them to change their own behavior. The sociologist Robert Merton called such activity "disinterested reform" (Merton & Nisbet, 1961). The magazine did not always condemn large kills but disapproved of the method and disposal of the game if it did not fit the English tradition. One issue listed the results of a contest held by the Potsdam Sporting Club (Table 1.4).

Those who shot the highest number of game received awards, a common practice of the time ("Pigeon Matches," 1879). Many of the

Figure 1.5. Sport hunters in the northern woods.
In 1880, a group of sport hunters posed in front of a collection of waterfowl and other game, some of it nailed to the side of a railroad car. Hunters such as these took advantage of plentiful wildlife and improvements in firearm technology to shoot huge quantities of game. Reproduced from Lee Bros./Minnesota Historical Society (No. 32035).

trap shoots at the gun clubs used passenger pigeons for targets (Kimball & Kimball, 1969, p. 80). When one reader asked about the difference between a "sports man" praised by the editors for his skill in killing 51 snipe in 90 minutes and a "pot [market] hunter" vilified for killing 21 quail in three shots, the magazine said the quail were scated and the snipe were flying ("The Sacrifice," 1884). The writer contradicted himself in the same issue when he said "we hear a great deal about the true sportsman, but it is the untrue sportsman who makes the biggest bags" ("The Sacrifice," 1884, p. 19). The creation of moral behavior—elite behavior—was a major goal of the publication. Hunting ethics and ideology were the issues. The ideology of the sportsmen emerged from a group that occupied a socially dominant role, although it (and its goals) were subject to pressures of the expanding industrial age.

Table 1.4 Reports of Game Killed by a Sportsman's Club in *Forest and Stream* in February 1879

Animal	Number Killed
Gray squirrels	34
Red squirrels	67
Chipmunks	1,372
Partridges	14
Crows	8
Ducks	1
Blue jays	13
Pigeons	3
Blackbirds	26
Meadowlark	1
Yellowhammer	1

Meanwhile, market hunters viewed sportsmen as less than ethical. One market hunter, H. Clay Merritt, felt sport hunting was inhumane and unethical "since it involved unnecessary slaughter for pleasure," whereas professional hunting was likened to farming (Kimball & Kimball, 1969, p. 78). Prior to the 1870s, American beliefs in common rights to wildlife were manifested in doctrines that rejected landowner claims of privilege and allowed free taking on private lands. Social position and land—two English qualifications for hunting—were considered inappropriate in the United States (Lund, 1980, p. 24).

By 1875, the magazine recognized the expanding markets for wild game in the eastern states and suggested a law prohibiting "exportation of game beyond the limits of states or provinces" ("Game Protection," 1875, p. 313), although even the writer doubted the constitutionality of such a law. Ten years later, New York City enacted a law restricting the amount of game to be sold by each dealer. When the dealers complained, the magazine said they were "no more sensible nor honest than they were in 1859" ("The Sale," 1885, p. 345). The magazine, noting disparities among regions and states, offered a model piece of legislation titled "Simplified Plan for Uniformity of Closed Season—Legislation Made Easy" ("Pigeon

Matches," 1879, p. 145). Finally, in 1894, Grinnell called for the total ban on the sale of wild game (Graham, 1971, p. 191).

Helping Grinnell in his crusade was the American Ornithological Union (AOU), founded in 1883 as a professional association of scientists studying birds. The AOU asked Congress to set up a new office to study birds, and Congress responded with a small appropriation for the Office of Economic Ornithology and Mammalogy, which would eventually become the U.S. Fish and Wildlife Service in the Department of the Interior.

REDEFINITION OF HUNTING

Forest and Stream's stand was unyielding. Readership increased and sportsmen began to mobilize with greater frequency. They exerted more power. Gradually, pressured by sportsmen in various statehouses and in line with the tone reflected in the magazine, states began to exert control over wildlife management. In 1887, the year Grinnell and Roosevelt founded the Boone & Crockett Club in New York, there were 47 bills introduced in the New York legislature dealing with wildlife regulations ("Game Protection," 1887). Ten years later, there were 97 such bills introduced ("Game Protection," 1897). The sportsmen urged regulations on sale, transportation, and storage of game, closed seasons, limited shooting hours, limits to hunting methods, protection of females and special access to landowners—all in the English tradition. In addition, states adopted statutes, including bag and possession limits[21] and hunting licenses (to pay for enforcement), that were peculiarly American.

Iowa enacted the first bag limit law in 1878. Home to one of the first Audubon clubs, the state limited hunters to 25 prairie chickens and other game birds per day. Wisconsin banned the hunting of deer with dogs in 1876, and Michigan limited the hunter to five deer per season in 1895. Many states, including Iowa in 1874, Arkansas in 1875, and Florida in 1877, although encouraging sport hunting, banned market hunting of some species altogether. California and New Hampshire set up game departments to regulate hunting in 1878, following the lead of Massachusetts. By 1911, 19 states had passed laws restricting the sale of game within their boundaries to varying degrees. Some regulations were too little, too late: Michigan enacted a 10-year closed season on elk in 1879; Wyoming passed a similar season on bison in 1890, after most of the species died out. One historian noted sarcastically, "It was a little like closing the season on saber-toothed cats" (Borland, 1975, p. 116).

Market hunters and sportsmen alike could take advantage of technological changes, but sportsmen were able to lobby for regulations limiting the hunt to their advantage, leaving their culture intact at the expense of market hunters. By 1901, 27 states banned big guns, swivel guns, or punt guns. Sixteen states limited the use of boats in waterfowl hunting, 22 states banned artificial lights, and 23 banned night hunting. Significantly, there were no regulations concerning sportsmen's guns, such as limiting the number of cartridges in a chamber or banning hand-held repeating weapons, or limitations on the caliber of bullets, which would have affected the market of the weapons manufacturers and the methods of hunting employed by sportsmen. The media legitimated certain uses of an invention (in this case, several weapons innovations) while condemning others, defining a pattern of ideas about how the weapons should be used and who should use them.

Lobbying efforts by the hunting groups, womens' clubs, and others succeeded in changing or creating federal law: The Lacey Act of 1900 banned interstate shipments of game taken in violation of state laws, which effectively put market hunters out of business. The Lacey Act may have been most effective on the illegal trade in plumed birds, but soon the federal government assumed a major role in wildlife management. The Federal Tariff Act of 1911 outlawed the importation of plumes of certain birds, and the Weeks-McLean Act of 1913 gave the Secretary of Agriculture power to regulate waterfowl seasons on the grounds that migration across state lines constituted interstate commerce. A treaty with Canada was followed by the Federal Migratory Bird Treaty Act of 1918, which made migratory birds the responsibility of the federal government because treaties took preference over state law. By the 1920s and 1930s, a persistent drought and more land use changes increased government intervention in wildfowl populations (Orsi, 1994). By the 1930s, game management was established in government and universities as a science (Dunlap, 1988, p. 37).

CONCLUSION

As the 19th century came to a close, most game populations continued to decline. By the late 20th century, wildlife management was the cultural norm and a central focus of the environmental movement; one hundred years previous, hunters were prevented from killing a certain species. By the 20th century, hunters needed permission to pursue a particular species of game, signaling a complete shift in thinking. On the other side of the conflict, market hunting ceased to exist in the United States by the middle of the century. In the Midwest, many of the market hunters became guides for wealthy sportsmen; on the East Coast, market hunters turned to crustaceans. Game dealers still functioned in a small wild fur trade, but much "wild" game was raised domestically for restaurants and other markets. Market hunting may seem wasteful, but part of the impact of market hunting may have been to illuminate the limits of wildlife populations, creating the idea of limits to growth that marks much of the modern discourse on the environment.

Specialty magazines usually preach to the choir, with the hopes of getting some in the congregation off their feet. They reach audiences with information and entertainment the audience wants to hear. *Forest and Stream* reinforced the English sportsman's culture regarding hunting ethics. The magazine targeted an elite audience, encouraged mobilization through its subscription and editorial policies, and ridiculed politicians and others who behaved in ways other than those it defined as sporting. There was a distinct role of social class in defining a particular view of hunting and the ensuing conflict. When the eastern elites practiced their hunting rituals in a certain way—for the purpose of sport—they clashed with the working-class midwesterners and southerners who viewed shooting game as a means to an end rather than an end in itself. At the same time, although the magazine played a socialization role in the conservation movement, the weaponsmakers supported the publications with advertisements, encouraged legislative limits on hunting ethics, and avoided any technological limits that would have restricted their markets.

In the case of hunting practices, as in most issues, a key event that shifted public thinking does not exist; rather, the media influence was gradual, over time, constructed by the continued reinforcement of one set of realities concerning the relationship of humans and wildlife. The role of the magazine and its editors was in defining and legitimating a new hunting ethic, along with mobilizing early conservationists, while delegitimizing a group of nonelites—market hunters. The sporting journals, which challenged the cultural assumptions of the freedom of the hunter (and, in a small way, freedom of private enterprise), established themselves in the marketplace and are now some of the oldest specialty publications in the magazine business.

The hunting controversy was an early environmental conflict—sportsmen versus market hunters—with larger forces, particularly changes in land use patterns and the weaponsmakers, at work ending market hunting as a profession. The only time market hunters could have existed was the mid- to late 19th century in the United States, when the factors of wild game, technology, market, and geography came together. Without game and certain geographic advantages, the equation fell apart. Hastening its demise was the role of the magazines, which not only reflected a change in the nature of leisure time activity but also provided a particular problem definition while serving as a socializing vehicle for upper-class hunters. Grinnell, Hallock, and other editors used the media to create and sustain conservation organizations and spread ideas. Although market hunting may have been doomed regardless, the style of hunting that replaced it was formed with the help of the early conservation movement and its publications. The social class battle was reflected in later green crusades, when the movement was criticized for being a middle- and upper-middle class collective, promoting issues at the expense of nonelites.

NOTES

1. Hays dealt with water, trees, and land—not wildlife. In his analysis, Hays did not mention the actions of hunters, which remains today a part of the movement and a source of conflict.

2. Market hunters had more impact in some state legislatures than others. Their legislative efforts focused on keeping the sale of game legal rather than hunting restrictions.

3. One distinctly North American hunting invention was the wooden duck decoy, developed by native tribes and adapted by market hunters. The decoys contrasted with the Old World custom of using live decoys. Among the more popular European techniques was to attach a long rope to a pigeon or other bird on a platform to attract others of the species—the "stool pigeon."

4. Battery boxes were almost completely submerged, with heavy iron decoys supported by canvas wings used for balance. Hunters would remain prone and rise to a seated position to fire. Punt guns or big guns, which weighed about 100 pounds, were used as weapons. Essentially, punt guns were small cannons, usually home-made from steam pipes, packed with 1.25 pounds of shot and a quarter pound of powder. Night guns were even larger—up to 150 pounds—and were said to be able to shoot 75 to 100 sleeping ducks at one blast.

5. Lower classes were prohibited from hunting in forest preserves by various local laws for many centuries before this.

6. "Hawking" was the practice of hunting with a bird of prey. One of the English hunting traditions that developed was the practice of not shooting females of the species. This probably stemmed from the earlier practice of training birds of prey to attack only males of the hunted species.

7. The magazine's full title was "Forest and Stream, a Weekly Journal Devoted to Field and Aquatic Sports, Practical and Natural History, Fish Culture, the Protection of Game, Preservation of Forests, and the Inculcation in Men and Women of a Healthy Interest in Outdoor Recreation and Study." Note the inclusion of women in the title.

8. Mott's exhaustive magazine history contains only one sentence on *Forest and Stream* and less than one page on sporting journals in general. Mott also erroneously states that George Bird Grinnell took over editorship of the magazine in 1885; Grinnell's personal papers establish the date at 1879.

9. As a circulation incentive during its first few months of publication, one of Hallock's books was offered to new subscribers. Hallock had published his first book, *The Recluse of Oconee,* when he was 20 years old.

10. Charles Hallock is not mentioned in any of the standard journalism reference biographies.

11. For example, *American Sportsman* (1874, p. 100) noted the poor conditions of the grounds, where "shooting is a farce and fishing is a sham."

12. Hallock raised $12,000 from eastern sportsmen for a hunting lodge-hotel on the St. Paul, Minneapolis and Manitoba Railroad with commitments from 600 members, but St. Paul railroad baron James J. Hill eventually froze out tourists after a dispute with Hallock. The journalist sought financial help from Hill's rival, Andrew Carnegie, but Carnegie refused. The sportsmen's hotel burned on Christmas Eve 1892, and there was no insurance. Hallock has been credited with making the first successful experiments in growing sunflowers for their oil product. For many years after he left *Forest and Stream,* he was engaged in field work and collecting specimens for the Smithsonian Institution. He died in Washington, DC, in 1919 at the age of 84 (see Hallock, 1913).

13. After his father retired, the younger Grinnell had dissolved the family business and went to Yale to work for Marsh.

14. Within the magazine itself, useful information on circulation and subscription numbers was published from time to time, particularly on December 12, 1878, April 11, 1878, and January 2, 1879. The circulation reports published in those

issues coincided with the time of the sale of the magazine from Charles Hallock to George Bird Grinnell, which may or may not have been coincidental.

15. The circulation figures cannot be certified as accurate in the days before auditing.

16. A significant question left for further research is how much financial support the magazine received from market hunters and game dealers.

17. Eventually, technology was legislated. For example, waterfowl hunters in the 20th century were limited to three shells per shotgun. High-powered rifles were banned in use for deer hunting in several states.

18. Sink boxes are holes dug in the ground in which the hunter stands, often covered with a camouflaged canvas tarp. Sneakboats, also called skullboats, ride extremely low in the water and operate as a floating sink box.

19. Tober (1981) noted that the law was amended in 1871 to exempt nonresident "sportsmen" who owned or leased land in North Carolina "and who do not kill game for a foreign market." In other words, wealthy members of North Carolina shooting clubs were exempt.

20. English hunters considered shooting a deer "in velvet" (before the breeding season) as unsporting.

21. A bag limit is the maximum amount of game that can be killed in one day. A possession limit (often double the bag limit) is the maximum amount of game one can have in his or her freezer.

2

MAINSTREAM MEDIA

The Radium Girls

ome social movements and organizations are better at mobilizing and communicating than others. As Max Weber would say, the production of ideas is not to be confused with their distribution. Some groups are too poor, unorganized, or otherwise disadvantaged to produce their own communication systems. Although the 19th-century hunters and anglers were helped by specialized publications—and powerful groups in society—other, less advantaged groups that dealt with environmental issues needed to wait until the mainstream media "discovered" their stories before they were able to effect any type of social change. The case of the Radium Girls is one example.

The Radium Girls lacked the union muscle or the political power to garner much media attention when they were stricken with radiation poisoning at their job; in fact, their lawyer did not seek media coverage, believing it to be harmful to his position. In addition, preconceived notions worked against the Radium Girls. Radium was seen by some as a miracle drug; if a few workers were martyrs to science, it was a small price to pay. Workplace hazards were not always defined as a social problem in the United States in the 1910s and 1920s, particularly if the workers were not organized in a union or represented by a political party. It was not until the Consumers League and a charismatic public health doctor named Alice Hamilton got involved that the Radium Girls attracted the attention of New York journalist Walter Lippmann, who wrote about the case of the sickened women in his newspaper. Lippmann was used by the league, Hamilton, and others to get the Radium Girls onto the public agenda; soon, Lippmann was able to use the judicial process as an accelerating agent for his stories.

GRACE FRYER

Grace Fryer and the other women at the radium factory in Orange, New Jersey, naturally supposed that they were not using anything poisonous. It was a little strange, Fryer said, that when she blew her nose, her handkerchief glowed in the dark. Everyone knew, however, that the stuff was harmless. The women even painted their nails and their teeth to surprise their boyfriends when the lights went out. They all had a good laugh, then got back to work, painting a glow-in-the-dark radium compound on the dials of watches, clocks, altimeters, and other instruments.

Grace started working in the spring of 1917 with 70 other women in a large, dusty room filled with long tables. Racks of dials waiting to be painted sat next to each woman's chair. They mixed glue, water, and radium powder into a glowing greenish-white paint and carefully applied it with a camel hair brush to the dial numbers. After a few strokes, the brushes would lose their shape, and the women could not paint accurately. "Our instructors told us to point them with our lips. . . . I think I pointed mine with my lips about six times

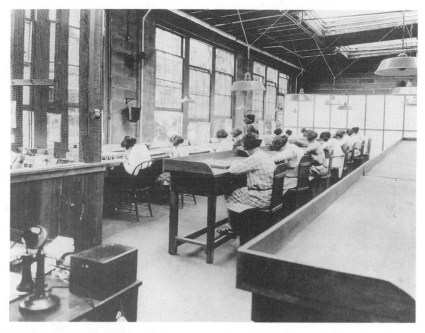

Figure 2.1. Radium Girls' workplace.
Radium dial painters worked in this shop at U.S. Radium Corp., in Orange, New Jersey. The photo was probably taken in the 1920s. The clock faces are visible in front of the woman at left. Reproduced from Argonne National Laboratory (No. 149-903).

to every watch dial. It didn't taste funny. It didn't have any taste, and I didn't know it was harmful" (Pfalzgray, 1928, p. 1) (Figure 2.1).

Nobody knew it was harmful except the owners of the U.S. Radium Corporation and scientists who were familiar with the effects of radium. In those days, most people thought radium was some kind of miracle elixir that could cure cancer and many other medical problems.

Grace quit the factory in 1920 for a better job as a bank teller. Approximately 2 years later, her teeth started falling out and her jaw developed a painful abscess. The hazel eyes that had charmed her friends now clouded with pain. She consulted a series of doctors, but none had seen a problem like it. X-ray photos of her mouth and back showed the development of a serious bone decay. Finally, in July 1925, one doctor suggested that the problems may have been caused by her former occupation.

As she began to investigate the possibility, Columbia University specialist Frederick Flynn, who said he was referred by friends, asked to examine her. The results, he believed, showed that her health was as good as his. A consultant who happened to be present emphatically agreed. Later, Fryer found out that this examination was part of a campaign of misinformation started by the U.S. Radium Corporation. The Columbia specialist was not licensed to practice medicine—he was an industrial toxicologist on contract with her former employer. The colleague had no medical training either—he was a vice president of U.S. Radium (*Fryer et al. v. U.S. Radium Corp.,* 1928).

Grace Fryer probably would have been another unknown victim of a bizarre new occupational disease if it had not been for an organization called the Consumers League and journalist Walter Lippmann, an editor with the *New York World.* Formed in 1899, the Consumers League fought for an end to child labor, a safe workplace, and minimum pay and decent working hours for women (Goldmark, 1953). Lippmann was a crusading journalist and former muckraker who represented a powerful New York newspaper at a time when New York newspapers were arguably the most influential in the country.

THE CONSUMERS LEAGUE

The request of a city health department official in Orange, New Jersey, brought the Consumers League into an investigation of the suspicious deaths of four radium factory workers between 1922 and 1924. The request was not unprecedented because league officials had been involved in many official state and federal investigations. The causes of death in the Orange cases were listed as phosphorous poisoning, mouth ulcers, and syphilis, but factory workers suspected that the dial painting ingredients had something to do with it.

New Jersey Consumers League chairman Katherine Wiley brought in a statistical expert and also contacted Alice Hamilton, a Harvard University authority on workers' health issues. Hamilton was on the league's national board and, as it turned out, she was already involved in another aspect of the same case. A few years earlier, a colleague at Harvard, physiology professor Cecil Drinker, had been asked to study the working conditions at U.S. Radium and report back to the company. Drinker found a heavily contaminated workforce, unusual blood conditions in virtually everyone, and advanced radium necrosis in several workers.

During the investigation, Drinker noticed that U.S. Radium's chemist, Edward Lehman, had serious lesions on his hands. When Drinker spoke to him about the danger in the careless and unprotected way he handled the radium, he "scoffed at the possibility of future damage. . . . This attitude was characteristic of those in authority throughout the plant. There seemed to be an utter lack of realization of the dangers inherent in the material which was being manufactured" (see "Blame Odd Deaths," 1925, p. 3). Lehman died a year later.

Drinker's June 1924 report recommended changes in procedures to protect the workers, but Arthur Roeder, president of U.S. Radium, resisted the suggestions. In correspondence with Drinker, Roeder raised several points that disputed the physiologist's findings and promised to send along facts to back up the assertions, which he never did. Roeder refused to give the Harvard professor permission to publish his findings about the new radium disease at the plant, insisting that Drinker had agreed to confidentiality. Eventually, U.S. Radium threatened legal action against Drinker.[1]

Roeder was also in correspondence with Wiley at the Consumers League. Wiley wanted U.S. Radium to pay some of the medical expenses for Grace Fryer and the other employees having problems. Roeder said that Fryer's condition had nothing to do with radium, saying it must be "phospho jaw or something very similar to it." He also accused Wiley of acting in bad faith, saying that a small amount of data from the company was shared with the league in confidence, and he claimed Wiley betrayed his confidence.[2]

In April 1925, Alice Hamilton wrote to Katherine R. Drinker, also a PhD and a partner with her husband Cecil in their U.S. Radium investigation. The letter, on Hull House stationery, stated,

> Mr. Roeder is not giving you and Dr. Drinker a very square deal. I had heard before that he tells everyone he is absolutely safe because he has a report from you exonerating him from any possible responsi-

bility in the illness of the girls, but now it looks as if he has gone still farther.... [The New Jersey Department of Labor] has a copy of your report and it shows that "every girl is in perfect condition." Do you suppose Roeder could do such a thing as to issue a forged report in your name?[3]

After this letter, Cecil Drinker realized why Roeder had been stalling him and trying to keep his report from being published. After the Hamilton letter, Drinker sent his original report to the Department of Labor and made arrangements to publish it in a scientific journal despite U.S. Radium's threats. While the Drinkers fought Roeder for permission over the data, a Consumer League consultant trumped the Drinkers by reading a radium necrosis paper at the American Medical Association conference (Hoffman, 1925).[4] The Drinkers finally published their paper later that year (Castle, Drinker, & Drinker, 1925), which concluded,

Dust samples collected in the workroom from various locations and from chairs not used by the workers were all luminous in the dark room. Their hair, faces, hands, arms, necks, the dresses, the under-clothes, even the corsets of the dial painters were luminous. One of the girls showed luminous spots on her legs and thighs. The back of another was luminous almost to the waist. (p. 373)

This casual attitude toward the green radium powder was not matched in other parts of the factory, especially the laboratory, in which chemists typically used lead screens, masks, and tongs. The company management, however, "in no way screened, protected or warned the dial painters," Fryer's attorney, Raymond Berry, charged (*Fryer et al. v. U.S. Radium Corp.,* 1927). The Radium Girls, like many other factory workers at the time, were expendable.

RADIUM'S DANGERS

The scientific and medical literature contained plenty of information about the hazards of radium. Even one of U.S. Radium's own publications, distributed to hospitals and doctors' offices, contained a section with dozens of references labeled "Radium Dangers—Injurious Effects." Some of the references dated back to 1906.

Figure 2.2. Dial painters' studio.
Radium dial painters worked on individual desks in a studio in Ottawa, Illinois. The clock dials are placed in crates next to the workers, and the radioactive radium paint is set on the tables in front of them. Reproduced from Argonne National Laboratory (No. 149-5074).

Despite the availability of information on the hazards of radium, it was often seen as a scientific miracle with enormous curative powers. The "radium craze" in America, which began around 1903, familiarized the public with the word radium. One historian stated, "The spectacular properties of this element and its envisioned uses were heralded without restraint in newspapers, magazines and books and by lecturers, poets, novelists, choreographers, bartenders, society matrons, croupiers, physicians and the United States government" (Badash, 1979, p. 25). Stomach cancer could be cured, it was imagined, by drinking a radium concoction that bathed the affected parts in "liquid sunshine" (Badash, 1979, p. 25). One of the medical drinks sold over the counter until 1931, "Radithor," contained enough radium to kill hundreds or possibly thousands of unsuspecting health enthusiasts who drank it regularly for several years ("A Most Valuable Accident," 1959, p. 49).[5] An overview of newspaper and magazine articles on radium in the first decades of the 20th century found their tone to be strongly positive (Weart, 1988) (Figure 2.2).

Even when hazards emerged in mainstream press coverage, the benefits usually outweighed the dangers. For instance, the death of

French scientist J. Bergonie in November 1924 provoked a spate of news articles extolling the "martyrs to science" who died experimenting with the element. The *New York World* counted 140 scientists who, like Bergonie, had given their lives for humanity. The sacrifice had been worthwhile, the newspaper stated ("Bergonie Is Latest," 1924; see also "Heroes," 1928, p. 2),

> Nowadays, tested precautions make the manipulation of radium or the use of x-rays as innocuous to both operator and patient as the pounding of a typewriter. . . . The exploration has cost many lives and untold agonies, but the martyrs would undoubtedly be the first to assert that the gain in knowledge had been worth the price. Both discoveries are now thoroughly established as safe, healing agencies of the utmost value. (Section II, p. 1)

Many scientists felt threatened by the idea that radium could cause, rather than cure, cancer. "If radium has unknown dangers, it might seriously injure the therapeutic use of radium," Charles Norris, chief medical examiner of New York, wrote Raymond Berry during Fryer's lawsuit.[6] An ore agent and former partner in U.S. Radium also wrote to Berry, "Thousands in Germany have been taking radium salts, admixed with bicarbonate of soda, as a vital stimulant." The bone afflictions of the Radium Girls were probably produced by the glue or another ingredient, but "radium could not produce the results ascribed to it."[7]

THE LAWSUIT

Although it meant flying in the face of some medical opinion, Grace Fryer decided to sue U.S. Radium, but it took her 2 years to find an attorney willing to take the case. On May 18, 1927, Raymond Berry, a young Newark attorney, took the case on contingency and filed a lawsuit in a New Jersey court on her behalf. Four other women with severe medical problems quickly joined the lawsuit. They were Edna Hussman, Katherine Schaub, and sisters Quinta McDonald and Albina Larice. Each asked for $250,000 in compensation for medical expenses and pain. The five eventually became known in newspaper articles carried in papers throughout the United States and Europe as "the Radium Girls."

The first legal hurdle was New Jersey's 2-year statute of limitations. Berry contended that the statute applied from the moment the women learned about the source of their problems, not from the date they quit working for U.S. Radium. Berry alleged that U.S. Radium's misrepresentation of scientific opinion and campaign of misinformation was the reason that the women were not informed and did not take legal action within the statute of limitations.

While Berry and the company skirmished in court, medical examiners from New Jersey and New York continued to investigate the suspicious deaths of plant workers. Amelia Maggia, a former dial painter and sister of two of the Radium Girls, McDonald and Larice, died in 1922 from what was said to be syphilis and was buried in Rosemont Cemetery in Orange. She had been treated by a New York dentist, Joseph P. Knef, who had removed Maggia's decayed jawbone some months before she died. Knef stated, "Before Miss Maggia's death I became suspicious that she might be suffering from some occupational disease" ("Exume Girls," 1927, p. 1). At first, he suspected phosphorous, which produced the notorious "phossy jaw" necrosis common among matchmakers in the early 18th century. Knef ("Exume Girls," 1927) stated,

> I asked the radium people for the formula of their compound, but this was refused. . . . After the girl's death so many other persons were sent to me with almost similar symptoms that I became more suspicious, and took up the study of radium with an expert. (p. 1)

In 1924, Knef wrapped the jawbone in unexposed dental film for a week and then developed the film. He also checked the bone with an electroscope to confirm its radioactivity and then wrote a paper with the Essex County medical examiner identifying radium necrosis (Martland, Conlon, & Knef, 1925). In the words of a Newark, New Jersey, newspaper, "Dr. Knef then described how radium, hailed as a boon to mankind in treatment of cancer and other diseases, becomes a subtle death-dealing menace" ("Exume Girls," 1927, p. 2).

An autopsy could confirm Knef's findings, and after a formal request by the Maggia sisters and Raymond Berry, Amelia's body was exhumed on October 16, 1927. An investigation confirmed that her bones were highly radioactive. Clearly, Maggia had not died of syphilis, but rather of the new and mysterious necrosis that was also killing her sisters.

THE MEDIA COVERAGE

Only after the case of the New Jersey women was legitimized in a courtroom setting—a formal structure for news gathering—did the larger media outlets pick up the story. They did so with a mix of sensationalism and muckraking, accelerating the issue. In the fall of 1927, an enterprising *Star Eagle* reporter found that U.S. Radium had reached out-of-court settlements with the families of other radium workers in 1926, paying a total of $13,000 in three cases ("Newark Pathologist," 1927).

Legal maneuvers filled 1927, and the medical condition of the five women worsened considerably. The two sisters were bedridden, and Grace Fryer had lost all of her teeth and could not sit up without the use of a back brace, much less walk. By the time of the first court hearing on January 11, 1928, the women could not raise their arms to take the oath. All five of the Radium Girls were dying.

"When pretty Grace Fryer took the witness stand, she said her health had been good until after she had been employed at the radium plant," one news account reported ("5 Women," 1928, p. 1). Fryer and the others bravely tried to keep smiling, but friends and spectators in the courtroom wept. Edna Hussman told the court about the financial troubles the medical bills were causing: "I cannot even keep my little home, our bungalow. . . . I know I will not live much longer, for now I cannot sleep at night for the pains" ("5 Women," 1928, p. 1). She was content, however, because her children would be cared for by relatives.

The news media suddenly found the story irresistible. Headlines included "Woman Awaiting Death Tells How Radium Poison Slowly, Painfully Kills" ("Woman Awaiting Death," 1928) and "Would You Die for Science? Some Would" ("Would You Die," 1928). The newspapers followed the twists and turns in the case, particularly the suffering of the women, the disappearing hope for a cure, and the company's defense. One of the macabre fascinations with the Radium Girls story was how—assuming the women won the lawsuit—one might spend a quarter million dollars with only a year to live. One enterprising newspaper asked 10 randomly selected women what they would do. Most of the responses involved spending sprees and charity donations ("Doomed to Die," 1928).

By April, the women were not physically or mentally able to attend a second hearing in court. Their attorney, Berry, was caustic, stating, "When you have heard that you are going to die, that there is no hope—and every newspaper you pick up prints what really amounts to your obituary—there is nothing else" (as quoted in Bedford, 1928, p. 1).

French scientist Marie Curie, the discoverer of radium, read about the case and told papers in her home country that she had never heard of anything like it, "not even in wartime when countless factories were employed in work dealing with radium." She stated that French radium workers used small sticks with cotton wadding rather than paintbrushes. Although the five New Jersey women could eat raw liver to help counteract the anemia-like effects of radiation sickness, they should not hope for a cure for radium poisoning. "I would be only too happy to give any aid that I could. . . . There is absolutely no means of destroying the substance once it enters the human body" ("Radium Poison Hopeless," 1926, p. 1). A local newspaper stated that Madame Curie had "affirmed the doom already sounded by leading medical authorities who have examined the girls." The predictable reaction, the paper said, was that "some of the victims were prostrated with grief last night when they received the news" (Bedford, 1928, p. 1).

Curie heard about the reaction and, on June 4, stated,

> I am not a doctor, so I cannot venture an opinion on whether the New Jersey girls will die. But from newspaper descriptions of the manner in which they worked, I think it imperative to change the method of using radium." ("Mme. Curie Urges Safety," 1928, p. 1)

Curie herself died of radium poisoning in 1934.

Time was running out, and Berry, Wiley, Hamilton, and others had long been concerned that legal maneuvering would delay justice until well after the women were dead. As anticipated, U.S. Radium did not hesitate to use delaying tactics. After the hearing on April 25, 1928, the Chancery court judge adjourned the case until September despite Berry's strenuous objections. Berry reminded the judge that the women were dying and might not live until September. Berry also found lawyers with cases scheduled in less than a month who were willing to take a September court date to give the Radium Girls their day in court. U.S. Radium attorneys, however, said that their own witnesses would not be available because many were going to Europe for the summer on vacation, and the judge insisted on continuing the case until September (Figure 2.3).

WALTER LIPPMANN
AND THE NEW YORK PRESS

The blizzard of publicity surrounding the case worried some medical consultants. One doctor wrote Berry, "Can you get the [newspapers] to agree to keep the women out of the paper henceforth? . . . We all agreed that this should be done and that the publicity has had a bad effect on the patients. One was quoted as seeing her body glow as she stood before a mirror."[8] Another doctor wrote, "I would certainly not like to have anything the matter with me and be told every few weeks that I was going to die. . . . Surely you realize what the psychological effect of that would be."[9] Berry protested, "I am absolutely unconnected, in any way, with newspaper articles which are published. I have endeavored to discourage publicity."[10]

Despite the general disdain for the press on the part of the plaintiffs, a moment arrived in the case when the Radium Girls needed a champion. Their physical condition was deteriorating and their financial situation was pitiful. Time was running out. Alice Hamilton had carefully laid out a strategy in the previous months with the editor of one of the nation's most powerful newspapers of the time, the *New York World*. An avowedly liberal newspaper founded by Joseph Pulitzer, the *World* championed public health causes as part of its mission to "never lack sympathy with the poor [and] always remain devoted to the public welfare" (*New York World*, May 19, 1928, p. 30).[11] Hamilton's long-time friend was *World* editor Walter

Figure 2.3. Five women from New Jersey.

The five Radium Girls stand before the barred doors of justice in this May 14, 1928, editorial cartoon from the *New York World*. Although they had only a few years to live, the former dial painters found their lawsuit delayed by court procedures and their former employer, the U.S. Radium Corp. Walter Lippmann called their situation "a damnable travesty of justice." ("Five Women Doomed," 1928, p. 28). Reproduced from Library of Congress/*New York World*.

Lippmann (Figure 2.4); Lippmann had already worked with Hamilton, ensuring that coverage of the ethyl leaded gasoline controversy in 1925 included both sides of the story, including large amounts of copy from university scientists critical of Standard Oil (Kovarik, 1993).

Hamilton had written to Lippmann in 1927 as she formulated strategy. She wrote, "There is a situation at present which seems to me to be in need of the sort of help which the World gave in the tetra-ethyl affair."[12] She got a response. Lippmann wrote to Berry, "Dr. Hamilton has asked The World to interest itself in this case and has told me that you have the necessary documents. I should appreciate it if you could let me see them."[13] When the judge continued the case until September, Lippmann stepped out of his normally cool and sober editorial pulpit. This, he stated in a May 10, 1928, editorial ("Five Women Doomed," 1928), was a

> damnable travesty of justice. . . . There is no possible excuse for such a delay. The women are dying. If ever a case called for prompt adjudication, it is the case of five crippled women who are fighting for a few miserable dollars to ease their last days on earth." (p. 28)

At this point, Frederick B. Flynn, the Columbia University consultant for U.S. Radium, called a press conference and proclaimed that the women could survive and that he found no radioactivity in his tests. Berry refused to comment, saying he would "prefer to try the case in court" ("5 Radium Victims," 1928, p. 1). Lippmann ("The Case of the Five Women," 1928) was furious:

> To dispute whether they can live four months or four years while lawyers wrangle over technicalities is to make the case more stupendously horrible than ever. The whole thing becomes a legal nightmare when in order to obtain justice five women have to go to court and prove that they are dying while lawyers and experts on the other side go to the newspapers to prove that they may live somewhat longer. (p. 23)

Noting that it was U.S. Radium that was holding up proceedings, Lippmann stated, "This is a heartless proceeding. It is unmanly, unjust and cruel. This is a case which calls not for fine-spun litigation but for simple, quick, direct justice" ("The Case of the Five Women," 1928, p. 23).

Figure 2.4. Walter Lippmann.
Editor of the *New York World* in the 1920s, Walter Lippmann was a close friend of activist and organizer Alice Hamilton. Lippmann and his newspaper covered worker and public health issues. Reproduced from the Collections of the Library of Congress (No. 43034).

Lippmann's editorials, Berry's maneuverings, the behind-the-scenes public relations work of Hamilton and others, and the accumulating outrage as represented in headlines convinced the New Jersey court system, and a trial was rescheduled for early June 1928.

Thousands of sympathy letters and quack remedies arrived at the women's homes and the office of their attorney. Inject tannin, said one. Drink Venecine health juice, said another. Drink "mazoon," an old world cure-all, said a third, but the author did not include the recipe for the potion. The *New York Graphic* wrote to offer the services of the famous nature healer Bernarr MacFadden in exchange for publicity rights:

> Since the medical doctors have given you up, you have nothing to lose and much to gain by trying natural methods. . . . Of course, we would expect you to be willing to cooperate with us to the fullest extent and to allow us to give full publicity to the case.[14]

THE SETTLEMENT AND ITS AFTERMATH

With Lippmann and the newspapers outraged and the legal system shifting in favor of the victims, pressure to settle the case built on U.S. Radium. In early June, a federal judge volunteered to mediate the dispute and help reach an out-of-court settlement. Days before the case was to go to trial, Berry and the five Radium Girls agreed that each would receive $10,000 and a $600 per year annuity while they lived, and that all medical and legal expenses incurred would also be paid by the company. The agreement also stipulated payment for all future medical expenses, which would be determined by an impartial panel of physicians.

Berry was not entirely happy with the settlement, feeling that "the corporation gets a great advantage," although he knew that the women's situation had grown desperate. He was also skeptical of the mediator, U.S. District Court Judge William Clark. "He is, I am sure, a very honorable man and genuinely interested in social problems, [but he is] a man whose circumstances in life place him in the employer's camp." Berry was informed that Judge Clark was a stockholder in the U.S. Radium Corporation.[15]

Meanwhile, the national president of the Consumers League, Florence Kelly, wrote to Alice Hamilton saying she was "haunted" by the "cold blooded murder in industry" that was taking place in the radium case. Kelly led other state chapters of the Consumers League in checking other radium dial plants, including those in Pennsylvania and Illinois.

Along with investigating other plants, Kelly and Hamilton agreed that another step needed to be taken. In a meeting in New York City, the medical examiners for New York and New Jersey sat down with Hamilton, Kelly, and Berry. The group agreed on a strategy for proposing a general conference on radium factory safety standards to Surgeon General Hugh Cumming of the U.S. Public Health Service. The medical examiners signed a letter proposing the conference, and the *New York World* supported it editorially. Kelly and her colleague, Josephine Goldmark, visited Lippmann, and Goldmark wrote the following account of the meeting (Goldmark, 1953):[16]

> The day we visited him in his small office high up in the dome of the old World building was not wholly propitious for detailing our plans. The political campaign of 1928 was in full swing and just at the moment when we reached his office, Mr. Lippmann, as I recollect it, was receiving the first wires from the Democratic National Convention in Chicago. He listened to us with interest, nevertheless, and promised his full aid as soon as the letter to the surgeon general had been sent. But he counseled delay . . . [as Kelly put it] Lippmann agreed to help us in every way possible, but warned us that we should injure our case if we attempted to present it publicly before July 4th, after the close of the second presidential convention. (p. 201)

All agreed to wait for Hamilton's signal, and Hamilton and Lippmann stayed in close contact during those weeks in July 1928. On July 16, as the letter went out, Lippmann wrote in an editorial, "In many aspects the disease is surrounded by mystery which only an expert, impartial and national agency can remove . . . clearly this is a task for the Public Health Service" (*New York World* as cited in Goldmark, 1953, p. 201).

Other endorsements followed, including one from Mrs. Franklin D. Roosevelt, a board member with Hamilton on the National Consumers League. Surgeon General Cumming agreed to the conference and called interested parties together on December 20, 1928.

The conference agreed that two committees should be set up: one to investigate existing conditions and a second to recommend the best known means of protection for workers. A U.S. Public Health Service official, James P. Leake, commended the Consumers League and others who had worked on behalf of public health and worker safety (as quoted in Goldmark, 1953), "By focusing public attention on some of these horrible examples . . . the broader problems of disease prevention . . . can be greatly reduced. It was so in the tetra-ethyl lead work. . . . The martyrdom of a few may save many" (p. 203).

CONCLUSION

The five Radium Girls died in the 1920s and 1930s. Their sad fate was sealed when they dipped paintbrushes into radium paint and sharpened the bristles with their mouths. There was a resistance to warnings about the dangers of radium in society—highlighting the importance in the relationship between ideas and social structure. In addition, radium was seen as part of the arena of science and medicine and, as such, enjoyed a certain legitimacy that made it almost beyond criticism. Science was seen as having all the answers, and people were reluctant to question it. It was not until Lippmann and other mainstream media outlets became involved in the story— and that involvement was accelerated by the legitimation of the legal system—that the Radium Girls finally settled their lawsuit, albeit for $10,000 plus—much less than the $250,000 they had hoped to receive.

The Consumers League and the news media as represented by Lippmann may have served the democratic process. Other dial painters from the era survived, and those who worked at radium paint factories in later years were better protected. Goldmark (1953) stated, "The hazards of another lethal industrial poison were over-come, and the democratic process of government by informed public opinion was again justified" (p. 204). The newspapers, with their preference for dramatic events, also served up the victims as part of a daily fare of murder, mayhem, and monstrosities. There exists an interesting parallel to the investigative journalism of later in the century. In the book *The Journalism of Outrage* (Protess et al., 1991), the authors note a "coalition building" process between journalists and government officials or interest groups or both in the 1980s. In one case, journalists from a Philadelphia newspaper coordinated their efforts with congressional staff from the very beginning of a project. The interactive nature of the process in the 1920s was evident when Walter Lippmann and Alice Hamilton used each other for their own ends. Lippmann's newspaper was considered "liberal" and catered to a working-class audience, which would appreciate a story such as the Radium Girls; Hamilton needed Lippmann and other journalists to meet her goals, including public awareness of workers' safety issues.

NOTES

1. Josiah Stryker to Cecil Drinker, June 20, 1925, Records of the National Consumers League, Raymond H. Berry files, Manuscript Division, Library of Congress, Washington, DC.

2. Arthur Roeder to Katherine Wiley, January 26, 1925, Records of the National Consumers League, Raymond H. Berry files, Manuscript Division, Library of Congress, Washington, DC.

3. Alice Hamilton to Cecil Drinker, April 4, 1925, Records of the National Consumers League, Raymond H. Berry files, Manuscript Division, Library of Congress, Washington, DC.

4. The first paper to identify radium necrosis was that of Theodore Blum (1924, p. 802).

5. Each bottle contained two picocuries of radium.

6. Charles Norris to Raymond Berry, June 7, 1928, Records of the National Consumers League, Raymond H. Berry files, Manuscript Division, Library of Congress, Washington, DC.

7. Thomas F. V. Curran to Quinta McDonald, May 24, 1928; Thomas F. V. Curran to Raymond Berry, May 21, 1928, Records of the National Consumers League, Raymond H. Berry files, Manuscript Division, Library of Congress, Washington, DC.

8. E. B. Krumbhaar to Raymond Berry, undated (probably June 17, 1929), Records of the National Consumers League, Raymond H. Berry files, Manuscript Division, Library of Congress, Washington, DC.

9. Robert E. Humphries to Raymond Berry, October 26, 1929, Records of the National Consumers League, Raymond H. Berry files, Manuscript Division, Library of Congress, Washington, DC.

10. Raymond Berry to James Ewing, June 6, 1929, Records of the National Consumers League, Raymond H. Berry files, Manuscript Division, Library of Congress, Washington, DC.

11. The paper's motto was carried in a box called a "Masthead" on the editorial page in all issues.

12. Alice Hamilton to Walter Lippmann, July 12, 1927, Box 12, Folder 496, Lippmann Collection, Yale University Library, New Haven, CT.

13. Walter Lippmann to Raymond Berry, July 18, 1927, Records of the National Consumers League, Raymond H. Berry files, Manuscript Division, Library of Congress, Washington, DC.

14. Various letters to Raymond Berry, including P. J. Leach, Advice Department, *New York Graphic,* to Raymond Berry, May 28, 1928, Records of the National Consumers League, Raymond H. Berry files, Manuscript Division, Library of Congress, Washington, DC.

15. Raymond Berry to Cecil Drinker, June 6, 1928, Records of the National Consumers League, Raymond H. Berry files, Manuscript Division, Library of Congress, Washington, DC.

16. Alice Hamilton to Cecil Drinker, June 19, 1928, Records of the National Consumers League, Raymond H. Berry files, Manuscript Division, Library of Congress, Washington, DC.

3

THE MEDIA AND
SOCIAL CHANGE

I. Mother of the Forest

he national park system of the United States, created in the latter part of the 19th century and institutionalized in the 1910s, may be seen as social change. In the late 1800s, the creation of federally controlled parks was part of a product of a new public perception about land and, additionally, the efforts of an alliance of business elites and government. In one sense, the park system—places away from the cities and (mostly) unchanged by human hands—was a societal response to the conflicts inherent in industrialization, urbanization, and the closing of the frontier in the 19th century. These structural influences on American society supported the notion of a system of national parks. The idea of the federal government withholding land from private development became ingrained into the system after a coalition of environmental groups, mainstream and specialized media, and powerful national business groups worked for its passage. In opposition stood some local business groups and the newspapers that represented them—groups that were not necessarily opposed to the idea of a park but wanted the land kept under local control. Such controversies flared up again in the mid-1990s debate in Washington, DC, over returning some federal power over natural resources to state and local governments.

The national park system is one prominent example of the type of social change that may occur when the mainstream media, powerful business and political groups, and the environmental movement are functioning together to control the direction of change. The question was twofold: what to do about wild and unusual lands and how best to cope with the loss of the frontier. One answer was to preserve some of it, eventually placing it in the bureaucratic structure and centralizing control at the federal level.

MOTHER

In the middle of the 19th century, many citizens of the United States knew California meant one word—gold. The discovery of nuggets in a creek near Sutter's Mill in 1849 and the rush of miners, businessmen, laborers, scalawags, hustlers, tinhorns, and journalists thrust the new state into the country's consciousness with the fever carried by precious metal. News accounts highlighted gold strikes, outrageous claims, and great fortunes made and lost. Back East, at the center of power, these news reports were important because a trip to California for a firsthand look was difficult at best and life threatening at worst. The country was a couple of decades away from transcontinental railroads: An overland passage could take 4 months or more and remained full of hardships; the sea route around South America was faster but risky and expensive.

In the 1850s, Americans learned about California through the pages of newspapers and magazines. A businessman named George

Gale and his partners provided the nation with its first big news story from California after the gold rush. In the process, Gale and his companions inadvertently assisted the forces that led to the protection of the natural wonders of the Sierra Nevada mountain range. Gale's vaudevillian stunt (Figure 3.1), which received press attention in the United States and Europe, has since slipped into the forgotten pages of history, but its by-product, the national park system, lives on.

The story begins in 1852 when miners looking for another lode in the boom-and-bust cycle of their existence stumbled across a grove of giant trees in a remote mountainous area in Calaveras County in northern California. In a moment of unimaginative nomenclature, the miners named the area the Calaveras Grove of Big Trees. Native American tribes knew of the region, of course, and white hunters saw the Calaveras giant trees in 1850. The Sierra region had received local publicity in 1851 when a battalion under trader James Savage invaded a valley south of Calaveras in Mariposa County and got into a skirmish with a tribe of Indians, the Ahwahnechee. Savage accused the tribe of raiding his trading posts and he and his men burned out the Indians, who escaped under the leadership of a brave named Tenaya. A surgeon in the battalion, Lafayette Bunnell, took time from his duties to serve as a diarist for the trip, and he remembered the scenery. Several years later, he wrote, "It seemed to me I had entered God's holiest temple, where that assembled all that was most divine in material creation" (Bunnell, 1890, p. 796). A second expedition, under John Boling, caught up with Tenaya and his band in May of 1851 and killed one of Tenaya's three sons. The following spring, the Indians attacked a group of miners, killing two. The regular army invaded the valley, killing five captive Indians (Runte, 1990, p. 11).[1] Newspaper stories of the battles in the valley, which was called by the Indian name Yo-Semite, did not travel beyond California. Meanwhile, rumors of a second grove of giant trees near Yo-Semite, bigger and more numerous than the Calaveras Big Grove, circulated among the local population.

As word of the huge trees in Calaveras County spread among folks scratching out a living in the region east of San Francisco, among those who rode out for a look was Gale. Some 20 or 30 miles from the mouth of the Klamath River, Gale stumbled into the grove. Among

Figure 3.1. Mother of the Forest.
An artist for *Harper's Weekly* drew this interpretation of George Gale and his workers cutting down the giant sequoia tree Mother of the Forest in the Calaveras Grove of Big Trees in 1852. The tree was 325 feet high and more than 2,500 years old and toured the East Coast and Europe, but its felling caused an uproar. Reproduced from the University of Minnesota.

the 92 giant sequoias in the 160-acre valley, Gale saw what he mistakenly thought was a cedar tree—not just a backyard cedar, but a tree measuring 300 feet high, 92 feet in circumference at the ground, and perfectly symmetrical from base to top. He called it "the Mother of the Forest" and sent to town for a team of five men to chop it down.

Gale was not a lumberjack, nor did he own a sawmill or a lumberyard. He was about to become involved in show business, and in the tree he saw the biggest attraction of his career. The Mother of the Forest, however, did not die easily. After Gale's men bored holes through the trunk of the giant sequoia with a long auger, they worked saw blades from one hole to the next. The sawyers, cautious of a 300-foot tree falling on them without notice, continued with great care. The five men worked 25 days to complete the task. According to one account of the event, the tree was so "straight and balanced" that it remained upright, even after it was sawed completely through. Wedges were forced into the cut with hammers and sledges; the trunk was smashed by a crude battering ram fashioned from nearby lumber, but the Mother of the Forest did not topple.

Not until a wicked gale blew up, in the dead of night, did the tree begin to "groan and sway in the storm like an expiring giant and it succumbed at last to the elements" ("The Big Trees," 1858, p. 372). Sounds of the crash of the giant sequoia carried 15 miles away to a mining camp; the tree buried itself 12 feet deep into the muck of a creekbed. Mud from the creek splashed 100 feet high onto the trunks of nearby trees. Later, forestry experts in the East estimated that the sequoia tree was 2,520 years old.

Gale's men stripped most of the bark—which was 2 feet thick in places—in sections so it could be pieced together like a grainy jigsaw puzzle for display in the sideshow. Reassembled, the bark section was 50 feet high, 30 feet in diameter, and 90 feet in circumference. Another portion of the tree was cut across the diameter, showing rings representing forest fires, drought, and rainy seasons over the previous 2½ millennia. Stripping of the bark was done "with as much neatness and industry as a troop of jackals would display in cleaning the bones of a dead lion" ("The Big Trees," 1858, p. 357). The rest was left to rot. The tree was so immense—and stored enough water in its system—that 5 years passed before its leaves turned brown and died. Gale shipped the bark to Stockton, on its way to San

Francisco, then to the Atlantic states and finally to London, to be seen "for a trifling admission fee" ("An Immense Tree," 1853, p. 217).

Sadly for Gale and his partners, reaction to the tree was of two kinds, and both doomed the sideshow. Citizens either thought the bark to be a fake, or, more surprisingly, were hostile to the killing of what was billed the largest tree in the world. The editors of *Gleason's Pictorial,* a widely read magazine published in Boston, stated, "To our mind, it seems a cruel idea, a perfect desecration, to cut down such a splendid tree . . . what in the world could have possessed any mortal to embark in such a speculation with this mountain of wood?" ("An Immense Tree," 1853, p. 217). Europeans cherish such trees, the editors said, and protect them by law. They hoped that two other American natural wonders, Niagara Falls and Kentucky's Mammoth Cave, would be safe from purchase and exploitation, and wryly asserted that the cave "is comparatively safe, being underground" ("An Immense Tree," 1853, p. 217). New York newspaperman Horace Greeley (1860/1964), after visiting the region a few years later, wrote,

> It is a comfort to know that the vandals who bore down with pump augers the largest of the Calaveras trees, in order to make their fortunes by exhibiting a section of its bark at the east, have been heavy losers by their villainous speculation. (p. 267)

Economic speculation in the Calaveras Grove did not end with the bark exhibition, however. Another entrepreneur, seeing a tourist opportunity in the rugged hills 240 miles from San Francisco, built a hotel next to Mother of the Forest. The Mammoth Tree Hotel opened for business in 1855, with dances and theatrical performances held on Mother's stump. Several dozen feet of the fallen tree's surface were shaved flat; a tavern and two bowling alleys, complete with 81-foot lanes, were built on the leveled area and soon were ready for customers ("The Big Trees," 1858). Tourists also traveled to another, larger tree in the grove called Father of the Forest that had died a natural death many years earlier; its corpse ran along the ground for 450 feet and, after a rain, held a pond in its trunk deep enough to hold a steamboat.

The publicity surely stimulated interest in the natural wonders of California. Historian Hans Huth said vandalism such as the killing of the Mother of the Forest caused easterners to ponder their duty to protect nature (Huth, 1948, p. 27). A more recent environmental historian, Donald Worster (1977), insightfully argued that ecological thought reflected not just discoveries (such as the Mother of the Forest) but the specific cultural conditions in which those discoveries arose. For example, the excitement caused by the felling of the giant tree caught the attention of one of the country's most popular philosophers and poets, James Russell Lowell. In an article for *The Spectator,* reprinted in other publications, the well-known social critic called for a society for the protection of trees. Lowell (1857) wrote, "The American seems to have an hereditary antipathy to Indians and trees, both having been the foes he had to first encounter in conquering himself a home here in the West" (p. 96). Lowell, who had succeeded Henry Wadsworth Longfellow as chair of modern languages at Harvard, wanted trees to be left alone, free of the interference of sideshow huckster and government forester alike. He wrote, "That is the best government for trees which governs least. . . . Nature knows better than any city forester" (Lowell, 1857, p. 96). Lowell's dislike of government foresters prevented him from extending his minimal interference notion to the idea of state protection. The idea had been on the books as early as 1817 in the United States, when the Secretary of Navy was authorized to reserve lands producing oak and cedar for the purpose of supplying lumber for ships (Muir, 1991, p. 255).

In 1864, 11 years after Gale felled the Mother of the Forest and 7 years after Lowell's call for a tree protection society, the federal government granted the State of California an area of about 8 square miles to be used as a park several miles south of the Calaveras Grove of Big Trees. Ironically, the Calaveras Grove of Big Trees was left out of the protected area, even after all the attention it received in the popular press.[2] The new park was in Yosemite Valley, which was home to more giant trees—the Mariposa Grove of Big Trees—in addition to spectacular and unusual granite formations, delicate waterfalls, and scenery unlike any other in the world. The process of making Yosemite Valley a park, which began with the discovery of the Mother of the Forest, worked its way through the political arena with unusual speed. Yosemite Valley provided a model for a new kind of land use—a state park—which was to be joined by another model—a federal park—at Yellowstone 8 years later.

SEEDS OF THE PRESERVATION IDEA

If one uses the works of writers such as James Russell Lowell as evidence, the seeds of environmental thought in the United States were in place by the end of the Civil War. Two of Lowell's contemporaries, Ralph Waldo Emerson and Henry David Thoreau, played critical roles in influencing the early environmental movement. Both had written and circulated significant works on the appreciation of nature before the end of the Civil War. Emerson (1883) wrote of the outdoors in 1836, "In the wilderness, I find something more dear and connate than in the streets or villages. . . . In the woods we return to reason and faith" (pp. 15-16). Thoreau (1950) was more specific in his writings, particularly in his private correspondence:

> National preserves, in which the bear, and the panther, and some even of the hunter race may still exist, and may not be civilized off the face of the earth—not for idle sport or food, but for inspiration and our own true revelation. (p. 51)

Thoreau's *Walden,* published in 1854, became a significant text for environmentalists in the 20th century.

Whereas Thoreau and Emerson were writers first and foremost, Lowell later served as ambassador to England and to Spain. His political interests were shared by George Perkins Marsh, a Vermont lawyer, U.S. representative, and ambassador to Italy. In 1864, near the end of his career, Marsh wrote a book titled *Man and Nature; or, Physical Geography as Modified by Human Condition.* In the book, Marsh (1864) said of the human condition, "The earth is fast becoming an unfit home for its noblest inhabitant" (p. 35). Furthermore, Marsh noted the need to preserve "American soil . . . as far as possible, in its primitive condition" (p. 228). A preserve could be "a garden for the recreation for the lover of nature" (p. 235). The national trend was in the other direction, however, as laws such as the Homestead Act of 1862 virtually gave land away to anyone with a small bank account and a desire to make a go of it on the frontier. Unscrupulous developers used the law to snatch large plots of land and resell them at enormous profits (Smith, 1950, pp. 168-173; see also Findley & Farber, 1988, pp. 335-336).

Although Lowell, Marsh, and Thoreau were aware of the western half of the nation, their personal lives did not include extended stays in the vast areas of the frontier. The task of conveying firsthand experiences of the West fell to explorers and storytellers such as Daniel Boone (through his biographer, John Filson), Osbourne Russell, Francis Parkman, and John Wesley Powell. Artists such as George Catlin worked in the Mississippi Valley from the 1830s; some historians credit Catlin with originating the preservation idea in 1833, although it is not clear whether he intended a protected reservation to be home for Indian tribes or as a national park for preserving nature.

A major in the Army who lost an arm at the Battle of Shiloh, Powell is probably most well-known for his 1869 rafting expedition down the Colorado River through the Grand Canyon. Magazines and newspapers of the day carried accounts of the expedition, including articles written by Powell. He later became familiar to readers of *Scribner's Monthly* after a series of his stories appeared in 1874 and 1875. Other writers contributed to and reflected the national mood. Popular fiction writer John Burroughs's first nature essay, "With the Birds," appeared in the *Atlantic Monthly* in 1865, with many more stories to follow until his death in 1919. By 1880, a writer for *Harper's* said that parts of the Rocky Mountains were becoming too popular with the press, crowded with visitors, and immodestly advertised (Hayes, 1880).

On March 1, 1872, President Ulysses S Grant signed into law an act designating more than 2 million acres of what is now northwestern Wyoming and parts of Idaho and Montana as Yellowstone National Park. In the words of national park historian John Ise, Yellowstone was "so dramatic a departure from the general public land policy of Congress that it seemed almost a miracle" (Ise, 1961, p. 17). Prior to the creation of Yellowstone, there had been two other instances of U.S. governmental protection of wild or unusual lands.

The first case came in 1832 with the establishment of the Arkansas Hot Springs as what was called a national reservation. Clearly, the rejuvenating waters of Hot Springs were saved not as a park, but because they were "thought to be valuable in the treatment of certain ailments" (Ise, 1961, p. 13). The second instance was the state model at Yosemite Valley.

THE YOSEMITE MODEL

On May 17, 1864, Congress enacted legislation that withdrew two tracts of land in Mariposa County from the public domain and transferred them to the State of California. Congressmen were familiar with the Yosemite region, having had the opportunity to read several accounts of the area in eastern newspapers after the stir caused by the Mother of the Forest exhibition in the 1850s and subsequent visits by leading eastern newspapermen. In 1856, a New York magazine, *The Country Gentleman,* reprinted an article from a California journal extolling the natural beauty of the Yosemite region, "the most striking natural wonder on the Pacific" (*The Country Gentleman,* 1856, p. 43). Other California publications wrote of the area and, in the manner of the day, eastern newspapers and magazines excerpted bits and pieces of the articles. Artists, including Thomas A. Ayres, a Californian whose lithographs toured the East, visited Yosemite. A travel guide published in 1857 included a brief section on Yosemite Valley.

One newspaperman who legitimized the idea of Yosemite Valley as a paradise worthy of protection by the state was Horace Greeley (Figure 3.2). The *New York Tribune* publisher and editor, well-known for extolling the virtues of the American West, visited the area in a highly publicized trip in the summer of 1859. Many historians mention Greeley's trip as a key event in the protection of the area, but an examination of the popular editor's notes shows a somewhat less glamorous experience than the myth that grew out of it.

Starting out from Sacramento, Greeley and his companions took the stage to Stockton, where they rested before a 75-mile carriage ride to Bear Valley in heavy August heat. As they bumped their way into the mountains, the group crossed the waters of the Stanislaus,

Figure 3.2. Horace Greeley, editor of the *New York Tribune.*
Horace Greeley was one of the most well-known and influential eastern newspapermen who supported the idea of land conservation. His brief trip to Yosemite and his account of the journey contributed to the national debate on preservation of the area. Reproduced from the Collections of the Library of Congress (No. 26716).

Tuolumne, and Merced rivers, all rendered a churlish brown by the mining operations in the hills. Over the objections of the natives, Greeley left Bear Valley for Yosemite at 6 a.m. on an arduous horse-back trip (in a saddle with a Mexican stirrup that was too small for his left foot) "not having spent five hours on horseback . . . within the last 30 years" (Greeley, 1964, p. 254). His guide was Hank Monk, whom Mark Twain later highlighted in his book, *Roughing It,* for his hell-bent and hurried pace (Twain, 1913, pp. 161-162).

The middle-aged editor made the entire trip in a single day but did not arrive in the valley until long after dark "riding the hardest trotting horse in America" (Greeley, 1964, p. 259). The bad stirrup caused his foot to swell, making walking impossible, so he had to remain on horseback in the roughest terrain while other members of the party led their horses. The descent into the valley on the 3-mile-long, steep, single-file trail took 2 hours under moonlight. Reaching a cabin after 1 a.m., Greeley went to bed without food or drink. Covered with boils from the trip, he estimated he had ridden 60 miles and climbed and descended 20,000 feet.

Greeley, stiff with age and travel, arose "early," rode into the valley, dined at 2 o'clock, and left. Despite the brevity and hardship of his visit, the journalist was unsparing in his praise of the region: "I know of no single wonder of nature on earth which can claim superiority over Yosemite" (Greeley, 1964, p. 262). He called on the State of California to protect the big trees, "the most beautiful trees on earth. [The mountains] surpass any other mountains I saw in the wealth and grace of their trees" (Greeley, 1964, p. 257).[3]

The eastern newspapermen, writers, and artists initiated a some-times uneasy business-intellectual union that continued in environ-mental issues through the 20th century. Beyond being a journalist, Greeley represented the major eastern business establishment and saw economic possibilities in westward expansion and land and mineral development. Many people, including other journalists, noted his reports in the New York newspaper. The next significant publicity Yosemite received came from the pen of Thomas Starr King, a well-known eastern author and journalist who had moved to San Francisco in 1860. Starr King wrote a series of eight articles from December 1860 to February 1861 for the *Boston Evening Transcript.* Starr King's articles, which were intended to be reprinted as a book, were full of lavish descriptions of the region and its wonders, includ-ing the sequoias, the mountains, and the valley. Starr King died in 1864 and was remembered as a champion of the region. One of the giant sequoias, measuring 366 feet tall, was named after him.

Media coverage made many, including some members of Congress, aware of the unique nature of the Sierra region. Senator John Conness of California introduced a bill to protect the Yosemite Valley in March of 1864 (S. Res. 203, 1864, p. 1310; Cong. Rec., 1864, p. 2300). President Lincoln signed the measure in June. There is little recorded debate over the measure, leaving an aura of mystery surrounding the process. One congressman asked Conness about the size of the property, and he was told the Mariposa Big Tree Area, as it was called, was "about a mile" (Cong. Rec., 1864, p. 2300). Conness also said that "certain gentlemen in California, gentlemen of fortune, of taste, of refinement" (Cong. Rec., 1864, p. 2301) suggested the bill to him. Conness did not name the gentlemen, but it is likely that state geologist J. D. Whitney, Judge Stephen Field, Professor John F. Morse, businessman Israel Ward Raymond, and landscape architect Frederick Law Olmsted (designer of New York's Central Park) were among them (Huth, 1948, pp. 29-31). During the debate, the senator recalled the death of the Mother of the Forest, and he was clear in his intent to protect the trees: "The object of this bill is to prevent their being cut down or destroyed" (Cong. Rec., 1864, p. 2301).

Historians have debated how and why the national parks were created, but the establishment of each park should be examined in its own social and cultural context. Certainly, the increase in leisure time in society after the mid-19th century played a role in the development of some parks, including Yosemite Valley, which did not appear to have much economic use in an agricultural or mineral sense. Preserving the unusual big trees and other unique scenery was another factor. Historian Alfred Runte said Congress protected only "economically worthless" lands—or lands Congress believed to be economically worthless—and the source of this belief may have been park supporters, who may have seen it as a way to get legislation passed amid the unbridled capitalism of the 19th century (Runte, 1979). Why the Yosemite land was deeded to the state is another matter of speculation. In the end, the deeding may have been judicious. Perhaps the lax enforcement and loose provisions of federal land laws would have made it easier for homesteaders and land speculators to snatch pieces of Yosemite property. The grant was given "upon the express conditions that the premises shall be held for public use, resort and recreation and shall be held inalienable for all times" (Cong. Rec., 1864, p. 2300).

The formation of the park increased the public's interest in the area. After Lincoln signed the bill, *Springfield Republican* editor Samuel Bowles and noted war correspondent Albert B. Richardson of the *New York Tribune* were in a parade of journalists who journeyed to Yosemite. Bowles and Richardson visited the area with Speaker of the House of Representatives Schuyler Colfax and 18 people during 4 days in August of 1865. On seeing the region for the first time, Bowles (1865) wrote, "All that was mortal shrank back, all that was immortal swept to the front and bent down in awe" (p. 223). The visitors saw an area home to nine species of pine, two species of silver fur, and five other conifer species, plus oaks, maples, poplars, and others. Olmsted, the first commissioner of the park, was seeking more state funds for the valley, and Bowles wrote in support of the park idea. Yosemite, he stated, "furnishes an admirable example for other objects of natural curiosity and popular interest all over the Union" (Bowles, 1865, p. 231). The park idea was popular. Bowles reported the number of visitors to the valley grew to 300 in the first 7 months of 1865, up from 100 for all of 1864.[4] The journalist suggested similar state government protection for Niagara Falls, the Adirondacks, and a Maine lake and its surrounding woods. Richardson echoed those sentiments in a report published on the trip in 1867.

THE YELLOWSTONE MODEL

In the Reconstruction years, laissez-faire economics represented the dominant ideational model as the country underwent an unprecedented period of business and industrial growth. Technological innovations in communication and transportation were making the nation known and conquered. Unrestricted competition was the rule of the day. With the completion of the Union Pacific Railroad in 1869, the West and all of its natural resources—for ranching, mining, timber, and farming—opened on a gigantic scale. Furthermore, progress became "synonymous with growth, development and the conquest of nature. The idea of living . . . harmoniously with nature was incompatible with 19th century American priorities" (Nash, 1989, p. 35; see also Marx, 1970).

The protection idea was revisited in 1872 but not at Niagara Falls or in Maine, as Richardson had hoped.[5] Instead, congressional leaders acted to preserve Yellowstone Park in the mountains of the western territories. Unlike the Yosemite model, however, no state government existed to assume title to the land; therefore, a federally controlled national park may have been seen as the only solution. In March 1872, President Grant, who would run for re-election against Horace Greeley in the fall, signed the Yellowstone National Park Act. Evidence suggests a coalition of media, railroad companies, government scientists, and conservationists led to its establishment. The signing of the Yellowstone bill was uncharacteristic of President Grant, who was no particular friend of the wilderness, nor did he favor federal intervention in any matter, much less conservation. For example, in 1875, the nation's first wildlife protection bill (including a measure designed to protect the vanishing buffalo herds of the West) passed Congress, but Grant vetoed the proposal. Congress failed to override the veto, and 10 years later, the buffalo were all but gone from the Plains (Udall, 1988, p. 58) (Figure 3.3).

Occupied by members of the Shoshone, Blackfoot, Bannock, and Crow tribes in the early 19th century, Yellowstone was explored by white trappers in the 1830s, including Osbourne Russell. A number of public and private expeditions explored the area from 1869 to 1872. The fledgling conservation idea, defined and publicized by writers and journalists, joined with major business interests and the government at Yellowstone in the person of U.S. geologist F. V. Hayden, who was a prominent park supporter (Huth, 1957, p. 153). Hayden traveled to Yellowstone in 1871, collecting geologic samples in his role as government scientist; on the same trip, he surveyed the area for the Northern Pacific Railroad (Runte, 1984, p. 22). Hayden, a physician, had "strong friends in Congress and the railroad lobby" (Chase, 1987, p. 266) and received $40,000 for his Yellowstone trip from Congress for a geologic survey of "the sources of the Missouri and Yellowstone rivers" (Chase, 1987, p. 266). The 20-man survey party included landscape artist Thomas Moran, who was in the employ of the railroad. Moran's job was to paint the vistas of the proposed park; his works were part of the lobbying effort, as were the photographs of expedition member William H. Jackson.

Figure 3.3. Buffaloes and hunters.
A lithograph drawn in 1850 illustrates a herd of buffaloes on the western plains, with hunters closing in. By the turn of the century, the 40 or so remaining wild buffalo in the United States lived in Yellowstone National Park under the protection of the army. Reproduced from the Minnesota Historical Society (No. 3056).

On returning to Washington, Hayden urged passage of the Yellowstone Park legislation in the halls of Congress. Joining Hayden in the lobbying effort was Nathaniel Pitt Langford, a Montana politician and among the 19-member Washburn Expedition of 1870, another Yellowstone trip partially funded by the railroad. Both Hayden and Langford wrote articles for the popular magazine *Scribner's Monthly* urging passage of a national park bill and favorably mentioned the railroad. Langford, who would become the park's first superintendent, wrote of a 2-month trip to the region in the May and June 1871 issues of *Scribner's*. The majesty and grandeur of what Langford and his party saw enchanted them, while at the same time the men were frightened by the unknown qualities of geysers, mud lakes, and sheer precipices (Langford, 1871a, p. 10). Langford, however, was not so frightened as to miss the possible economic benefits of the area. He stated,

> By means of the Northern Pacific Railroad, which doubtless will be completed in the next three years, the traveler will be able to make the trip to Montana from the Atlantic seaboard in three days, and thousands of tourists will be attracted to both Montana and Wyoming in order to behold with their own eyes the wonders here described. (Langford, 1871b, p. 128)

Coming upon the gigantic rock formation later called Devil's Slide, Langford wrote, "In future years, when the wonders of Yellowstone are incorporated into the family of fashionable resorts, there will be few of its attractions surpassing in interest this marvelous freak of the elements" (Langford, 1871a, p. 7). The Washburn Expedition shot venison, grouse, antelope, and deer and caught and dried several hundred brook trout for provisions along their journey.

Langford, a descendent of Salem, Massachusetts, settler John Langford, was a native of New York who came to St. Paul, Minnesota, in 1854 to work as a banker. He continued west in 1862, becoming tax collector for the Montana territory. A politician, he was appointed territorial governor of Montana but was never seated due to a dispute with President Andrew Johnson. One of his friends called him "the John the Baptist of the National Park idea, crying aloud both in the wilderness and out of it" (Wheeler, 1915, p. 661). Another leader of the Yellowstone trip, a Harvard-educated judge named Cornelius Hedges, was an easterner by upbringing, prompting one historian to write, "The men who were responsible for conceiving the national park idea and pushing it through Congress in 1872 were, without exception, nature importers from eastern states" (Nash, 1982, p. 350). Local residents were slow in coming around to the idea of a park "until it became clear that Yellowstone Park would attract money-spending tourists. The realization that park development might help, rather than hinder, development, won over the locals" (Haines, 1977, p. 74).

Langford's descriptions of the natural wonders of Yellowstone inspired Hayden to travel to the region the following year. Hayden detailed his journey in *Scribner's Monthly* February 1872 issue in an article titled "More About Yellowstone." Although Hayden's article spoke mainly of the unique geologic nature of the region, claims by a couple of homesteaders in an area of hot springs also caught his eye. Hayden (1872) stated,

> With a foresight worthy of commendation, two men have already preempted 320 acres of land covering most of the surface occupied by the active springs, with the expectation that upon the completion of the Northern Pacific Railroad this will be a famous place of resort for invalids and pleasure-seekers. (p. 390)

Hayden urged Congress to act to make a park, although how he thought a park could coexist with homesteading is unclear. Hayden (1872) wrote,

> The intelligent American will one day point on the map to this remarkable district with the conscious pride that it has not its parallel on the face of the globe. Why will not Congress at once pass a law setting it apart as a great public park for all time to come, as has been done with that not more remarkable wonder, the Yosemite Valley? (p. 396)

A few weeks after Hayden's article, President Grant signed the Yellowstone National Park Act. Unknown to the general public, Langford and Hayden were in the employ of the railroads. Jay Cooke, owner of the Northern Pacific Railroad, partially funded Langford's Washburn Expedition and sponsored Langford on a 20-lecture tour of the eastern United States. Hayden heard a Langford lecture in Washington, DC, and was inspired to travel to the park; soon, Cooke asked him to survey the area for a railroad (Runte, 1984, pp. 20-22).

When the park bill was up for debate, the railroad, in a "lobbying blitzkrieg," engaged Hayden and Langford to set up shop in the capitol rotunda, displaying geologic samples, Moran's sketches, and photographs of the area taken by Jackson (Chase, 1987, p. 266). Congressmen received copies of *Scribner's Monthly*. The railroad company "quite probably paid the expenses necessary to insure a speedy passage of the park bill through Congress" (Nash, 1982, p. 111). After formation of the park, the railroad funded the first concessionaire fees, and Langford was named the park's first superintendent, although he was not paid (Chase, 1987, p. 267). A coalition of media, business, government, and conservation members was born.

Following the creation of the park, *Scribner's* praised the act in May 1872, noting the utilitarian value of the property, in keeping with 19th-century values. Calling the area a "pleasure ground" and "junketing-place," the anonymous author of the article said the park "aims to ensure that the region in question shall be kept in the most favorable condition to attract travel and gratify a cultivated and intelligent curiosity" ("The Yellowstone," 1872, p. 120). Noting the flow of Americans to Europe on vacations, the magazine ("The Yellowstone," 1872) went on to point out,

> When the Northern Pacific railway, as we are led to hope to be the case, drops us in Montana in three days' journey, we may be sure that the tide of summer touring will be perceptively diverted from European fields. Yankee enterprise will dot the new park with hostelries and furrow it with lines of travel. (p. 121)

The Yosemite model, a result of a call to save 2,000-year-old trees, may or may not have been carried out for idealistic reasons, but the Yellowstone model was definitely in keeping with the economic views of the day, primarily the relatively new business of tourism. Placing the park under federal protection was a departure from the Yosemite idea, and it left the nation with a pair of experiments.

THE 1890 YOSEMITE EXPANSION

Yellowstone represented an alternative to the Yosemite model, and both were tested by economic and political pressures buffeting the parks in their formative years. Yosemite's overseers, the California Commission to Manage Yosemite Valley, met only a few times a year to supervise park operations. The first commissioners on the eight-member board were genuine and straightforward in their dealings about the park, but politicians in Sacramento soon took control of the appointment process, beginning a period of mismanagement. In Yosemite, sheep (and to a lesser extent, cattle) overgrazed the land,

and loggers raided the forests. In the 1870s and 1880s, many trees were felled, some only for their seeds. Hay planted in the valley fed the horses bringing tourists into the park after livestock chewed up much of the valley's natural grasslands.

Yellowstone had its share of problems. The Department of the Interior was charged with protecting and maintaining the property, but Congress did not provide money for upkeep nor enforcement provisions for poaching. Park officers ate park buffaloes, and unusual rock formations were quarried and sold for cash. Park superintendent Phileton W. Norris estimated that 7,000 big game mammals—elk, bighorn sheep, deer, antelope, and moose—were killed in the spring of 1875 alone. One of the first concessionaires, the Park Improvement Company, signed a contract in 1882 with professional hunters to kill 20,000 elk, bison, deer, and mountain sheep to feed its employees because wild game was cheaper than beef (Chase, 1987, p. 16).

Enter the cavalry. Administration of the park was turned over to the U.S. Army in 1886, and the military ran Yellowstone until the 1916 creation of the National Park Service (see Hampton, 1971). The Army cracked down on poaching, sent scouts to drive big game back into the park, and put up several miles of 7-foot-high fencing to keep them there. Army details fed elk and antelope in the winter and left garbage for bears to forage. The army replaced the depleted stocks of native cutthroat and grayling with imported game fish from all over the world—German brown trout, Lake Superior salmon, Lock Levens from Scotland, brook trout and salmon from the eastern United States, and coho salmon, rainbow trout, and mountain whitefish from other western regions. Soldiers also stocked black bass and yellow perch (Figure 3.4).

The Army had better luck replenishing animals than fish. Many of the salmon, rainbow trout, and black bass died quickly; the brown trout crowded out the native species and the yellow perch in Goose Lake multiplied and were poisoned to keep the population under control. Meanwhile, most of the animals, particularly elk, bred and prospered. Wilderness lover John Muir wrote in his journal, "The best service in forest protection—almost the only efficient service—is that rendered by the military. . . . Blessings on Uncle Sam's soldiers. They have done the job well, and every pine tree is waving its

Figure 3.4. The cavalry in Yellowstone.
An army detail picks its way down a steep trail in Yellowstone National Park in 1895 in this illustration in *Harper's Weekly.* The army was given charge of the park in the 1880s when other management efforts failed and successfully restocked fish and some wildlife. Reproduced from the Collections of the Library of Congress (No. 50762).

arms for joy" (as quoted in Wolfe, 1938, p. 352). The Lacey Act of 1894, which prohibited hunting and trapping in the park, aided animal populations. For several years, the cavalry resisted political pressure from farmers, ranchers, and the U.S. Biological Survey to kill predators—wolves, coyotes, and mountain lions. The only mammalian failure was in the park's mountain bison herd, which dropped to 25 animals by 1901. Plains bison were imported from Texas and crossbred with the remaining mountain bison; a buffalo ranch was built, and grains were planted for feed in some of the valleys. By 1912, the hybrid herd recovered. Yellowstone, particularly after the frustrated Interior Department turned protection of the park over to the Army, became representative of the federal centralization of power that marked the Progressive era and its ideas about the conservation of natural resources (Hays, 1959).

As the Army got control of Yellowstone, the Yosemite Valley still bent under the political winds of the State of California. Six bills were introduced in Congress between 1879 and 1886 to expand the protection of the Yosemite region around the smallish California park, but all failed. Finally, in 1890, legislators created a 1-million-acre federal reserve around Yosemite Valley. The Yosemite National Park amendment passed both houses of Congress in 2 days behind a coalition of railroad lobbyists and conservationists strikingly similar to the Yellowstone group.

Century magazine journalist Robert Underwood Johnson was an important figure in the 1890 Yosemite issue, along with the Boone & Crockett Club and the people who would create the Sierra Club, particularly Muir, who had become nationally known as a geologist through his magazine articles (Johnson, 1923). Muir's theories of the glacial activity in Yosemite gained fame after a series of articles in 1874 and 1875 in *Overland Monthly* that were "the first scientifically accurate description of the formation of the Sierra Nevada, and threw Muir to the forefront of the scientific world" (Weber, 1964, p. 64). In addition to his work as a geologic theorist, Muir was well-known as a writer, philosopher, and naturalist and an expert in publicity. Greeley hired him to write on the Yosemite Glaciers in the *New York Tribune* in 1871, the first of 65 newspaper and magazine articles he wrote over the next 20 years. A native of Scotland, his family immigrated to Wisconsin when John was 11 years old. He spent much of his young adulthood wandering North America, from Canada (where he went to avoid conscription during the Civil War) to Florida. By the 1860s, he journeyed into Yosemite, where he made a home until his death in 1914. A highly moral man, Muir saw the

Creator in nature; he believed wilderness existed for its own sake, not necessarily to serve the needs of humans. Heavily influenced by Emerson and Thoreau, Muir spent most of his life attempting to protect wild places, and Yosemite was his passion.

Muir and the preservationists ran into trouble with three groups when they tried to set aside a Yosemite park in 1889: local entrepreneurs—for example, the Yosemite Stage and Turnpike Company, which brought tourists from the railroad station to the park; cattlemen, sheepherders, and loggers; and California politicians, who were under the influence of Leland Stanford, head of the railroad. Muir had been attempting to get parts of California preserved since the late 1870s; in 1881, he helped draft a bill based on the Yellowstone model to preserve the Kings River region in the southern Sierras, but it died in committee. Congress also stymied his attempt to enlarge the region around Yosemite Valley and the Mariposa Grove (by giving more property to the state) (Wolfe, 1945, pp. 227-228).[6] Muir's attempt to protect Mount Shasta met a similar fate in 1888.

Muir could not win legislative relief on his own. Johnson, *Century*'s associate editor, was emerging as a leading figure in the preservationist movement by 1890, and he had important friends in Congress. Johnson knew his way around Washington after he spent nearly 2 years successfully lobbying for an international copyright law in the late 1880s. As the park crusade heated up, Johnson wrote two articles in the January edition of *Century*. The lead article, titled "The Care of Yosemite Valley," took the members of the Yosemite Valley Commission to task for a plan to chop down all trees less than 30 years old. Johnson, who took 100 pictures of the "mismanaged" park, wrote about "the moral claim of all humanity to an interest in the preservation of the wonders of the world" (Johnson, 1890, p. 474). The article contained the beginnings of a favorite theme of *Century*'s over the years, that of asking for turning control of the state park over to the national government. For these efforts, several California newspapers, many of which were indignant over the possibility of federal control of the entire Yosemite region, attacked Johnson and his friends. This was one time that the media did not uniformly favor the park idea—California media supported local control of the park, whereas the media centered in the eastern

United States favored national control. This was predictable, based on theoretical notions that mass media tend to represent their local interests first and foremost (Tichenor et al., 1980). On one level, the San Francisco newspapers represented the interests of the business and political elites of northern California; the eastern newspapers and magazines would not be concerned about California per se, but were concerned about their own interest groups and constituents, who were interested in vacationing grounds and nature preservation.

Johnson talked Muir into writing two articles glorifying Yosemite for *Century* in August and September of 1890. Muir wrote in the manner of the transcendentalism of Emerson, who visited Muir at Yosemite in 1871, and Thoreau: "No temple made with hands can compare with Yosemite. Every rock in its walls seems to glow with life" (Muir, 1890a, p. 484). In describing one view from a mountain peak, Muir wrote, "[It is a] view that breaks suddenly upon you in all its glory, fair and wide and deep; a new revelation in landscape affairs that goes far to make the weakest and meanest spectator rich and significant even more" (Muir, 1890a, p. 488).

Muir also criticized the ability of the state commission to manage Yosemite Valley, where slapdash saloons, clapboard hotels, and a fragrant butcher shop, complete with pigpen, stood cheek to jowl. Muir proposed an alternative: "Steps are now being taken toward the creation of a national park about the Yosemite, not only for the sake of the adjacent forests, but for the valley itself" (Muir, 1890a, p. 487). The following month, Muir was more specific: "The bill cannot too quickly become law. . . . By far the greater part of the destruction of the fineness of wildness is of a kind that can claim no right relationship with that which necessarily follows use" (Muir, 1890b, p. 667). In the same issue, a *Century* editorial also urged the passage of protective legislation. The editorial stated, "The Yosemite is too great a work of nature to be marred upon by the intrusion of farming operations or of artificial effects" ("Amateur Management," 1890, p. 798). The editorial also criticized the commission when it claimed a "hope for the good name of the state that will not be necessary to transfer to the halls of Congress the scandals of California's capitol" ("Amateur Management," 1890, p. 798). Muir's writing inspired Representative William Vandever of California to introduce a park bill, whereas Olmsted wrote letters to newspapers urging its passage. Johnson appealed to a pair of influential politicians, Representative William S. Holman of Indiana, a Democratic member of the House Committee on Public Lands and an old family friend, and Senator Preston B. Plumb of Kansas, Republican chair of the equivalent Senate committee. Both men had clout: Holman was serving in his 26th year in Congress, and Plumb was first elected in 1877.

The bill signed by President Harrison on October 1, 1890, was very different from the one introduced by Vandever in March as HR 8350. The bill did not come to the floor of the House until September 30, whereupon Vandever deftly substituted another measure, HR 12187. There was a major difference between the two bills, although the substitution happened with only a minor amount of political grousing. That difference was in the size of the proposed park—the substitute bill offered a park five times larger than HR 8350. The new bill looked suspiciously like a park proposal Muir made in 1889, although no congressman noticed it at the time. After passing the House, Plumb brought HR 12187 to the Senate floor the next day, the penultimate day of the session. Senator George Edmunds of Vermont raised the only protest to the bill, saying that he did not understand it. Someone drew Edmunds aside, spoke to him quietly, and he withdrew his objections.

No one ever admitted drafting the substitute bill, and the congressional archives do not even contain the original bill (Dilsaver & Tweed, 1990, p. 69). Who was behind the measure that increased the original park plan by five times, to 1,500 square miles? Circumstances point to the Southern Pacific Railroad. The critical moment may have come when Stanford, who rejected pleas for help from editor Johnson in 1889, was forced out as railroad president in favor of Collis Huntington, who announced that Southern Pacific was "withdrawing" from politics, perhaps as part of a public relations move. Huntington then may have directed Southern Pacific lobbyists to help Muir win approval of the park bill. Historian Stephen Fox (1981) stated, "All but invisibly, so as not to burden the Vandever bill with the SP tarnish, the railroad's lobby moved behind the measure" (pp. 106-107). The railroad's reasoning may have been twofold— tourists and timber. At about the same time, Congress established

Sequoia National Park and General Grant National Park—both areas were rich in timber, which could not have been logged and transported without the services of the railroad. The railroad also ran a spur to Raymond, one of the pick-up points for the Yosemite Stage and Turnpike Company.

In any event, Yosemite provided the conservation movement with an important victory. The cavalry was given charge of Yosemite, as it was in Yellowstone, and forced out the sheepherders. The model established by the Wyoming park wound up as the dominant system of large-scale land protection in the United States. At Johnson's urging, the Yosemite campaign led to a permanent coalition of elite members of San Francisco society, as two University of California professors, William D. Armes and Joseph LeConte, joined with San Francisco attorney Warren Olney to form the Sierra Club in 1892. They persuaded Muir to become its first president (Fox, 1981, p. 107).

THE RECESSION
OF YOSEMITE VALLEY

Muir published a series of articles in the *Atlantic* that became the book, *Our National Parks,* in 1901. The Scotsman began to gather support for the idea of re-ceding Yosemite Valley, which he called "frowzy and forlorn" in his journal, to the federal government (as cited in Wolfe, 1938, p. 349). Among those he persuaded was President Theodore Roosevelt, with whom he camped in Yosemite in 1903, and California Governor George C. Pardee, both Republicans. Historians remembered the Roosevelt camping trip for the jubilance with which the president greeted the dawn after an evening's snowfall, but events of the day also illustrated attitudes toward nature were different in the beginning of the century. Late one evening, when Muir and Roosevelt camped away from the rest of their party, Muir quietly arose from his bedroll and set fire to a tall, dead pine in a meadow. The tree erupted in flame. Roosevelt shouted, "Hurrah! That's a candle it took five hundred years to make. Hurrah for Yosemite!" (as quoted in Wolfe, 1945, p. 291).

A bill to recede the valley, drafted by a Sierra Club member, was introduced into the California assembly in early 1905 to heated debate. On one side were a few local newspapers and elected representatives of the valley's business interests who fought the "giveaway." The Sierra Club, which began a letter and telegraph campaign, and Pardee's administration took the opposite view. After passing the state House, the bill ran into trouble in the Senate with Senator John Curtin, Democrat from Sonora. Curtin, an attorney for the stageline and hotel interests in the valley, had once tried to graze cattle in the area. One of his arguments against recession was that firearms were not allowed in the national park. He stated, "I would not live under a government that would not let me carry a gun" (as quoted in Wolfe, 1945, pp. 302-303). One newspaper headline read "Those Who Would Vote for Recession of Yosemite Must be Traitors" (as cited in Wolfe, 1945, p. 302). Among the newspapers opposed to the recession was William Randolph Hearst's *San Francisco Examiner,* which resisted the idea of federal control of a state treasure. The *Examiner* printed petitions in December and January that the newspaper claimed resulted in 62,890 signatures protesting the recession plan ("Sign This," 1905).[7] Hearst also fought the railroads at every turn, so any issue favored by Southern Pacific, Hearst reflexively would oppose. With a very close vote looming, Muir appealed to the railroads for help.

The Southern Pacific had landed in the empire of New York financier E. H. Harriman, who had known Muir since an eventful 1899 trip to Alaska. Harriman financed the Alaskan expedition, which included Harriman and his family, Muir, John Burroughs, and several dozen scientists, poets, photographers, hunters, and artists. On the trip, Muir named a glacier in Glacier Bay after Harriman. "Mr. Harriman came to thank me for proposing the name," Muir wrote in his journal (as quoted in Wolfe, 1938, p. 387). Six years later, Harriman agreed to help Muir in the Yosemite Valley matter. The railroad, the largest and most powerful political force in the country, again kept its role secret: Its legislators were told to speak out against the bill in the California Senate, then vote for it. "California and the country are much indebted for the success of this [Yosemite] measure of retrocession to Edward H. Harriman," Johnson (1923, p. 291) wrote in his memoirs. The state board of trade joined the coalition by coming out in favor of the bill to save itself the annual $13,000 appropriation for park upkeep. A sudden shift of a few votes allowed the measure to pass by a single vote (Johnson, 1923, pp. 127-128).

The battle, however, was not over. Congress required federal legislation to accept the receded grant. Muir and Johnson, with the railroad's help, went to Washington to get Congress to act. State Senator Curtin and other stockmen worked to carve a slice of the park for grazing. Timber companies fought for a pair of rich groves of sugar pines, and the city of San Francisco asked for water rights in the Hetch Hetchy valley and Lake Eleanor. Joseph Cannon, the powerful speaker of the House of Representatives, held up the bill because of its costs—more federal dollars would be needed for roads, maintenance, staff, and other expenses.

Muir wrote Harriman, asking him to get involved. The railroad magnate penned a personal letter to Cannon, enclosing a copy of Muir's letter (as cited in Wolfe, 1945, p. 304). Cannon reversed field and the acceptance bill passed the House in May. In the Senate, the bill stumbled again before Harriman applied more pressure and Roosevelt announced he would not agree to a bill with changes in the park boundary. The measure passed in June; Roosevelt signed it on June 11, 1906. After 42 years as a state park, Yosemite Valley was under federal control again.

CONCLUSION

One political impact of the media publicity given to Yellowstone, Yosemite, and wilderness preservation ideas was that by the turn of the century, the nation entered a new era of land management. The changes included the following: The Adirondack Forest Preserve was created in 1885; in 1891, the federal government created the first comprehensive Forest Preserve Act; and President Harrison set aside 13 million acres in 2 years of his administration. In 1894, the Lacey Act passed Congress in response to the poaching at Yellowstone. The act provided for a $1,000 fine and up to 2 years of incarceration—a jail was built in the park—for anyone caught removing mineral deposits, cutting timber, or poaching game. President Grover Cleveland closed national forest preserves to unrestricted mining in 1897 to the outrage of westerners. The Sierra Club played an informal, advisory role in the 1897 passage of the Forest Management Act, which established the federal Division of Forestry, with Gifford Pinchot as its head (Schrepfer, 1989). Mount Rainier National Park was established under federal auspices in 1899.

The media-savvy Roosevelt and his administration increased national awareness of conservation by solidifying and increasing the federal government's role in the protection of natural resources, particularly land preservation. During his terms as president, Roosevelt set aside 150 million acres in forest reserves, national parks, and national monuments. Land preservation was not the only area in which the young conservation movement was flexing its muscles. Birds, fish, and wild game had already been the subject of extensive conservation efforts and a class-based social conflict by the time Roosevelt assumed national prominence (see Chapter 1). The social system of the United States became more accepting of the ideas of the conservationists and the nation's media—with some local exceptions—went along for the ride. The coalition of power groups, the mass media, and the environmentalists continued in the case of the Alaskan land affair.

The issue of local versus national control, reflected in the newspapers that represented each interest, did not go away. Similar controversies flared up again in the mid-1990s debate in Washington, DC, over returning some federal control over natural resources to state and local governments.

NOTES

1. Tenaya was killed in 1853 in a dispute with the Mono Indians at Mono Lake, where he had fled from the soldiers.

2. The Calaveras Grove, which was split into northern and southern sections, was not protected by the state until 1931 (northern) and 1954 (southern).

3. John Muir did his first newspaper writing for Greeley's paper, publishing an article on Yosemite glaciers in the *New York Herald Tribune* in 1871.

4. In 1869, more than 1,100 visitors traveled to Yosemite after the Central Pacific Road reached Stockton. In 1900, after the area was expanded, 5,000 persons visited the park. By the early 1990s, the park hosted 3 million visitors per year.

5. For more information on Niagara Falls, see Dow (1921) (especially Chapter 11, Preservation of the Falls).

6. The Kings River region eventually became the home for Sequoia and General Grant National Parks.

7. Another factor in the *Examiner*'s opposition may have been the paper's chief legal counsel, J. J. Lerman, who was also secretary of the board of commissioners of the park. The recession bill would cost him his job.

4

THE MEDIA AND
SOCIAL CHANGE

II. The Great Alaskan Land Fraud

ne social problem well established in American life by
the turn of the 20th century was the management of
federal land. The withdrawal of public lands from private exploitation concerned the citizenry, the emerging
groups associated with conservation, and the leadership of the politically powerful Progressive movement. The Alaskan
land fraud controversy of 1903 to 1911—known in some quarters as
the Ballinger-Pinchot feud after its two primary participants—
represented how deeply the idea of the conservation and use of public
land had ingrained itself into the American psyche in a relatively

short time. The mass communication phenomenon known as muckraking journalism—investigative, crusading, in-depth reporting for
magazines and newspapers during the Progressive era—played a
key role in the exposure of the Alaskan conflict. A complex mixture
of conservation as part of the ideational system of the era, a split in
the leadership of the Republican party, and a search for direction
among the Progressives was inspired and highlighted by the muckraking of the Alaskan land deal. Powerful sources fed information to
the journalists, who amplified the controversy and sustained it with
conservationists and politicians working with the press. Reporters
and editors played an active role in the political process. As in the
national park system episodes, the Alaskan issue was defined by
conservationists and key members of the political system and accelerated by the press.

LAND CONSERVATION
IN THE UNITED STATES

The word *conservation* has undergone several meanings, including "preservation" and "protection," but the word also meant "wise
use of natural resources" to its proponents during the Progressive
era (1898-1920). A useful definition of conservation comes from Max
Nicholson, the head of the British Nature Conservancy, who said
conservation meant a "positivist, interventionist approach in the
theater of the natural environment" (Nicholson, 1970, p. 186).

In the colonies, Virginia farmer and future president Thomas
Jefferson experimented with contour plowing to prevent soil erosion.
A nagging problem for Jefferson and other founders of the new nation
was what to do with federal land—a problem that would plague
policymakers more than 200 years later. The basic argument remained the same—who should use the public land, and for what
purpose? Jefferson's view of an agrarian nation is well-known—land
sold (or given away) to small farmers was one of the building blocks
of a democratic system in his view. He was opposed by Alexander
Hamilton and others, who wanted to sell federal land to corporations
and aristocrats, in keeping with Adam Smith's conception of the
worth of land. In *The Wealth of Nations,* Smith (1977) merged the

capitalistic economic system and the use of nature through its technological domination. Smith believed that by conquering land, a more fair, efficient, and productive life would be provided for everyone. In addition, nature could be worked not only to meet individual needs but also to create goods to trade with others. Land was a resource to be used as a commodity for acquiring private fortunes. Environmental historian Donald Worster stated, "Agroecosystems were rationally and systematically reshaped in order to intensify, not merely the production of food and fiber, but the accumulation of personal wealth" (Worster, 1990, p. 1,101).

The central government, throughout U.S. history, acted as a real estate broker. In 1795, the federal government sold land in 640-acre and 160-acre segments to pay Revolutionary War debts. The trend continued in laws such as the Homestead Act of 1862, which enabled settlers to earn title to 160 acres by living on and working the property for 5 years or by purchasing it for $1.25 per acre. Developers and speculators took advantage of lax enforcement provisions and legal loopholes to obtain huge amounts of land, sometimes reselling it for a large profit (Smith, 1950, pp. 160-173). Tens of millions of acres were given to the railroads as incentive to lay track; the railroads then offered land to settlers to build a customer base near their right-of-ways. The government agency charged with issuing land grants was the General Land Office, which became known as bureaucratically inept and sometimes outrageously corrupt.

In the Reconstruction years, laissez-faire economics fueled a period of business and industrial growth, technological innovation, and communication and transportation revolutions. With the driving of the golden spike in the final rail of the Union Pacific Railroad in 1869, land west of the Missouri River was open to all manner of speculators, farmers, ranchers, miners, and lumber companies. As the land was eaten up, structural strains appeared between Western business interests and eastern conservationists. It was not a coincidence that Richard Ballinger, the secretary of the interior whose actions were at the core of the Alaskan land fraud issue, was a westerner. Nor was it a coincidence that his primary nemesis, U.S. Forest Ser- vice director Gifford Pinchot, was an easterner.

Public health laws had established a pattern of governmental intervention in the environment. Issues of public health first emerging in England in the mid-19th century influenced American Progressives in the latter part of the century. The writings and speeches of the intellectuals in the conservation movement—James Russell Lowell, Henry Thoreau, George Perkins Marsh, George Bird Grinnell, John Burroughs, and many others—contributed to the emergence of shared beliefs on natural resources that sustained the movement and its goals through the mid- and late 19th century. By the 1890s, the conservation movement had recorded significant gains in land and wildlife issues. National parks were established throughout the country, and the number of special interest groups concerned with nature issues continued to grow. Clearly, conservation was established as a social problem by the late 19th century.

THE PROGRESSIVES AND CONSERVATION

Because the use of natural resources by humans is a given throughout recorded history, why would the conservation movement record gains in certain periods? One possible answer in the Progressive era is in the structural strains caused by the growth of the trusts in the latter part of the 19th century. The campaign against the trusts contributed to the campaign for conservation by associating the possibility that the financiers would assume control of all the natural resources of the country.

Historian Clayton R. Koppes identified three themes in the American conservation movement that became focused during the Progressive era: (a) efficiency, or the technical management of wild lands and rivers; (b) equity, or the distributed benefits of nature, such as irrigation projects; and (c) aesthetics, or the preservation of scenic wonders (Koppes, 1988). Koppes wrote, "The ideas, politics, and policies that emerged at the turn of the century set the tone of intellectual and political debate for the next half century and laid the basis for the environmental movement of the late 20th century" (p. 231). Theodore Roosevelt had a hand in bringing all three themes together. Before becoming president, Roosevelt was involved in organizing conservation groups. He was a charter member of the Boone & Crockett Club (membership was limited to 100), an exclusive group that also included Grinnell, Elihu Root, Henry Cabot Lodge, and Madison Grant. To qualify for membership, a man must have bagged at least three trophy heads (Roosevelt had eight). The Boone & Crockett Club was credited with making a hunting refuge in Yellowstone Park, the formation of the New York Zoological Park (the Bronx Zoo), and the National Zoological Park in Washington, DC (Graham, 1971, p. 103).

The conservation movement enjoyed a close relationship with the government in the Roosevelt era. As in many social movements, as its membership became more professional, the conservation movement became co-opted by the government. Efficiency was the cornerstone of the Roosevelt plan, and the individual who made it work was Gifford Pinchot. Late in the 19th century, Marsh's (1864) book, *Man and Nature,* inspired Harvard botanist Charles Sprague Sargent to survey the nation's forest for the federal government as part of a forest protection idea. A forest protection bill passed Congress in 1891, and 13 million acres were set aside in the next 2 years (Fox, 1981, p. 109). Pinchot, a recent Yale graduate, accompanied Sargent on his forest survey. In December 1894, the 29-year-old Pinchot, Sargent, and journalist Robert Underwood Johnson met in New York to devise a plan for a federal forest commission. The New York Board of Trade and the Chamber of Commerce were among those business groups endorsing the idea, and the forest commission was created in 1897 with Pinchot appointed as its head. Pinchot, who was fond of political power and a master of public relations, eventually received his own department within the federal bureaucracy. "One of the great promoters in the history of bureau politics" (Penick, 1968, p. 5), Pinchot succeeded in persuading Congress to transfer the forest reserves from the Interior Department to the Agriculture Department. Roosevelt, who recognized the growing power of the conservation movement (because he was a part of it), put Pinchot in charge of conservation during his administration, and in 1905, the U.S. Forest Service was created. In 10 years, its budget increased 100-fold (Fox, 1981, pp. 114, 119).

During Roosevelt's administration, only a handful of environmental laws were passed, but the president used existing legislation to greatly enlarge protected federal holdings. Under Roosevelt and

Pinchot, the national forests were expanded from 42 million acres to 172 million acres, 51 national wildlife refuges were created, and 18 areas of special interest, including the Grand Canyon and the Petrified Forest, were preserved under the Antiquities Act of 1906 (Fox, 1981, p. 134).

PINCHOT, BALLINGER, AND GARFIELD

Under Roosevelt and Pinchot, one of the goals of the conservation movement was to keep monopolistic trusts from complete control of the nation's natural resources (Hays, 1958). Pinchot's background was similar to Roosevelt's: He was trained at an Ivy League school, came from a wealthy eastern family, and, like many men of wealth in his era, became an outdoorsman. When no American college could offer him training in forestry, he went to Europe. Tall and slender, Pinchot, the grandson of one of Napoleon's officers, was in Roosevelt's famous "tennis cabinet" and probably held more power than any bureau chief and some cabinet officers. *Current Literature* referred to Pinchot as "A Millionaire With a Mission" ("Pinchot: A Millionaire," p. 388) (Figure 4.1).

Pinchot's nemesis, Richard Achilles Ballinger, was born of a different set of social circumstances. Son of a middle-class Calvinist abolitionist newspaper editor, Ballinger, who was named after his father, graduated from Williams College and eventually carved out a career as a lawyer, judge, and mayor in Seattle, winning election in 1904 on a clean government platform (Penick, 1968, pp. 20-23). Seattle struggled with the problems of urban growth after the Klondike gold rush of 1898, and Ballinger became one of the reform mayors of the era. He retired from the mayor's office in 1906 and continued a correspondence with James Garfield, son of the murdered president, who was a college friend. Garfield, appointed by Roosevelt to be secretary of the interior, eventually hired Ballinger to reorganize the General Land Office, which was badly managed, disorganized, and bereft of morale. Ballinger, who was the administration's third choice for the job, streamlined the land office, hired new employees, and won high praise from Garfield and Roosevelt in

Figure 4.1. Gifford Pinchot.

President Theodore Roosevelt's chief forester and his leading adviser on conservation matters, Gifford Pinchot became involved in a bureaucratic dispute with Secretary of the Interior Richard Ballinger, a Taft appointee, that came to a head in the Alaskan coal deal. Ultimately, Taft fired Pinchot, angering Roosevelt and other Progressive Republicans. Reproduced from the Collections of the Library of Congress (No. 21919).

March 1908 on his resignation to return to his Seattle law practice. Despite the praise of the president, not all was smooth for Ballinger in the nation's capitol. While at the land office, the relations between the two division heads, Ballinger and Pinchot, were strained as each engaged in the usual bureaucratic fighting and turf wars. In an act he would come to regret, shortly before he left office, Ballinger hired 23-year-old Louis Glavis as chief of the Portland division.

Garfield, in a previous job as head of the Bureau of Corporations, was the architect of Roosevelt's antitrust policy. He and Pinchot enjoyed close relationships with the president, which was unusual for department heads. "No two men have been as closely identified with so many of the policies for which this administration has stood," Roosevelt (as quoted in Wanners, 1969, p. 105) wrote at the end of his term. When Garfield became head of the Interior Department, he brought the same philosophy of bureaucratic control to the conservation of natural resources.

Before Garfield's transfer, 100,000 acres of Alaskan coal lands were withdrawn from public use in 1906, and the U.S. Geologic Survey began classifying them and opening them up for sale at market value. (Previously, federal coal land sales were based on a flat price set by statute, which allowed speculators to make enormous profits.) Garfield wanted to ensure government ownership and control of the virgin lands. Roosevelt and Garfield indicated that the coal properties would be turned over to the small miner and the pioneer, rather than the huge Wall Street trusts.

With the election of William Howard Taft as president in 1908, Ballinger returned to Washington as Garfield's replacement as secretary of the interior, even though Garfield had assumed he would be reappointed—he had even renewed the lease on his Washington house (Wanners, 1969). During the previous year, the Roosevelt-Garfield-Pinchot conservation agenda had suffered a series of legislative setbacks, including the failure of bills relating to the Inland Waterways Commission and the National Conservation Commission. After Garfield found out that he would be replaced by Ballinger, he began withdrawing water sites from all development except water power, partly as a way to regulate the water companies (see Filler, 1976, p. 328; Penick, 1968, p. 7). The last of the withdrawals was made only 48 hours before Taft was to take the oath of office.

Politically, Ballinger was a better bureau chief than a cabinet member. Although he thought of himself as a Progressive—he favored civil service reform, city planning, tariff reform, the income tax amendment—Ballinger brought a 19th-century westerner's view of natural resources to Washington. He disliked eastern conservationists and favored business interests and the rights of the individual over the collective good. He supported the outright selling of coal and grazing lands to private individuals and companies and opposed the Roosevelt method of leasing the lands for limited periods for fair royalties. When Ballinger spoke out against certain other programs of the Roosevelt years (including the creation of the Chugach National Forest in Alaska) and began restoring the withdrawn water sites for possible development, he was looked on as a traitor by the Progressives. Garfield's land preservation work was being undone by Ballinger, his former subordinate.

Pinchot remained as head forester, and his infighting with Ballinger continued. "The burden of the fight for the Roosevelt policies under this administration will fall on Gifford's shoulders," Garfield (as quoted in Penick, 1968, p. 47) wrote in his dairy on April 3, 1909. Pinchot intervened with President Taft to force Ballinger to withdraw the water sites again, which hurt Ballinger politically, only 6 weeks after the transfer of power from Roosevelt. It was a temporary victory, however, for the forester. Ballinger was clever enough to withdraw the water sites from all forms of entry, which exacerbated structural strains and bloomed in the form of an anticonservationist backlash, particularly in the West, where control of water meant power.

Beginning in June 1909, Garfield and Pinchot plotted to overthrow the secretary, which reflected not only their disgust with Ballinger but also their disappointment with Taft. Garfield and Pinchot began leaking information critical of Ballinger to the newspapers, particularly the *New York Sun*. Ballinger knew where the leaks were coming from, but he was not nearly as media savvy as Pinchot and the Progressives; nor was his boss, Taft, interested in cultivating the press (Ponder, 1994). The story may have disappeared into history as a typical bureaucratic struggle if it had not been about conservation, and if not for the Alaskan coal scandal, Louis Glavis, and the muckrakers.

Figure 4.2. Coal ships in Alaska.
Coal is loaded into the Dora Bluhm in St. Michaels, Alaska, around the turn of the century in this stereocard image. A controversy arose over the disposition of the lands in the Taft presidency, when the Interior Department was accused of favoring the big eastern syndicates. The coal land turned out to be much less valuable than originally thought. Reproduced from the Collections of the Library of Congress (No. 5119).

THE ALASKAN DEAL

Rumors of the rich mineral fields of Alaska inspired rich and poor alike to speculate in land claims. A 1904 law stating that a claim could only cover 160 acres and the number of possible consolidated claims could be no more than four limited all speculators. The claimants or the association of four claimants were required to swear that no further consolidation would take place. The system was fraught with fraud. Small speculators would stake a claim (at $10 an acre) and secretly resell the claim to huge financial interests at a healthy profit.

Among the first to prospect for minerals in Alaska in the era was Clarence Cunningham, a better prospector than businessman who found promising coal samples in 1902 and staked out claims in 1903 (Figure 4.2). Cunningham, who acted as an agent on behalf of a group of 32 people, paid $10 per acre for rights to the coal claims in 1907, for a total of $52,800. Eight of Cunningham's partners were from Seattle and were political allies of Ballinger. Because the Cunningham claims were filed before the 1904 law, the General

Land Office was ordered to investigate and approve the claims if its findings warranted. Among those thinking the Cunningham claims were illegally bound for an eastern syndicate was Louis Glavis, who should be remembered in history as one of the 20th century's early whistle-blowers.

The Morgan-Guggenheim syndicate was the most powerful economic force in the Alaskan territory. Charges, rumors, and accusations circulated that the syndicate would supply the money to develop the Alaskan coal fields in return for an uninterrupted 25-year supply of coal. If true, the railroad run by Morgan-Guggenheim, the Copper River and Northwestern, would have controlled virtually the entire estimated $1.5 billion Alaskan coal market. Among the prominent accusations was that Clarence Cunningham was secretly working for the syndicate. A General Land Office investigation of the Cunningham arrangement, under the direction of Horace T. Jones, was hastily completed under pressure from the head of the land office, Ballinger, who needed the finished reports to support his testimony before Congress (Penick, 1968, pp. 84-85).

Shortly thereafter, Glavis was appointed head of the Portland office and began to round out the report started by Jones. Before Glavis could finish his investigation, Ballinger clearlisted (recorded as valid) the claims so the Cunningham group could begin mining coal. Ballinger was lobbied by former Washington governor Miles Moore, one of the Cunningham claimants. On January 7, 1908, Glavis was informed that the claims were clearlisted and asked Ballinger to halt the clearlisting, which was within his power. Ballinger complied, but he lobbied for a bill before Congress that would have legalized the claims.

Glavis, concerned about the rumors of Morgan-Guggenheim control, found evidence of fraud in Cunningham's 1903 dairy, which Cunningham was attempting to use as a defense. Glavis forwarded the damning document to Washington (Penick, 1968, p. 88). The investigator discovered more incriminating evidence, including a contract between the Morgan-Guggenheim syndicate and the Cunningham group dated July 20, 1907 by which David Guggenheim agreed to buy half the claims (Mowry, 1958, pp. 250-258). On May 2, 1908, however—two months after Ballinger resigned to return to Seattle— Glavis was ordered to drop his investigation of the Cunningham claims and return all his men to Oregon to look into claims of fraud in that state.[1] In the meantime, Ballinger, in private law practice in Seattle, was hired as counsel by Cunningham. Ballinger prepared a brief for the land office on behalf of the Cunningham group and wrote letters to his replacement, Fred Dennett, urging approval of its claims (Mason, 1941, p. 54).

His attorney-client relationship with the Cunningham group would pose a problem for Ballinger. By representing Cunningham, and accepting a fee for doing so, Ballinger was breaking an administrative rule that forbade a former officeholder from appearing before his old department in the interest of a claim pending before his resignation. Back in Washington as secretary of the interior in March 1909, Ballinger disqualified himself from acting on the Cunningham claims and appointed his assistant, Frank Pierce, to rule on the coal cases. Glavis, who had restarted the Alaskan investigation a few months earlier, was ordered to Seattle from Portland to be closer to the scene.

In his report, Glavis said the Cunningham claims were clearly fraudulent and hinted that political ambitions played a role in his being pulled off the investigation in 1908. Glavis asked for more time to complete the work but was given only 60 days. Glavis became convinced that the Cunningham group was receiving favorable treatment from someone in Washington (Penick, 1968, p. 99).[2] When Glavis complained to Ballinger about the rushed nature of the investigation, he was removed from the case again.

Glavis then went to Pinchot, heating up the jurisdictional battle between the land office and the forest service. Why Glavis approached Pinchot is not known—perhaps because some of the coal lands were in the Chugach National Forest—but he handed the chief forester ammunition of no small caliber in his fight against Ballinger. In a letter written in late July, Glavis gave the impression that he believed a public investigation on the order of the Oregon land trials would take place, with Glavis acting as chief witness and prosecutor (Penick, 1968, p. 105). Pinchot provided Glavis with letters of introduction to President Taft, and the young man took his evidence to the chief executive. The most damaging charge was that Ballinger used his public office for private gain: The secretary had personal friends and clients in the Cunningham group and twice rendered them assistance with rulings at the land office. Taft remained silent after Glavis's visit, whereas Spokane and Denver news- papers published sketchy accounts of the charges and the wire services distributed the story across the country. Taft forwarded Glavis's charges to Ballinger for comment. Pinchot's forest service continued to leak information to the press, and Ballinger was not helped by his friends, one of whom told the Roosevelt-friendly press that "perhaps Roosevelt thought he was the Lord; he acted that way for many years around this place" (as quoted in Penick, 1968, p. 124).

Taft received reports from those involved by September, but his ruling was delayed, adding to the atmosphere of conspiracy surrounding the case. Taft finally exonerated Ballinger of all charges, while privately urging Pinchot to stay out of the affair. Louis Glavis was fired on September 16, 1909.

THE MUCKRAKING

Rebuffed in bureaucratic channels, Glavis turned to the muckrakers. Writing an article with considerable help from media-savvy members of Pinchot's forest service, Glavis went to Norman Hapgood, the muckraking *Collier's* magazine editor known to dislike Ballinger. In October, Hapgood's magazine said Ballinger "is, at the most moderate statement, grossly unsuited to his post, and if Mr. Taft retains him it will be an error from which he will never recover" ("Editorial," 1909, p. 9). Glavis was offered $3,000 for his story from another magazine, but he refused the money (Hapgood, 1930, p. 182). He also refused payment from Hapgood.

The article, factual and detailed in the muckraking tradition, charged that the majority of the land claims in Alaska, including the Cunningham claims, were fraudulent (Glavis, 1909, pp. 15-17, 27). Glavis repeated his contention that Ballinger knew the claims "were under suspicion" when he ordered them approved, that Ballinger urged Congress to approve the fraudulent claims, that he worked for Cunningham's group as its attorney, and that he favored the Cunningham group as secretary of the interior (Glavis, 1909, p. 15). If the land claims went through, Glavis said the Cunningham group would realize 91 million tons of coal. (The going rate for coal was between 50¢ and $1 per ton.) Glavis wrote that Cunningham's diary revealed evidence of the alleged collusion with the Morgan-Guggenheim group, which also was committing fraud by attempting to consolidate more land than the law allowed. Glavis was careful not to accuse Ballinger of any criminal behavior, saying "I made no such charge, nor do I make it now" (Glavis, 1909, p. 27).

A story of robber barons stealing pristine public land with the help of shady government henchmen touched a nerve among conservationists and muckrakers alike. Other magazines took up the crusade, helped by leaks from Pinchot's men, "and they had done it with remarkable effect," Pinchot wrote in his autobiography (Pinchot, 1947, p. 446). Muckrakers John Lathrop and George Kibbe Turner covered the topic for *McClure's,* and John Mathews did the same for *Hampton's* (Lathrop & Turner, 1910; Mathews, 1909). Mathews, a muckraker expert in conservation issues, argued that Ballinger was a pawn of the trusts, "the land grabbers, the water grabbers, the coal land grabbers" (Mathews, 1909, p. 674). Among his charges was that those in control of the railroads in Alaska—and the coal to run them —would ultimately control the rich copper mines of the state. Mathews also named Taft as a participant in the conspiracy. Ballinger called the muckrakers "apostles of vomit," "scoundrels," and "assassins of character" (as quoted in Penick, 1968, p. 130).

In muckraking style, *Collier's* seized the issue as its own and attempted to make the most of it (Figure 4.3). In December, the magazine's editor all but accused Ballinger of lying when the secretary told *Outlook* editors he did not know of the charges of fraud against the Cunningham group when he left the General Land Office in March 1908. *Collier's* reported a meeting between Glavis and Ballinger in late 1907 over the same matters ("Achilles," 1909). One basis for the *Collier's* article was the extensive records of the case, conveniently supplied to the magazine by the forest service. Two weeks later, the magazine charged that Ballinger's election as mayor of Seattle in 1904 was set up by James J. Hill, the railroad magnate, and it attempted to make connections between the former mayor and the Morgans, Guggenheims, and Standard Oil ("Can This Be," 1909).[3]

The muckraking of the Alaskan land controversy changed the nature of the issue from a bureaucratic infight to a vote of confidence in the Taft administration and its conservation policies. The charge

Figure 4.3. The muckrakers and conservation.
Collier's magazine was a leading muckraking journal in the 1900s, and one of its top issues was the conservation of public lands. The magazine accused Interior Secretary Richard Ballinger (insert) of a conflict of interest in his dealings with an eastern syndicate over Alaskan coal lands. Reproduced from the Collections of the Library of Congress (No. 51500).

beneath the rhetoric was that Taft was not adhering to the Roosevelt agenda, particularly in matters of conservation. "Politically, they involve the future relation between the Taft policy and the Roosevelt policy and, possibly, the future relations between the two men," wrote one editor of the day ("A Review of the World," 1910, p. 119). Taft was never as progressive as Roosevelt on conservation matters, and those differences were highlighted in the muckraking of the Alaskan deal. Taft, once he supported Ballinger, could not easily withdraw that support for political reasons. This left him more at odds with the Progressives, whose former leader, Roosevelt, was kept informed of the situation by letters from Pinchot while the ex-president was on an African hunting trip. The issue moved to the congressional arena when the insurgent Republicans, already unhappy with Taft over tariff questions, demanded an investigation of Ballinger. In a countermove, the interior secretary also asked for hearings, but he wanted a complete probe of Pinchot's forest service as well as his own department.

THE CONGRESSIONAL HEARINGS

On conservation matters, the muckrakers and the Progressive movement were on the same page. The Alaska charges were revived after the congressional investigation, fueled by the insurgent Progressives in Congress and framed in public debate by the muckrakers. Evidence of the close relationship between the media and the movement came from accounts of a December meeting between Hapgood, Henry L. Stimson, Pinchot, magazine publisher Robert Collier, and Garfield. Hapgood and Collier were concerned about a possible lawsuit by Ballinger against *Collier's* and wanted to participate in the congressional hearings. The magazine editors feared the congressional hearings would turn into a whitewash if the committee were loaded with conservative Republicans. Ballinger, exonerated, would sue the magazine for $1 million, according to the rumors. A worried Collier hired Boston attorney Louis Brandeis to serve as counsel for the magazine and for Glavis (Hapgood, 1930, pp. 183-186). *Collier's* had no formal standing before the committee, but Glavis did.

Pinchot drafted a letter to Senator Jonathan Dolliver of Iowa, one of the insurgents, accusing Taft of abandoning Roosevelt policies in conservation issues. The letter also confessed that the forestry department was the source of the media leaks to the muckrakers. By writing the letter, Pinchot purposely disregarded Taft's executive order not to comment on the Ballinger case. After Dolliver read the letter on the Senate floor, Taft instructed Secretary of Agriculture Jim Wilson to fire Pinchot. "By your own conduct you have destroyed your usefulness as a helpful subordinate of the Government," Taft (as quoted in Penick, 1968, p. 142) wrote Pinchot the next day. Pinchot knew what he was doing; Taft, too, knew he was making a martyr for the Progressive cause out of Pinchot. "I would not have removed Pinchot if I could have helped it," Taft said (as quoted in Penick, 1968, p. 142). Roosevelt, writing Pinchot from Africa, said simply, "I cannot believe it" (as quoted in Wanners, 1969, p. 122). The forester forced the firing to keep the issue in the public arena.

Taft also struck back at the magazines, although indirectly. In late 1909, he instructed his postmaster general, Frank H. Hitchcock, to draft legislation that would rescind the favorable postage rates enjoyed by the magazines since 1879. Hitchcock, under whom the Post Office department was running a deficit, proposed to eliminate the debt by raising the postage on magazines from 1¢ to 4¢ or 5¢. Magazine editor Benjamin Hampton asked why Taft did not simply list the muckraking magazines to be destroyed and skip the facade of a postage increase (Filler, 1976, p. 362). The proposal failed, but not before it cemented the muckraking magazines' low opinion of the president.

Against this backdrop, *Collier's* and *Hampton's* continued to investigate Ballinger and the General Land Office. In the January 8, 1910, *Collier's,* muckraker Christopher Connolly said the land office was controlled by the railroads and that Ballinger's assistant, Oscar Lawler, was a stooge for the Southern Pacific machine (Connolly, 1910a, pp. 18-19). Connolly accused Speaker of the House Joseph Cannon of being one of the "railroad-controlled" senators who received money from the corporations in exchange for votes. Connolly (1910a) wrote, "The way of the General Land Office has been the way of a serpent on a rock" (p. 19). Bashing the Senate and the railroads was a familiar and successful path for muckrakers, and the circulation of *Collier's* appeared to reflect the public's interest in the story. According to its own figures, the magazine's circulation increased 14% from June 1909 (before the Ballinger controversy was public) to 545,000 in December 1909, when the issue was in full bloom.[4] At *Hampton's,* circulation rose from 125,000 in 1908, before it began muckraking, to 450,000 by 1910 (Mott, 1938b, p. 151).

The investigation, with seven regular Republicans and four Democrats plus one insurgent Republican on the committee, lasted from January 26 through May 20 because a total of 45 sessions were held. By all accounts, Brandeis was brilliant in his representation of Glavis and *Collier's.* He held daily press briefings and was such an expert in press relations that the committee chair, Knute Nelson of Minnesota, said in frustration, "It might help Senators to understand that counsel is trying this case for the other table, the press table, and not this one" (as quoted in Mason, 1941, p. 107). The 26-year-old Glavis was calm and professional on the witness stand. The lawyer for Pinchot, George Wharton Pepper, recognizing the power of the conservation issue, succeeded in labeling Ballinger as an enemy of conservation. Pinchot, who gained much of his power through the effective use of public relations, in March commissioned an unmarked flyer distributed to newspapers around the country as a "summary of the testimony" (see Ponder, 1986a). Part of the flyer was undoubtedly the basis for the April 2 story in *Collier's* titled "What the Investigation Has Proved" (1910, pp. 18-19). "Publicity, like every other great power which is capable of good use, may be grossly misused," Garfield had written, but that was "no good reason for failing to use it" (Garfield, 1909, p. 391). Ballinger's efforts to get his case presented in the media were "puny and ineffective" in comparison (Penick, 1968, p. 152).

Ballinger's counsel and testimony were nearly as poor as his public relations efforts. After going without a lawyer during the first couple of days of the hearings, Ballinger was given Tennessee attorney John Vertrees, an ardent anticonservationist who only served to reinforce Pepper's argument. Vertrees, a Democrat, also defended Ballinger by pointing fingers at the Roosevelt administration and at Ballinger's own subordinates. The first tactic served to further establish the debate as Ballinger versus Roosevelt.

The muckraking of Ballinger continued throughout the hearings, the threat of a libel suit notwithstanding. In March, *Collier's* dug up a story from Decatur, Alabama, where Ballinger, as a young attorney, had sold stock in a nail company that subsequently went out of business ("Some Lighter Aspects," 1910). The magazine article stated, "Decatur became an undesirable residence for Ballinger, and, gathering his family together, he disappeared" ("Some Lighter Aspects," 1910, p. 22). Ballinger repaid one banker only after he became a candidate for judge in Seattle and the banker threatened to go public with the story. The most hard-hitting story appeared in early April under the headline "Ballinger-Shyster" in *Collier's* (Connolly, 1910b, pp. 16-17). The story, written by Connolly, was culled from Ballinger's enemies in Seattle. Connolly said that Ballinger's election as judge was helped by alleged ballot-box stuffing, that he was a poor lawyer, and that "if Ballinger ever selects a coat-of-arms, it ought to be a whitewash brush couchant" (Connolly, 1910b, p. 17).

On the other side of the fight, Pinchot was called an "ineffective" witness by one of his biographers—he admitted mistakes and lacked evidence to support his adamant conclusions (Fausold, 1961, p. 27; see also Mason, 1941, pp. 115-116). His technical differences with Ballinger on bureaucratic issues made for poor cross-examination.

The muckraker Connolly was personally attacked in the hearings while his editor, Hapgood, was both observer and participant throughout. Brandeis suspected that the Ballinger forces had backdated a key piece of evidence—a refutation of a charge against Attorney General George Wickersham that appeared in *Collier's* on November 13, 1909—and mentioned the possibility to Edward C. Finney, an important witness, during cross-examination. Brandeis placed Hapgood in the audience to carefully watch Finney and his aides; the two men agreed that the panic in Finney's eyes confirmed their suspicions, although there were denials all around. Pinchot (1947) stated, "Finney's face gave him away to Hapgood and Brandeis and they pressed ahead with that line of questioning" (p. 484). Brandeis found more proof in an event mentioned in the Wickersham report that had not occurred until after the date on the document. Brandeis asked the committee for more detailed records of the backdating incident but twice was voted down (Penick, 1968, pp. 179-180).

Brandeis won more points in the press after Frederick M. Kerby, 24, a stenographer for Ballinger, went to the *Washington Post* with the backdating story when it became obvious to Kerby that a key document called the Lawler memorandum was not forthcoming from the department. Newsmen told Kerby it was his patriotic duty to divulge the facts, and he was promised a job at a newspaper company. Kerby told of copying a draft of Taft's letter exonerating Ballinger; the letter, however, was not written by Taft, but by Ballinger, Lawler, Finney, and Pierce. In an exciting bit of testimony, Kerby told of the burning of the drafts of the letter in an office fireplace rather than simply discarding them in a wastebasket (Mason, 1941, pp. 160-161). The story appeared in the *Washington Post* on May 14 and Kerby was dismissed on May 16. The results of backdating a piece of evidence and ghostwriting a presidential letter left the impression that the Taft administration had something to hide. As often happens in politics, lying to cover up the event was more damaging than the event itself.

Proving or disproving the Glavis charges became secondary. Given the makeup of the committee, the 7-to-5 vote exonerating Ballinger was predetermined. As an example of the bureaucratic phase of the process, the committee hearings were a classic case of the bureaucracy attempting to control the direction of change. In the process, Ballinger was shown to be anything but a conservationist. The Taft forces won the battle, but the Progressive conservationists were winning the war.

CONCLUSION

Collier's was not sued, and Hapgood was not finished with his muckraking of the affair. In June 1910, he commissioned an article by a young Radcliffe graduate named Myrtle Abbott, who charged that Taft and Ballinger had conspired to turn the Alaska claims over to the Morgan-Guggenheim syndicate. Hapgood, unsatisfied with Abbott's evidence, declined to publish the story. Abbott turned the material over to the United Press wire service and the Newspaper Enterprise Association, both of which distributed it to their members. Abbott wrote the article from files obtained from the government, but one of her key pieces of evidence was found to be a forgery. Although nothing came of the allegations, the story kept the issue in front of the public for several more months (Penick, 1968, pp. 179-180).

Ballinger, his career and reputation at stake, remained as secretary of the interior throughout 1910, despite calls for his resignation. Taft knew Ballinger was a political liability, but refused to fire him out of sympathy for the man. For not dismissing Ballinger, muckrakers made Taft look like he was afraid of, or in the pocket of, the monopolists whom the secretary allegedly represented. Ballinger finally resigned in March 1911, citing poor health and financial reasons. The Cunningham claims continued to plague the Taft administration until they were canceled in mid-1911 by Walter Fisher, Ballinger's successor and a friend of Pinchot's. Ironically, the Alaskan coal lands turned out to be of little value.

Taft, seeking to regain support from the conservationists, ended up removing more public lands from private entry than did Roosevelt in a comparable length of time (Mowry, 1958, p. 258). The president, however, made few other efforts to appease the Republican Progressives and lost the House to the Democrats in 1910, and his margin in the Senate was narrowed to 10 votes. Senator Robert La Follette of Wisconsin emerged as the political leader of the Progressives in Washington.

Taft's attention to the conservation issue was a response to the place held by the idea of land management in the social system. The well-chronicled split between Roosevelt and Taft, which came to a climax in 1912, did not result from the Alaskan land affair. There were other, serious policy differences between the two men, including Taft's support of the Payne-Aldrich tariff. A similar bureaucratic split was represented by the career of Dr. Harvey W. Wiley, the chemist who had been canonized by the muckrakers in the pure food and drug fight, when he was condemned by Secretary of Agriculture Jim Wilson at a meeting of the National Food Conference. Whether it was true or not, the press portrayed the circumstances of Pinchot and Wiley as the punishment of Roosevelt men by the Taft administration. The departmental battle between Pinchot and Ballinger was thrust center stage by the machinations of Pinchot and the assistance of the muckrakers. As a result, it was transformed from mere bureaucratic infighting to a sign of the growing gap between Roosevelt and Taft and the power of federal control of public lands as a social problem, an issue which continued to bother politicians a century later. The idea of collaborative efforts among journalists and politicians was solidified by the muckrakers; that association began to be questioned by some in the media, who preferred an "information messenger" function. Still, as David Protess and coauthors (1991) pointed out, investigative journalists in the 1980s continued to contact government policymakers to discuss reforms that might result from the publication of a story. They were following a media-source relationship path that began years earlier.

NOTES

1. Timber frauds in Oregon first came to light in 1903, and 26 convictions were won by the government in 5 years, including that of Senator John H. Mitchell.

2. Some historians claim one of Pierce's sons was a Cunningham claimant, but this research could find no evidence of that statement.

3. Several years later, the muckraker Gustavus Myers, who never gave up the genre, said the Guggenheims had already invested $15 million in Alaska and won the election of one of the family, Simon Guggenheim, to a U.S. senate seat from Colorado (see Myers, 1939, pp. 212-214).

4. Figures reported in the April 2, 1910, issue of *Collier's*.

5

MEDIA AND COMPETING POWER GROUPS

A Big Dam Controversy

n the cases of the national park system and the Alaskan land grab affair, the three-way coalition of environmentalists, the mass media, and important members of the business and political establishments controlled the direction of change so that the goals of the environmentalists were met. When the three-way coalition came apart, as happened in the Hetch Hetchy dam controversy in California, the issues of the environmentalists were lost. In this case, as was the case of the ethyl leaded gasoline controversy in the 1920s, conflicting problem definitions came from the power structure, and important interest groups were working against the environmentalists. The green crusaders retained their specialty publications and alternative forms of media, pushing their definition of the problem, but the response of the mainstream media was mixed. In the case of the local media, they supported the power structure in northern California, much as they did in the instance of the formation of the parks. The results of the conflict were disappointing to the environmentalists.

AN EXPENSIVE COMMODITY

In 1847, 2 years before the California gold rush, the community of Yerba Buena, recently won from the Spanish, changed its name to honor St. Francis. The residents of San Francisco relied on springs for their fresh water, which was a suitable solution until the forty-niners flooded the city. Water rapidly became an expensive commodity. An enterprising man named Juan Miguel Aguirre opened a water distribution company with a burro and two large barrels in his fleet. Aguirre dipped water from three sources—the Presidio, Mountain Lake, and a spring on Washington Street near Montgomery. The man and his burro carried water to San Franciscans who paid $1 per bucket; in flush times, Aguirre pocketed $30 per day (Taylor, 1926, p. 10).[1]

On November 23, 1852, an earthquake struck northern California. At Lake La Merced, near the city, the quake ripped open a channel to the sea and water poured forth, dropping the level of the lake by 30 feet. The La Merced discharge illustrated the geologic problems of a young, growing city sitting on a major fault line without enough fresh water to meet its commercial and residential needs. The city had other problems as well. Almost all of the buildings—and many of the roads—were made of wood, a plentiful and cheap building material but a flammable one. At least six times during the first few years of the settlement, a significant part of the city caught fire; newspaper stories highlighted the area's water shortage after each blaze. Enterprising citizens sometimes put out fires with water substitutes: One man saved his warehouse by throwing 80,000 gallons of vinegar on it (Taylor, 1926, p. 14).

Water shortages plagued the city throughout the 19th century. Eventually, San Franciscans turned to a water source in Yosemite National Park in a valley called Hetch Hetchy, named by Indians in reference to its grassy meadows. The long fight over the Hetch Hetchy dam cannot be separated from the importance of water in the settlement of the region and the status of conservation as a social movement. The conflict was among the first of many 20th-century confrontations between the interests of government, businesses, and groups concerned with the environment. The national media reported the goings-on between the city of San Francisco, the water companies, and nature lovers with zeal. Historian Hans Huth (1957) wrote, "One of the remarkable things about the case was that, though the subject of the debate was a remote valley in California which few in the East had seen, interest in it became nation-wide" (p. 183). The issue aroused the nation because it was communicated coast to coast and reflected common concerns—about water rights and the role of the national parks—among the public. Fights between (and among) environmentalists and dam builders became commonplace in the years to follow; in many ways, Hetch Hetchy is the granddaddy of those disputes.

Hetch Hetchy is often seen as representative of an emerging fissure in the conservation movement between the protectionism ideas of John Muir and Robert Underwood Johnson and the utilitarianism of Gifford Pinchot and Theodore Roosevelt (Jones, 1965; Nash, 1982, pp. 161-181). Others view the issue as an antimonopoly dispute at a time when one private water company controlled most of San Francisco's supply (Taylor, 1926). To some degree, these interpretations are correct. The construction of a reservoir in Yosemite National Park was a complex political and social fight about water, national parks, and public utilities between the city of San Francisco, competing private interests, political groups, and environmentalists. That environmentalists joined the fray after it had begun is not as important as their failure to rebuild coalitions—coalitions of big business, mass media, and government agencies that were powerful forces in the successful debates at Yellowstone National Park and Yosemite Valley.

WATER NEEDS OF SAN FRANCISCO

By the mid-1850s, San Francisco's need for water was outpacing Juan Miguel Aguirre's burro and the rest of the city's independent entrepreneurs. Aguirre's judgment on the best places to dip water was confirmed in 1858 when more sophisticated transportation systems grew up around his sources. Water first flowed along a new 5-mile-long redwood-plank aqueduct from Mountain Lake to a reservoir at Black Point in 1858. That year, the Spring Valley Water Works (later called the Spring Valley Water Company) opened using water from Aguirre's spring on Washington Street. Spring Valley hired a young, German-trained engineer named Hermann Schussler, who recommended that the firm acquire the rights to 100,000 acres of watershed property for dams, reservoirs, and aqueducts. Spring Valley bought out its major competitor, the San Francisco Water Works, in the 1860s and announced it would begin charging the municipality for water other than water to fight fires. The city refused to pay, beginning an 11-year legal battle and decades of hard feelings among politicians, taxpayers, and the Spring Valley Water Works, which began to resemble a water monopoly and became known for high rates and bad service (Taylor, 1926, p. 17).

The squabble between the water company and the city escalated in the 1870s when Spring Valley bought water rights in Calaveras County that the city wanted. The company offered to sell its holdings to San Francisco for $15.5 million, but the city refused. In turn, the city hired U.S. Army engineer George H. Mendell to look for water in 1876 and 1877. Mendell surveyed nine sources, including far-flung areas like Lake Tahoe, Clear Lake, and the Mokelumne River, but did not consider the Tuolumne River in Hetch Hetchy significant enough to examine. The city did not act on any of Mendell's surveys, perhaps because several years of wet weather had eased the water crisis, whereas Spring Valley opened a new reservoir and the city attorney advised against a municipal water works (Jones, 1965, p. 87). In 1877, Spring Valley rejected a counteroffer of $11 million from the city. Bitter feelings between the city and the private water company escalated in 1880 with the ratification of the California state constitution, which forced the city to pay for its water. City politicians passed on three fourths of the municipal water cost to the citizens, beginning an extended fight over water rates between the water company, businesses, politicians, and taxpayers.

THE HETCH HETCHY SITE

By April 1894, San Francisco's power structure tired of Spring Valley, and the board of supervisors published an advertisement in the *Examiner,* the *Post,* and the *Daily Report* asking for proposals from parties desiring to furnish water to the city and county. Replies came from everywhere, including one from George M. Harris, who suggested the city buy his land. Harris claimed he owned the water rights for the entire length of the Tuolumne River, which included the Hetch Hetchy Valley in the newly opened Yosemite National Park. His price: $200,000. Harris, who said he had mined the river since the first wave of gold fever in 1849, told of offering the water rights to San Francisco Mayor E. B. Pond in 1888. Pond had dismissed him, Harris said. During the discussion, at least one engineering map of the river turned up. An engineer named J. P. Dart, who was working for the Tuolumne and San Francisco Water Company, had surveyed the area in 1882. The board of supervisors rejected Harris's offer, but the debate established the Tuolumne River as a possible water source for the city (Taylor, 1926, pp. 29-31).

Hetch Hetchy was a valley in the Sierra Mountains about 20 miles north of Yosemite Valley in Yosemite National Park. Much more remote than Yosemite, Hetch Hetchy had no wagon road access and few visitors, which probably made it less appreciated than more popular areas. A writer for *Outing* magazine, Xenos Clark, noted in 1885 that Hetch Hetchy "is one perfectly cut little gem," although a trip there was only for "genuine outdoor people. The skin must be a little toughened to the wilderness, and the heart must be entirely on the nature side" (Clark, 1885, p. 151).

San Francisco's engineers and hydrologists found Hetch Hetchy to be perfect for a dam. The valley, which featured a flat floor and steep cliffs, narrowed at the west end, making it convenient and inexpensive for a dam. The site resembled a 3½-mile-long bathtub, through which a crystal-clear mountain stream flowed. Further-more, the "bathtub" was only 150 miles from the city. San Francisco city engineer Marsden Manson, an important figure in the Hetch Hetchy conflict, said (as quoted in Jones, 1965) he liked the site for several reasons, including

> absolute purity by reason of the uninhabitable character of the entire watershed tributary to the reservoirs and largely within a forest reservation . . . abundance, far beyond possible future demands for all purposes . . . largest and most numerous sites for storage . . . free-dom from complicating "water rights" and . . . power possibilities outside the reservation. (p. 88)

The protection provided by the national park supplied several of the site's benefits.

The federal government entered the conflict in 1899 when an engineer working for the U.S. Geological Survey (USGS) calculating stream flows measured the Tuolumne River in Hetch Hetchy Valley. J. H. Quinton took the results to the city, where he suggested a Hetch Hetchy site could provide an "unfailing supply of pure water" to San Francisco. Quinton produced USGS surveys from 1889 and 1890 at Lake Eleanor, 2 miles northwest of Hetch Hetchy, and 1891 at Hetch Hetchy to support his claim (Taylor, 1926, p. 33). The city, as it established Hetch Hetchy as its optimum site, relied on the federal reports written by Quinton.

The Progressive movement was under way at the turn of the century, and one of its reforms was a new city charter in 1900 for San Francisco—a document requiring the city to own its utilities. The charter required San Francisco's government to recommend a new water supply in place of the privately owned Spring Valley Water Company, which held the rights to all nearby water sources. The city briefly considered condemning the Spring Valley properties, but the engineers doubted whether—even if a fair price could be reached—the private firm controlled enough property to fill San Francisco's future needs (Clements, 1979, p. 187). After rejecting Lake Tahoe and the snowpack of Mount Shasta, the city engineer offered the Quinton report, adding cost estimates for canals, dams, tunnels, pipes, roads, a power station, and all the rest of a water supply's requirements. The price was $38.2 million. There was a jurisdictional matter to overcome, however, because most of the property in question was in Yosemite National Park.

In 1900, the national parks did not have a strong bureaucratic structure to protect themselves (the National Park Service was formed in 1916), amplifying a decade of federal ambivalence about the Hetch Hetchy project. The few national parks were under the purview of the Department of the Interior, which attempted to slow the project as best it could. Secretary of the Interior Ethan A. Hitchcock criticized the report on the use of Hetch Hetchy as a water supply as an "unauthorized invasion" of a national park by San Francisco (Graham, 1971, p. 161).

San Francisco's representatives pressured Congress for relief. Representative Marion DeVries of Stockton, who had failed on several earlier attempts to exploit park resources, authored Hetch Hetchy legislation in February 1901. The Right of Way Act of 1901 legalized San Francisco's attempts to use the park for a water supply, providing the city got the Interior Department's approval for the project. The Right of Way Act, according to park historian John Ise (1961), was "perfectly tailored for looters of the parks, for it authorized the Secretary to grant rights of way through government reservations of all kinds" for water conduits, dams, reservoirs, and other projects "in the public interest" (p. 85). None of the conservation groups, including the Sierra Club, fought the passage of the bill. William Colby, president of the Sierra Club, said later that "we were probably not vigilant enough, but we certainly did not lack the desire to know of all that was going on" (as quoted in Jones, 1965, p. 90). The act, which only applied to California parks, may have been written by DeVries on behalf of his farm constituency in the Central Valley, which needed water for irrigation. No matter what DeVries's motives were, Hitchcock would have none of it. The secretary turned down the city's request to build a reservoir on the site, claiming the request was not in the public's interest.

Hitchcock's opposition did not stop the city from moving ahead. In 1902, the board of supervisors recommended Hetch Hetchy and Lake Eleanor as the best possible supply sites. Quietly, the city retained a USGS engineer to survey the area again and file claims for water rights under the name of James D. Phelan, who was San Francisco's Democratic mayor and an antimonopoly progressive. Word of the

activity leaked to an angry Hitchcock, who complained to President
Theodore Roosevelt. San Francisco engineer Marsden Manson re-
plied that there was no requirement in the law that his office notify
the Department of the Interior before performing such work. Be-
sides, Manson said, Phelan filed the claims as a private citizen, not
as mayor. In April 1902, Phelan applied to the Department of the
Interior for right-of-way and reservoir sites for Hetch Hetchy and
Lake Eleanor. Hitchcock denied Phelan's request in January 1903.
The mayor then transferred his rights to the city and county, but
Hitchcock blocked the city's request in December 1903. Supporting
the interior secretary were irrigation districts in the San Joaquin
Valley representing Waterford, Modesto, and Turlock; those agencies
wanted the federal government to keep Tuolumne River rights so
they could obtain them later. One of the administrators of the
Modesto irrigation district was Lewis L. Dennett, whose law partner,
James C. Needham, was a congressman. The Spring Valley Water
Company also spoke out in favor of Hitchcock. An appeal by San
Francisco city attorney Franklin Lane failed in early 1905.

POLITICAL CHANGE
AND DRAMATIC EVENTS

The Democrats lost control of city government to the spoils-
dominated Union Labor Party. E. E. Schmitz replaced Phelan as
mayor in 1902, and engineer Manson was not reappointed to the
board of public works in 1904.[2] After the rejection of Lane's appeal
in 1905, the new mayor and board of supervisors said they were
weary of the Hetch Hetchy fight; they adopted a resolution early in
1906 formally abandoning the project, which they called "illusory"
(Taylor, 1926, p. 61). Party boss Abe Ruef then accepted an offer to
fill the city's water needs from the Bay Cities Water Company,
another private firm. The events of the coming months, however,
shortened the political careers of the mayor and 16 members of the
board. At the ensuing graft trial of Ruef and his cohorts, testimony
revealed that the Bay Cities's proposal came with a promise of a
million-dollar bribe (Bean, 1952, p. 270).

The water problems of the entire region became national news when the devastating earthquake of April 18, 1906, struck San Francisco. Fire swept through the streets, destroying much of the city. The Spring Valley reservoirs held fast, but the company's distribution system was severely damaged in the blaze, which burned out of control for hours partly due to a shortage of water. The fire mobilized the campaign for a new water supply and redefined the problem in the local media in terms of public safety (Cohen, 1988).[3] After the graft trial of Ruef and associates, the Democrats returned to office in 1907 with a powerful political issue.

In late 1906, Hitchcock resigned as interior secretary. He was succeeded by James R. Garfield, son of the late president and a Roosevelt favorite. Garfield, a close friend of chief forester Gifford Pinchot, favored the water project after viewing the results of the earthquake and fire. Pinchot liked the Yosemite dam, but his reasons for supporting the project were kept to himself on the basis of his utilitarian concept of conservation (he did not mention Hetch Hetchy in his autobiography). Pinchot endorsed the plan in a letter to Manson in May 1906, urging him to continue to work for a dam permit. Pinchot wrote (Gifford Pinchot to Marsden Manson, May 28, 1906, as cited in Wolfe, 1946),

> I was very glad to hear from your letter of May 10th that the earthquake had damaged neither your activity nor your courage. . . . I hope sincerely that in the regeneration of San Francisco its people may be able to make provision for a water supply from the Yosemite National Park. . . . I will stand ready to render any assistance which lies within my power (p. 312)

Manson had visited Washington to lobby for the proposal as a private citizen in 1905, winning over Pinchot and meeting with Roosevelt.

With the Schmitz decision to drop Hetch Hetchy discredited by the graft trials, the city reinstated its claim in the summer of 1907. Garfield traveled west in 1907, opening a hearing on the subject in San Francisco on July 27, 1907, in front of the city's new mayor and a mostly new board of supervisors. No opponents of the project appeared at the hearings. Park lovers, including the Sierra Club, had spent the previous few years fighting to get Yosemite Valley turned over to the federal government and may not have been prepared for another effort to raid Hetch Hetchy by the city. It was probably no coincidence that the hearing was scheduled at the same time the Sierra Club camped in the mountains on an annual trip. In addition, many of the Sierra Club's members lived in San Francisco and could see the appeal of both sides. Warren Olney, one of the Sierra Club's founders who had lost a reelection bid for a board of directors seat, was a project supporter. John Muir, of course, was not. He asked the Sierra Club to send a delegation to Washington, DC, to monitor activity on Hetch Hetchy in Congress and the executive branch. In a September letter, Muir appealed directly to Roosevelt, but the president, torn between political reality and his environmentalist leanings, refused to intervene and instead turned the issue back to Garfield. Roosevelt said he did not want to hinder the growth of California: The results of using Yosemite "so as to interfere with the permanent material development" of the state were undesirable (Theodore Roosevelt to John Muir, September 16, 1907, as cited in Morison, 1951, p. 793). In effect, Roosevelt endorsed the multiple muse concept of wilderness areas, the idea vigorously promoted by Pinchot. The forester (as quoted in Nash, 1982) wrote the president in October,

> I fully sympathize with the desire of Mr. Johnson and Mr. Muir to protect the Yosemite National Park, but I believe the highest possible use which could be made of it would be to supply pure water to a great center of population. (p. 164)

Muir, undaunted, considered re-forming his coalition with the railroad companies. The old Scotsman was unable to use railroad help on Hetch Hetchy, however, because powerful antimonopoly Progressives stood behind Roosevelt and the railroads were not interested in the issue (Cohen, 1984, pp. 324-325). Muir feared more political backlash from the Progressives, who were already lining up in favor of San Francisco's position. Muir instead appealed to Johnson, editor of *Century* magazine in New York City, and Theodore Lukens, a resident of San Bernardino who had helped Muir in his Yosemite fights. Muir also asked other clubs for help, includ-

Figure 5.1. John Burroughs and John Muir.
Two of the most well-known of the early preservationists, John Muir (right) and John Burroughs, wrote newspaper stories, magazine articles, and books promoting wilderness protection ideas. Muir's biggest defeat came with the building of a dam at Hetch Hetchy in Yosemite National Park. Reproduced from the Collections of the Library of Congress (No. 64265).

ing the Mazamas, the Appalachian Mountain Club, the Saturday Walking Club, and the American Civic Association. He wrote an article for *Outlook* magazine titled "The Tuolumne Yosemite in Danger" in which Muir defended the natural beauty of the valley and noted other water supplies outside the park (Muir, 1907, p. 489). Muir received encouragement from the Spring Valley Water Company, which naturally wanted to prevent the city water services from becoming a public utility (Fox, 1981, p. 142). A dam at Hetch Hetchy would put Spring Valley out of business (Figure 5.1).

Outlook magazine, a journal of opinion, became one of the media forces behind the preservationists. Editor Lyman Abbott's magazine served an upper-class audience, a group that viewed the rising ride of industrialism, immigration, and urbanization with some alarm. American culture was midway down a slippery slope, according to Abbott, and the emphasis of big business values over more genteel ideas was part of the problem. Abbott viewed the dam as an effort "to turn every tree and waterfall into dollars and cents" (as quoted in Nash, 1982, p. 166). *Outlook*'s editorials and articles focused on similar themes throughout the battle over Hetch Hetchy.

The conservationists sailed in rough seas. The city of Los Angeles recently tapped a distant water source in Owens Valley, and many Californians were acutely aware of the importance of water rights. The president of the University of California, Benjamin I. Wheeler, wrote Johnson that the damage to the valley would be slight and that opponents of the plan were led by Spring Valley, which had its own economic interests at heart. Furthermore, Wheeler said Muir did not speak for the entire Sierra Club (as cited in Richardson, 1959, p. 251).[4] Important members of the Progressive reform movement in California began lining up behind the construction of the reservoir, many objecting to the monopoly position of the Spring Valley Water Company or the bossism of Ruef, or both. H. L. Atkinson, a San Francisco attorney, wrote to Sierra Club president Colby (as quoted in Jones, 1965),

> I must earnestly protest against the Sierra Club for being used as a cat's paw to pull chestnuts from the fire for the Spring Valley Water Company, or for the grafters who have taken up the Sierras' water rights with the object of selling their rights to San Francisco. (p. 97)

The mixed signals sent from the splintered Sierra Club muddied public debate on the subject and weakened the environmentalists' position.

One of the unspoken aspects of the plan was the possible use of the Tuolumne as a source of electric power for the city. Phelan, Pinchot, and other Progressives favored municipal water and power; this may explain why alternate sites were not fully explored. Hetch Hetchy, with its natural reservoir and high elevation, was a natural hydroelectric power plant. Other sites in the lowlands had less to offer.

The opponents of the dam focused their efforts on Garfield, who had not seen the valley. Sierra Club members William F. Badé and Colby thought that if they could get the secretary to visit Hetch Hetchy, perhaps the scenery would help change his mind (Richardson, 1959, p. 251). Congressman Needham also approached the secretary, voicing the objections of the irrigationists. Their arguments did not carry the day. Garfield approved the request on May 11, 1908, inserting a clause that Lake Eleanor be fully developed as a water source first, with Hetch Hetchy held in reserve. In his decision, Garfield noted the pure water and electric power possibilities of the site. He stated that the scenery, which he had not seen, would not suffer from a reservoir and might be enhanced by the project. Garfield stated (as quoted in Jones, 1965), "The prime change will be that, instead of a beautiful but somewhat unusable 'meadow' floor, the valley will be a lake of rare beauty" (p. 99). Two days later, Pinchot opened an historic meeting in Washington, the White House Conference on the Conservation of Natural Resources, with the nation's governors and other leaders taking part. The theme of the event emphasized Pinchot's utilitarian views on conservation—the multiple-use idea—and the Garfield action illustrated that position. (Muir was purposely excluded.) The Garfield permit also quieted Roosevelt's congressional critics, who were complaining that too many natural resources were being shielded from development by the conservationists (Clements, 1979, pp. 189-190).[5]

A DAM SETBACK

Fourteen members of the board of supervisors, accompanied by Manson (newly reappointed as city engineer), six newspapermen, and several others visited Hetch Hetchy on August 19, 1908. The group, few of whom had ever seen the region before, traveled in three stagecoaches from Yosemite Valley to Hetch Hetchy. The party came upon a forest fire near Hog Ranch. A huge pine tree stood in the way of the blaze, but the men formed a bucket brigade at a spring 100 yards away and doused the blaze, saving the tree. Several miles from Hetch Hetchy, where the trail narrowed, the group left their coaches in favor of mules and horses. Several minutes later, another forest fire appeared, this one fought by Army troops stationed at Yosemite. The politicians and reporters dashed around and through the fire, leaving it to the troops, and found their way to the valley. The remoteness of the area was obvious to the group, but the hazards of fire were made clear too. The supervisors issued a favorable report on the proposed dam site, reported on with approval by the media involved in the trip (Taylor, 1926, p. 82).

San Franciscans hoped to get most of the land for the project for free because the national park was already in the public domain. Voters passed a bond issue in November approving $600,000 for the purchase of private property near the site. Garfield's stipulation that the city first explore Lake Eleanor slowed the project because the city did not own water rights at Lake Eleanor. The election of 1908 did not bode well for the city either. William Howard Taft, Roosevelt's choice, won the presidency, but among his first acts was to dump Garfield in favor of former Seattle mayor Richard Ballinger as secretary of the interior.

Meanwhile, a bill was introduced in Congress to allow San Francisco to exchange property it purchased from homesteaders in Yosemite Park—as Garfield requested in his decision—with the federal property needed for the dam project. The House Committee on Public Lands scheduled a hearing for December 16, 1908. The nation's important newspapers covered the 2-day session, as Muir, Johnson, Spring Valley's lawyers, and members of other groups, including the American Civic Association and the Appalachian Mountain Club, testified. Opponents of the dam started a direct mail and telegram campaign. Phelan testified that Muir "would sacrifice his own family for the preservation of beauty. He considers human life very cheap, and he considers the works of God superior" (as quoted in Wolfe, 1945, p. 316). When the hearings reconvened on January 9, 1909, antidam groups flooded the committee with letters, cards, telegrams, and other messages. Clubs associated with the environmental movement from Washington, Utah, Massachusetts, Iowa, Nevada, Illinois, California, and New York communicated with the committee—filling over 100 pages of the Congressional Record with telegram messages alone. Muir, using alternative and mainstream media when he could, published a pamphlet with the now-famous statement, "Dam Hetch Hetchy! As well dam for water tanks the people's cathedrals and churches, for no holier temple has ever been consecrated by the heart of man" (Muir, 1909). The House committee voted 8 to 7 to approve the issue, but several key senators opposed the proposal. Sensing defeat, San Francisco's representatives withdrew the bill.

The Appalachian Mountain Club, along with the Society for the Preservation of National Parks, made formal requests to Ballinger in April asking him to revoke Garfield's grant. A month earlier, Ballinger had assured Phelan that he would uphold Garfield's ruling, but several political events caused him to change his mind. The widely publicized battle with Pinchot over the Alaskan coal leases weakened the new secretary politically; perhaps he saw preserving Hetch Hetchy as a way to mend fences. Ballinger's rejection of Garfield's position may have been a simple act of vengeance in his bureaucratic turf war with Pinchot. Taft and Ballinger visited the 71-year-old Muir at Yosemite in October in a party of 200 people, and Muir took the interior secretary to Hetch Hetchy for a tour as the 300-pound Taft declined to camp in the valley. "Everything in the Hetch Hetchy Yosemite Park battle looks fine for our side & black for the robbers," Muir (as quoted in Clements, 1979, p. 192) wrote Johnson.

Supporters of the dam, led by Manson, focused on the theme of the need for a public utility to combat the monopoly of Spring Valley. Manson, no stranger to the power of publicity, published a pamphlet on the subject and supplied a writer for *Collier's,* Agnes Laut, with material for a series of four stories (Laut, 1909). Meanwhile, in a pair of seemingly contradictory moves behind the scenes, Manson appealed to an organization of elite businessmen, the Commonwealth Club, for an endorsement of the project. Also, a purchase agreement with Spring Valley was near. Manson convinced himself that Spring Valley was the power and the money behind the preservationists' efforts; he thought buying out the company would shut down the opposition. A special city election was scheduled for January 1910 with two questions on the ballot: a $45 million bond issue for the Lake Eleanor phase of the project and a $35 million bond issue to buy the water monopoly. The Lake Eleanor bond passed, but the water company buyout failed when the mayor and others complained that the price was too high (Clements, 1979, p. 194).

In 1910, shortly after Taft fired Pinchot, Ballinger reviewed the project, ordering the city to show why Hetch Hetchy should not be cut out of the affair entirely, leaving Lake Eleanor as the lone water source. Conservationists rejoiced. E. L. Bickford of Napa, California, wrote to Colby, "Secretary Ballinger's document sounded so much like Sierra Club literature you couldn't tell the difference with your eyes shut!" (as quoted in Jones, 1965, p. 123). Two Reclamation Service engineers, Louis C. Hill and E. G. Hopson, submitted a report to the secretary stating that San Francisco's plan was technically weak. The report went on to say that the region was more valuable as a campground than a water supply, that adequate water was available from other sources, and that the entire plan was a scheme by the city to force Spring Valley to lower its rates (Clements, 1979, p. 196). Taft told San Francisco mayor P. H. McCarthy that the Garfield permit of 1908 "was not worth the paper upon which it was written" (as quoted in Taylor, 1926, p. 103). The events signaled the high point of conservationists' effort to block the dam. Ballinger scheduled hearings for May 18, 1910. The usual suspects trotted back to Washington, DC, for more testimony, which was delayed until May 25.

Preparing for the hearings, Manson, irritated at the Hill-Hopson report, had been investigating the background of the two engineers. He found that the two had visited the proposed dam site only once; in fact, their report relied on a survey done by another engineer, Philip E. Harroun of Berkeley. This was a common practice among engineers, but the fact that Harroun was in the employ of the Spring Valley Water Company at the time interested Manson a great deal. The knowledge that much of Harroun's report came from data supplied by the Bay Cities Water Company also interested him greatly. Harroun's apparent conflict of interest raised doubts about the accuracy of his report. The environmentalists' position was damaged further when they decided to hire an engineer to support their notion that the city could use alternate sites for its water needs. The engineer they hired to attend the Washington hearings was Philip E. Harroun, who apparently neglected to inform them of his previous associations with Spring Valley and Bay Cities (Clements, 1979, p. 197).

Imagine Manson's glee when he saw Harroun representing Muir and the dam opponents at Ballinger's hearings. As historian Kendrick Clements suggested, however, the city engineer did not expose Harroun in public. Instead, Manson took Ballinger aside and told the secretary of the developments. Publicity about Harroun's conflict of interest and Ballinger's reliance on the Hill-Hopson report would have damaged the secretary politically and may have cost him his job. Ballinger was of more use to Manson as secretary of the interior, where he held power over the Garfield permit. Whether Ballinger would have revoked the Garfield permit is not clear; he certainly led Muir and the others to believe he favored their position. In the end, with the specter of another muckraker-driven conflict-of-interest scandal hanging over his head on the heels of the Alaskan coal deal, Ballinger appointed another commission to restudy the matter.[6] A special advisory board of the army engineers would review all the data and advise the secretary. The selection of the prodevelopment army engineers was a serious setback for the nature lovers, as was the committee's reliance on the city's data. The city's engineers, led by John Freeman, made little effort to explore alternate sites. Freeman's report, sent to every member of Congress, expanded the project considerably and influenced the army board a great deal.

The antidam forces suffered another loss in March 1911 when Ballinger, beset from all sides and in poor health, resigned. Taft appointed Walter L. Fisher, a friend of Pinchot, as his new interior secretary in an attempt to appease Progressives from California. Fisher visited Hetch Hetchy later in the year but made no pronouncements on where he stood on the issue. J. Horace McFarland, president of the American Civic Association, went along, as did Manson, and both lobbied the secretary while verbally sparring with each other. McFarland wrote Colby, "I taxed Mr. Manson at once with not intending to use the Lake Eleanor supply unless he could get Hetch Hetchy, and he admitted this was his intention" (as quoted in Jones, 1965, p. 129). It may have been the first public sign that Hetch Hetchy was the city's prime target, not Lake Eleanor.

The California Progressives, still unhappy with Taft, lined up solidly behind the Democrats and Woodrow Wilson in the election of 1912. Fisher held 6 days' worth of hearings in late November, and both sides felt they had convinced the secretary of the soundness of their position. All parties waited for the report of the army board, which was released in February. The Army recommended to Fisher that the dam be built because it was the most cost-effective solution to the city's water needs.

Perhaps as a last slap at the Progressives, 3 days before the Wilson inauguration, Fisher ruled that the dam could not be built without specific congressional authorization. The secretary said he did not believe the 1901 Right of Way Act gave him the authority to grant the permit if cost was the primary question, which the Army report said it was (Jones, 1965, p. 146). Fisher was also acting on behalf of the defeated Taft, who had stuck to the notion that the executive branch could act only with a legislative mandate throughout the Alaskan affair (see Chapter 3). Among Wilson's first appointees was the former city attorney of San Francisco, Franklin K. Lane, who became secretary of the interior. Fisher's decision left Lane powerless to rubber-stamp the matter; the issue moved to the congressional arena, where both sides began lining up their people one more time.

THE RAKER ACT

Congressman John E. Raker of Alturas, whose district included Hetch Hetchy, introduced a bill to confirm the Yosemite grant, HR 112, on April 7, 1913, shortly after the new president took office. Several more bills followed. Raker, a former California Democratic state committee chair, was a close friend of James Phelan and an early supporter of Wilson. The proposed legislation placated the irrigation districts by forcing San Francisco to sell them water at cost. Meanwhile, Spring Valley's political power, weakened over the years, rendered the company ineffective in Congress. Only the conservationists remained to fight the bill. Johnson and Muir sent out form letters to influential citizens all over the country asking them to mail cards to Congress. The Society for the Preservation of National Parks began a mass mailing campaign to more than 1,400 newspapers across the country. Among the mailings were leaflets designed for use by editorial writers or as drop-in fillers in the newspapers. Johnson published and circulated a pamphlet in which he called Hetch Hetchy "a veritable temple of the living God" and declared that "again the money changers are in the temple" (as quoted in Nash, 1982, p. 170). Muir also enlisted the help of politically powerful and well-organized women's clubs (Richardson, 1959, p. 254).

Many of the national media stood behind the city. *San Francisco Examiner* publisher William Randolph Hearst used his paper to secure 15,000 signatures to present to Congress. The *Examiner* published a special edition on December 2, 1913, that included a half-page drawing of the proposed reservoir and an editorial beneath it headlined "The Real Facts About Hetch Hetchy." On the front page, the *Examiner* quoted powerful men who approved of the project, including Secretary of Agriculture D. F. Houston, Secretary of State William Jennings Bryan, Vice President T. R. Marshall, and Secretary of the Interior Lane ("The Real Facts," 1913, p. 1). Every member of Congress received a copy of the *Examiner.* Muir and Johnson soon discovered that the Raker bill was an administration measure, probably agreed on before the election (Richardson, 1959, p. 255).[7]

Ironically, the old adversaries, Muir and Manson, were too ill to carry on the fight. Manson retired as city engineer in the summer of 1912 in poor health, probably due to overwork. Muir, who suffered from an infected lung, could not testify. He wrote his wife Helen, "Anyhow I'll be relieved when it's settled, for it's killing me" (as quoted in Wolfe, 1945, p. 340). The only well-known conservationist to testify was Edmund Whitman, who headed the eastern office of the Society for the Preservation of National Parks. The committee was not sympathetic to Whitman, who had not seen Hetch Hetchy in person (Clements, 1979, p. 209). Muir wrote two letters accusing the Sierra Club of not helping enough (Jones, 1965, p. 160). Disorganized and dispirited, the conservationists did not put up an effective fight on what was to be their last chance at saving the valley. The city, meanwhile, seized its opportunity and paraded an impressive roster of politicians, engineers, businesspeople, and others to Washington. Among the city's star witnesses was William Denman, a San Francisco judge and charter member of the Sierra Club. Denman, who had visited Hetch Hetchy, said the Club's actions were not in "perfect candor" and that the group was not united on the preservation of the valley (Jones, 1965, p. 157). Pinchot also appeared on behalf of the project, calling the need of the city "overwhelming." The final version of the Raker Act, HR 7207, passed Congress by a vote of 183 to 43 in August.

Mail flooded the offices of senators who took up the issue. Senator Reed Smoot of Utah estimated receiving 5,000 letters against the bill. Many of the nation's newspapers and magazines ran articles and editorials opposing the plan. *The Independent* stated, "The existence of one of the world's beauty spots is trembling in the balance against commercial greed. . . . There is no doubt the enlightened sense of the whole country is against this unnecessary profanation" ("Save Hetch Hetchy," 1913a, p. 8). Among those writing newspaper articles was Frederick Law Olmstead Jr., son of the famous landscape architect and Yosemite champion ("The Hetch Hetchy Bill," 1913). The *Boston Transcript* stated, "If San Francisco succeeds in stealing the Hetch Hetchy valley no doubt she will next want to cut down the redwood trees to obtain timber with which to dam it up" (as quoted in "Save Hetch Hetchy," 1913b, p. 204).[8] Some newspapers in Southern California opposed the plan, including the *Pasadena News,* which said San Francisco's worn-out arguments gave its editors the impression that "unless the Hetch Hetchy bill was passed our northern compatriots must perish from thirst" ("Save Hetch Hetchy," 1913b, p. 204). Elsewhere, the *Chicago Inter-Ocean,* locked in a circulation battle with Hearst's *Chicago American,* stated, "It looks as if every good American who thinks our national parks are worth while [*sic*] should bestir himself in defense of Hetch Hetchy" ("Save Hetch Hetchy," 1913b, p. 204).

While the preservationists were fighting a very public battle in the mass media, San Francisco's representatives were quietly working the hallways of the capitol, counting votes and culling favors. Among the public messages delivered by dam supporters came from Hearst's *Examiner,* which published a special edition on December 2, with stories and drawings showing the benefits of a new reservoir, marinas, and roads in the mountains ("The Real Facts," 1913). Although the debate was sometimes spirited, the Senate approved the measure in December by a 43 to 25 vote at 3 minutes before midnight on December 6, 1913. Eighteen southern Democrats provided the margin of victory for their Democratic president. Meanwhile, the Society for the Preservation of National Parks held a protest meeting asking the president to veto the bill. The protesters engaged in wishful thinking. Wilson signed the act on December 19, 1913.

The position of Wilson, Lane, Pinchot, and Garfield, which upheld the utilitarian view of conservation, received the support of the rest of the Progressives, who would have taken most any position opposite Taft and Ballinger. McFarland, who once called the utilitarians "ugly conservationists," wrote Colby, "I have had the feeling from the moment Mr. Lane was put into the cabinet that we were absolutely lost, because the San Francisco people had operated so cunningly as to get political influence at the right spot" (as quoted in Jones, 1965, p. 167). The city of San Francisco, in exchange for the water from Yosemite National Park, agreed to pay the federal government $15,000 per year for 10 years, $20,000 each year for the following decade, and $30,000 per year thereafter.

CONCLUSION

The Hetch Hetchy dam remained unfinished for several years. Muir, bitter at the defeat, died after catching pneumonia in 1914, before the dam flooded the valley. "As for the destruction of the Hetch Hetchy Valley, California and the Government owe him penance at his tomb," wrote Robert Underwood Johnson (1923, p. 315). World War I slowed construction, but the completion of what was called O'Shaughnessy Dam came on July 7, 1923. Other parts of the reservoir, vital to its use, went unfinished for several more years. Also left undone for years were the fire roads and other facilities San Francisco promised to build to accommodate tourists at the new lake. The aqueduct opened in 1934, but the city had no means to distribute the electricity generated by the dam, so it was sold to a private group, the Pacific Gas and Electric Company. The dam cost more than $100 million—more than twice the original estimate. In an ironic twist, cities in the East Bay, weary of waiting for Hetch Hetchy to help meet their water needs, developed the Mokelumne River as a source—the same river rejected by San Francisco—at a cost of $36 million by 1931. Technological progress triumphed over the aesthetic arguments of the environmentalists.

Hetch Hetchy's effect on the conservation movement divides scholars and politicians. Many take a lost-the-battle, won-the-war view. On the winning side: No part of a national park has since been appropriated for such a project. Frank Graham, Jr. (1971) stated, "The conservation movement came out purified and strengthened, better prepared for similar confrontations in the years ahead" (p. 167). The Hetch Hetchy fight, which further legitimized the movement in the governmental arena, was a key mobilization point for conservation groups. Hetch Hetchy became a valuable symbol of the worst that could happen to national parks, a martyr for the cause. Many of those groups were involved in the successful push for the establishment of the National Park Service in 1916. On the other side, the Sierra Club, which was defeated, did not fare as well. During the conflict, Olney and about 50 members of the club resigned (Cohen, 1988, pp. 30-32).[9] Torn by the controversy and the death of Muir, the club's power faded and, according to former Interior Secretary Stewart Udall, became "little more than a regional hiking club, preoccupied with the resources in its own backyard" until the 1950s (Udall, 1988, p. 206).

The performance of the mass media in the controversy was what one would expect given the nature of the groups involved and the events. Nearly all the local media, led by Hearst's *Examiner,* supported local control and business interests. It is common for local media to focus their reporting on conflict in an us-versus-them fashion. External threats to the local structure are taken very seriously by the media. Certainly, the intense nature of the conflict— a water supply for a major metropolitan area—meant that nearly all groups in the local community, including the media, would have an interest in the issue and tend to be more cohesive than in a less important event. The national Progressive leadership gave mixed messages on the issue, and those signals were reflected in the press: Some national media stood behind the environmentalists, whereas others favored the dam. Muir and colleagues used some alternative media methods—pamphlets and mass mailings—but those strategies were echoed by dam supporters. In the end, the environmentalists were frustrated in their attempts to control the conflict as the media reflected the competing interests involved. Media, when reporting on conflict, are dependent on the relationships between powerful groups more than individuals or organizations.

NOTES

1. Taylor was a reporter for the *San Francisco Examiner* (the newspaper owned by William Randolph Hearst), a long-time supporter of municipal utility ownership and the Hetch Hetchy project.

2. Although out of office, Manson continued to press the case for Hetch Hetchy with Roosevelt. He visited the president in 1905, and Roosevelt showed the engineer Hitchcock's letter turning down the city's request. Manson, city attorney Franklin Lane, and others asked Roosevelt to reopen the case; the president requested an opinion from his attorney general on the legality of such action and was told those rights rested with the secretary of the interior.

3. Cohen said the earthquake spurred San Francisco to an aggressive program of business growth. Dam supporters saw the project as necessary to the development of the West and an answer to water monopolies.

4. In 1910, the Sierra Club polled its members on the issue and Muir's position carried, 589 to 161.

5. Muir was not invited to the conference, which was a signal of the differences between he and Pinchot. When Johnson complained to Pinchot about Muir's absence, he was told there was "no room" for the famed nature lover.

6. Ironically, the American Civic Association and others opposed to the dam had asked Ballinger to appoint an impartial commission to study the question as a delaying tactic. Their suggestion left Ballinger with a safe way out.

7. Wilson's Democrats controlled the senate.

8. The magazine reprinted editorials from newspapers and magazines across the country, and added, "The San Francisco dailies alone seem to favor the project" ("Save Hetch Hetchy," 1913b, p. 204). The issue included four pages of photographs from Joseph LeConte, including a two-page view of the valley.

9. Cohen noted that it was 40 years before the club participated in another national battle—in the fight over Dinosaur National Monument.

6

CONFLICT MANAGEMENT AND SCIENTIFIC UNDERSTANDING

The 1920s Ethyl Leaded Gasoline Controversy

 Like the Hetch Hetchy controversy, the conflict over Ethyl leaded gasoline ended in disappointment for public health advocates but altered the terms of future debates. The news media mapped political postures over the scientific questions, with the liberal *New York World* often championing public health interests and the conservative *New York Times* usually defending industry and the sale of leaded gasoline. Although editors at both newspapers were concerned with scientific issues in general, none were able nor inclined to penetrate the dense fog of partisan rhetoric. The oil and automotive industries were free to narrowly define the problem of high octane "antiknock" fuel, and their scientists went unchallenged in their assertions that leaded gasoline was the only solution. The newspapers reported the claims of public health advocates who said plenty of alternatives were available, but the media and Ethyl opponents were not able to learn enough about the alternatives to directly contradict industry claims. Government took on a deliberately symbolic role in the ab- sence of any legal authority to regulate chemicals. A Public Health Service conference in May 1925 and a study commission of university experts, which met from June 1925 through January 1926, created two conflict management mechanisms dutifully reported by the newspapers. Reporting all but ended after the conference and commission released its study. Thus, the leaded gasoline conflict faded so quickly from the front pages and so completely from human memory that when public health opposition to the product again surfaced in the 1970s, many activists believed such concerns were entirely new.

THE HEART OF THE CONFLICT

Alice Hamilton's eyes blazed; her voice shook with emotion (Figure 6.1). "You are nothing but a murderer," the Harvard University scientist declared to General Motors research head Charles F. Kettering. The private confrontation took place in the hallway of a government office building as Hamilton and Kettering took a break from a Public Health Service hearing on leaded gasoline one morning in May 1925. Hamilton was America's leading expert on worker safety and lead poisoning, and she believed that Kettering was to blame not only for the strange deaths of 17 chemical refinery workers in the preceding year but also for many more that she was sure would follow if General Motors (GM), E. I. du Pont de Nemours Corporation, and Standard Oil Company of New Jersey continued to sell "Ethyl" brand leaded gasoline.[1]

Figure 6.1. Alice Hamilton.
The first woman to join the Harvard University faculty, Alice Hamilton was a tireless advocate for public health and worker safety. She was opposed to the widespread use of Ethyl leaded gasoline because of its public health impacts. Hamilton was inspired by Jane Addams and the Hull House settlement movement of Chicago. Reproduced from the Collections of the Library of Congress (No. B2 5068-14).

"There are thousands of things better than lead to put in gasoline,"
Hamilton said. Kettering answered with detached amusement: "I
will give you twice your salary if you will name just one such
material" (as quoted in Boyd, 1943, p. 276).[2] Later, in testimony
before the Public Health Service conference and in interviews with
news reporters, Hamilton insisted that there were many alternatives, whereas Kettering and other General Motors researchers
continued to claim that there were none.

Newspapers wrote about both kinds of claims, but not one journalist attempted a detailed examination of the conflict even though
many contemporary materials could have been illuminating. A glance
at old newspaper reports, technical publications, chemical abstracts,
patents, and indexes to periodical literature all would have shown
high octane fuel alternatives to leaded gasoline, such as catalytic
reforming and blends of other fuels and metals. Walter Lippmann's
newspaper, the *New York World,* would come closest to uncorking the
technological and political mystery of leaded gasoline by listening to
public health advocates; even Lippmann, however, believed that the
press did not begin to have the resources to understand scientific
controversy. Although the media reported the basic facts of the controversy, it was not analytical or explanatory.

The oil and automotive industries have long framed the news
coverage of the 1924 to 1926 Ethyl controversy as a case of sensationalism and yellow journalism. Industry historians have accused
the news media of "sensational publicity" and "wild stories" that
caused "panic." The media were said to have printed "lurid details"
and "shocking cartoons depicting Ethyl [Corp.] . . . squeezing blood
from an innocent public." In addition, the news media was presumed
to have "invented" the term *loony gas* for leaded gasoline (Young,
1961, p. 162; see also Robert, 1983, p. 122). In the absence of other
interpretations, mainstream historians have by and large accepted
the industry perspective (Leslie, 1983, p. 165; see also Rosner &
Markowitz, 1989, p. 125).[3] In fact, there were no cartoons of Ethyl
killing innocents and no evidence of panic. The stereotype of a
sensational press, however, fit conveniently over the embarrassing
facts of this early environmental controversy. An important step in
conflict management for GM, du Pont, and Standard was to ensure

that only their version of history would be accepted (Kovarik, 1993, 1994b).

ETHYL LEADED
GASOLINE IN PERSPECTIVE

The gasoline additive tetraethyl lead, whimsically dubbed "ethyl" by Charles F. Kettering in 1921, is the same leaded gasoline that the Environmental Protection Agency (EPA) began to phase out in 1975, when automakers grudgingly manufactured new exhaust control systems and the oil industry reluctantly began selling "unleaded" gasoline. It is the same additive that many cities banned in 1925 and again in 1984 and 1985. It is the same additive that the EPA banned nationwide in 1986 amid debate over the public health issues that alarmed the Workers' Health Bureau, Alice Hamilton, and other scientists in 1924 and 1925.

Leaded gasoline was invented at GM's research facility in Dayton, Ohio, in December 1921. GM research director Kettering and his research associate for fuel, Thomas Midgley, discovered leaded gasoline as one of many ways to raise the "octane" or antiknock rating of gasoline.[4] A gasoline that does not "knock" (or predetonate in the cylinder) burns more efficiently and allows smaller engines to produce more power. Tetraethyl lead was simply ordinary metallic lead suspended in ethyl alcohol,[5] but the manufacturing process involved an extraordinarily dangerous chemical reaction with the explosive element sodium and the poisonous liquid ethyl chloride under severe temperature and pressure conditions.

At the time leaded gasoline was discovered, oil reserves were thought to be running low, and a complete exhaustion of American oil wells was expected by the 1940s or 1950s. By developing a fuel additive that would allow a switch to higher compression engines, GM was trying to ensure the future of automobiles even if gasoline became scarce or prohibitively expensive. Higher-compression engines could burn alternative fuels, especially ethyl alcohol from farm crops and cellulose, when oil supplies ran out (Kovarik, 1994a). GM marketed leaded gasoline in 1923 under the brand name Ethyl with limited success, but in 1924, Kettering and GM president Alfred Sloan developed partnerships with several oil companies, especially Standard Oil of New Jersey (now Exxon).

Public health experts began to worry as leaded gasoline came into wider use. U.S. Surgeon General Hugh Cumming wrote to the du Pont Corporation in 1923 asking whether tests had been performed to ensure the new product's safety. Midgley answered with bland assurances about the safety of the substance. Working behind the scenes, Alice Hamilton and other university experts pushed for an investigation. In late 1923, 8 months after Ethyl gasoline had been on the market, GM asked the U.S. Bureau of Mines to conduct a small study of the effect of exhaust fumes on test animals.

Meanwhile, GM and Standard Oil executives worried about competition in the antiknock fuels business. Engineers who were designing new factories got "war orders" insisting that they proceed very rapidly. This denied the engineers the time to develop safety features. In September 1924, Standard completed an open-air tetraethyl lead process inside an existing oil refinery in Bayway, New Jersey. Du Pont engineers visited the plant and were "greatly shocked at the manifest danger of the equipment and methods [and] at inadequate safety precautions" (Wescott, 1935, p. 21). Although they said that Standard's safety precautions were "grossly inadequate," the du Pont engineers' warnings were "waved aside" (Wescott, 1935, p. 21). Although half a dozen GM and du Pont workers had already died from exposure to concentrated lead, Standard engineers insisted on operating a process that exposed workers to direct fumes and molten lead. The refinery system opened in September 1924 and closed less than 2 months later after a mass poisoning of workers and the outbreak of a vehement public controversy.

LEAD POISONING IN HISTORY

Although many newly understood health hazards surfaced in the 1920s, such as radiation, carbon monoxide gas, and asbestos, lead poisoning was one peril that had been well appreciated from antiquity. Lead has been known as the "assassin of empires" because of its extremely poisonous nature. The Bible notes the use of lead as a poison, and Egyptian hieroglyphics record its use as a "succession powder" to promote the replacement of various heirs to the throne (Nriagu, 1983, p. 12). A heavy and brittle metal, lead was not widely used until the time of the Roman Empire. Beginning around 200 B.C., however, and lasting through around 300 A.D., enormous amounts of lead were mined and smelted. Atmospheric lead deposits from the Roman lead and silver mining operations in Spain and Wales are reflected in ice core samples in Greenland (Hughes, 1994, p. 127; see also Patterson, Boutron, & Flegal, 1985, pp. 101-104). One estimate of mining activity from archaeological surveys is about 70 to 90 million tons of mining slag (Hughes, 1994, p. 127).

The Roman engineer Vitruvius (as quoted in Hughes, 1975) was aware of the health impacts of lead on workers in the mines and smelters:

> We can take example by the workers in lead who have complexions affected by pallor. For when, in casting, the lead receives the current of air, the fumes from it occupy the members of the body, and burning them thereon, rob the limbs of the virtues of the blood. Therefore it seems that water should not be brought in lead pipes if we desire to have it wholesome. (p. 5)

Lead water pipes and utensils made from lead were a source of lead poisoning for Roman citizens. Far more damage, however, was probably caused by extensive use of grape sweeteners made in lead vessels. Because the Romans did not have sugar, they frequently boiled down grape pulp from the wine presses in lead-lined vessels. They used it as a condiment to sweeten their food and called it "sapa" or "difrutum." According to historian and toxicologist Jerome Nriagu (1983),

> One teaspoonful of sapa per day could cause chronic lead poisoning, and countless Romans would have consumed more than this dosage from their foods and drinks. . . . The Roman fondness for sweet and sour flavors is well known, and the cooks made common use of the cheap . . . sapa in their sauces and seasonings to assuage the appetites of their patrons. (p. 332)

The sterility and high infant mortality rates experienced by the ruling class during the Empire period, as well as reports of rapid increase of cases of gout in which the symptoms directly mirror chronic lead poisoning, are consistent with foods sweetened with "sugar" of lead.[6]

Historically, the fall of Rome has been linked to lead poisoning since 1909 (Nriagu, 1983, p. 323), and it has been commonly suspected since at least the mid-19th century. For instance, in 1857, *Scientific American* noted,

> It is remarkable that this metal (lead), when dissolved in an acid, has the property of imparting a saccharine taste to the fluid. Thus the common acetate of lead is always called "sugar of lead." It was perhaps on this account that the Greeks and Romans used sheet lead to neutralize the acidity of bad wine—a practice which now is happily not in use since it has been found that all combinations of lead are decidedly poisonous." ("Sugar of Lead," 1875, p. 403)

An early modern concern about lead poisoning as a public health problem was documented in the 18th century when a British physician named George Baker became curious about the "Devonshire colic." Each autumn, there was an infestation of colic that tended to be more severe with the age of the patient. In 1767, Baker examined conditions in Devonshire and traced the colic back to apple cider made by presses lined with lead. He also noted that no similar colic attended the apple harvest in the cider drinking counties of Hereford, Gloucester, and Worcester. The presses there had wooden sides without the lead linings. Baker's paper to the Royal College of Physicians also showed that Devonshire cider itself contained lead. Rather than the praise that might have been expected, Baker was condemned by the clergy, by mill owners, and even by fellow doctors (Smith, 1986, p. 20).

American journalist and scientist Benjamin Franklin also worried about lead poisoning. In 1724, when Franklin worked as a printer's apprentice, he observed that the practice of heating lead type while cleaning off ink seemed connected to what was called "the dangles," an extremely debilitating paralysis of the hands that "dangled" uselessly from the wrists for the rest of the worker's life. In 1745, Franklin also published a paper on the "dry gripes," or stomach cramps—an epidemic that plagued America that he traced to drinking rum distilled in vessels with lead coils and other parts.

Franklin and Baker corresponded on scientific matters, and in 1768, Baker said his suspicions that lead might be the cause of Devonshire colic "had been greatly confirmed by the authority of Dr. Franklin of Philadelphia" (Smith, 1986, p. 20). Also around that time, Franklin investigated lead poisoning in France. He obtained a list of patients in La Charite Hospital in Paris who had been hospitalized for symptoms that would one day be diagnosed as lead poisoning and showed that the patients were involved in occupations that exposed them to lead (Smith, 1986, p. 20). In 1786, he wrote a long letter to a friend following a conversation on the effects of lead. He concluded, "The Opinion of the mischievous Effect from Lead is at least above Sixty Years old, and you will observe with Concern how long a useful Truth may be known and exist before it is generally receiv'd and practic'd on" (as quoted in Smith, 1986, p. 21; see also McCord cited in Smith, 1986, p. 21).

Tales of the disasters endured by England's working classes helped motivate a generation of reformers to study and regulate the effects of industry on workers and public health. In Germany before World War I, a system of permits and regulations governed air and mining pollution (Johnson, 1917, pp. 199-204). In the United States, concerns about worker health and public health seemed to carry a flavor of "sentimentality if not socialism." When workers in the lead trade came up with typical problems such as paralysis of the hands, they were usually attributed to drinking or to a wife's cooking (Hamilton, 1929). It was difficult even to understand the scope of the problem—no law forced industries to allow researchers to conduct their studies. Many did so only after a considerable amount of persuasion and assurances that the results of a study would not be reported individually but rather about an industry in general.

SPECIFIC WARNINGS
ON TETRAETHYL LEAD

GM, Standard, du Pont, and Ethyl Corporation officials received warnings about the use of lead compounds in gasoline. As the first plans were made to develop and market tetraethyl lead in 1922, alarming letters arrived from four of the world's experts in the field: Robert Wilson of Massachusetts Institute of Technology, Reid Hunt of Harvard, Yandell Henderson of Yale, and Charles Kraus of Pottsdam, Germany. Kraus had worked on tetraethyl lead for many years and called it "a creeping and malicious poison" that had killed a member of his dissertation committee. Hunt had informed Henderson about the work at GM because the Yale researcher was considered America's leading expert on automotive exhaust (Kovarik, 1993). Another warning came from a lab director in the Public Health Service who had heard about tetraethyl lead and wrote an October 1922 memo to the assistant surgeon general warning of a "serious menace to public health." Several other memos traded hands and in November, Surgeon General Hugh Cumming wrote to Pierre S. du Pont about the public health question. The surgeon general's letter was referred to Midgley, who answered that the problem "has been given very serious consideration . . . although no actual experimental data has been taken."[7]

Because of laboratory explosions at GM and other mishaps, Midgley himself was suffering from lead poisoning by late 1922. He wrote, however, a subcontractor who was doing some chemical research at Cornell University,

> It would not surprise me if in the course of using tetraethyl lead for a year that some of your men would experience a slight case of painter's colic. This is nothing to worry about as several of our boys have it.[8]

Yet, within two years, 17 would die and hundreds would be hospitalized.

Alice Hamilton was America's expert on lead poisoning in 1924. She was an MD who had done postdoctoral work at the Universities of Munich and Leipzig in Germany, at the Pasteur Institute in Paris, and at Johns Hopkins University in the United States. Her interest in what was called "occupational disease" was sparked by her years working with social activist Jane Addams at Chicago's Hull House, a settlement house in the middle of Chicago's working-class slums in which activists lived and worked for progressive causes.

In 1910, the labor department of the State of Illinois hired her to look into the question of workers' compensation claims from the lead industry trades. Hamilton found appalling conditions and 578 cases of outright lead poisoning, some of which were quite severe, or as Hamilton (1929) stated, "equal to those described by French authorities of the early 19th century" (p. 581). Shocked that Illinois was a century behind Europe, the state legislature quickly passed a law requiring ventilation and other safety standards for workers. The Illinois study brought Hamilton to the attention of the U.S. Department of Labor, where she worked from 1910 to 1919 as a special investigator of industrial poisons. She was then invited to join the faculty at Harvard University. This was not out of egalitarian academic impulse but simply because she was by far the best occupational toxicologist in America, according to biographer Barbara Sicherman (1984).

Hamilton worked with tact to popularize the views of social reformers among labor leaders, fellow physicians, and industrialists while attempting to avoid any hint of Marxism (Sicherman, 1984, p. 33). In a speech to the superintendents of the National Lead Company, she praised their efforts to safeguard worker health while at the same time noting that their factories were "so dangerous . . . that they would be closed by law in any European country" (as quoted in Sicherman, 1984, p. 5).

In 1920, she managed to obtain funding from the American Institute of Lead Manufacturers to study lead metabolism in the human body at Harvard. The study found that lead did accumulate in the bones and tissues of people who were exposed to it and was not quickly or fully metabolized and excreted. As a result, lead manufacturers were disappointed in their attempts to evade workers' compensation claims and civil damage suits (Sicherman, 1984, p. 238). A few years later, when General Motors began to put lead into gasoline, Hamilton and others—including Surgeon General Cumming—felt that this study had already laid the key scientific issue to rest. With the cumulative nature of the poison, no one could reasonably advocate the sure, slow public poison from the use of lead in gasoline (Hamilton, Reznikoff, & Burnham, 1925).

THE PUBLIC CONTROVERSY

The first time the public heard of leaded gasoline[9] was after a series of incidents at Standard's New Jersey refinery at the end of October 1924. State health officials told news reporters about a "mystery gas" that was driving workers at the Standard Oil refinery in Bayway "violently insane." The refinery was located just across New York Harbor from what was then the world's largest and most competitive newspaper market. The story, as one du Pont lawyer said later, was a "natural" (Wescott, 1935, p. 23).

The first Standard worker died Saturday, October 25. When the county coroner finished with the autopsy, he was so alarmed at the unusual symptoms of insanity and severe convulsions that he called the district attorney's office. Both the coroner and the district attorney contacted Standard Oil, but company officials refused to discuss their employee's death with them. The story was leaked to news reporters, who tracked down the chief chemist of the Bayway refinery works, Dr. Matthew D. Mann, on Sunday. Although he was also suffering from lead poisoning, Mann produced the following statement in writing: "These men probably went insane because they worked too hard." The *World* noted that Mann wrote out the statement after 15 minutes of deliberation in another room; the *Times* found the statement so extraordinary that Mann was quoted in a secondary headline on the front page.[10]

W. G. Thompson, Standard's consulting physician, claimed that he had no knowledge of what had happened. Thompson, who was based in Manhattan, also insisted, "Nothing ought to be said about this matter in the public interest" ("Odd Gas Kills," 1924, p. 1). This represents more than just a narrow view of the public interest. Thompson was articulating the alarm felt by industry leaders and scientists as their homogeneous community of science and chemistry was thrown into the public arena via the newspapers.

Times and *World* reporters may have found officials somewhat unresponsive, but they found workers all too aware of the dangers lurking at the Bayway plant. Those who volunteered for higher-paying jobs in the leaded gasoline section of the refinery were given mock farewells and funerals, according to reports in both papers. The workers—not the press—called the leaded gasoline additive loony gas because it caused hallucinations and delusions of persecution. Later, reporters would find that du Pont workers called tetraethyl lead production facilities the "Butterfly Factory" because of hallucinations of winged insects (Bent, 1925).

Headlines from the first reports on Monday, October 27, reflected a high level of alarm. "Odd Gas Kills One, Makes Four Insane," stated the top *Times* headline. The *Times* interviewed workers, relatives, state officials, Mann, and Standard's physician. "Gas Madness Stalks Plant; 2 Die, 3 Crazed" read the headline in the *World,* which scooped the *Times* on the second worker's death. The *Herald Tribune* headlined a story, "Mystery Gas Crazes 12 in Laboratory," following up on the new additions to the hospital sick list that the *Times* and *World* missed.

Aside from Mann and Thompson, Standard officials would not discuss the mystery gas, and the news media reflected the uncertainty. New Jersey government officials were quoted as saying the poison was "ethylene" and "ethyl chloride." The *Times* double-checked this information and cautioned that ethylene gas was an unlikely poison because it had been proven safe as an anesthetic. This attention to scientific detail is consistent with *Times* managing editor Carr Van Anda's reputation as a scientific expert. The *World* and most other newspapers simply reported ethylene gas was the cause of the "gas madness." The *Herald Tribune* came the closest to reporting the true compound, reporting "ethylchlorid" as the cause.[11]

On Monday, Thompson continued to be the lone Standard spokesman. At a press conference at Standard's headquarters at 26 Broadway, New York, Thompson confirmed that two men were dead and five others seriously ill as a result of chemical "experiments" at Bayway. He said that the chemical poison was some kind of gasoline additive, but said he could not tell reporters its exact nature nor could Standard tell local physicians. Thompson also said Standard "has given a great deal of attention to safety measures and no expense has ever been spared to safeguard employees against illness or accidents" ("Company Denies," 1924, p. 1). Although Thompson feigned ignorance, he was, in fact, the chairman of a committee of company doctors from Standard, du Pont, and General Motors specifically charged with investigating at least seven previous deaths and more than 300 poisonings at GM's Dayton, Ohio, plant and du

Pont's Deepwater, New Jersey, plants (Wescott, 1935, p. B3; see also Bent, 1925).

Thompson's stonewalling approach contradicted the "public information" model of open information sharing advocated by Standard Oil's famed public relations consultant Ivy L. Lee (Hiebert, 1966). His story was cast in doubt later the same day when a small public interest labor group named the Workers Health Bureau (WHB) called a press conference at its offices at 799 Broadway, New York. The bureau was established by labor organizer Grace Burnham after World War I and would last until 1927. During its short life, the bureau provided the media and the public with information about occupational disease and trade hazards that companies and public health institutions did not provide. For example, it published a warning to garage workers in 1924 titled "Carbon Monoxide: Poison Gas War on the Job" (Young, 1983).

The WHB press conference was called to alert the news media to the link between the New Jersey refinery deaths and Ethyl gasoline. At the press conference, reporters were given a copy of a telegram to the bureau from Yandell Henderson, a Yale University professor who identified the mystery gas as tetraethyl lead and linked it to Ethyl gasoline being sold by Standard and other oil companies. Henderson said that the gas was "one of the most dangerous things in the country today." A car with problems on Fifth Avenue could "cause gas poisoning and mania to persons along the avenue." Someone exposed to the gas would not know it from the odor, and "the damage may take place later," Henderson said in the telegram ("Another Man Dies," 1924, p. 1).

In the initial confusion surrounding the accidents, Henderson had believed that the public would be exposed to the full-strength tetraethyl lead compound, which had driven some refinery workers violently insane, instead of a blend diluted 1,000 to 1 in gasoline. His inaccurate view had been formed 2 years earlier when Henderson was approached as a consultant and had learned about GM's plans to market tetraethyl lead. In these discussions, GM officials told Henderson in 1922 that they were going to use full-strength tetraethyl lead in a second gas tank to be installed in every car.[12] Henderson realized his mistake a few days after the first news articles came out and sent another telegram revising his view of the immediate danger. The *World* quoted him saying that if all cars used leaded gasoline, a ton of lead powder would be discharged on Fifth Avenue per day. This alone would create gradual lead poisoning and represented a grave threat to public health, he insisted.

With Standard still refusing comment, one newspaper turned to published scientific information. The *Herald Tribune* noted that, some 10 months earlier, GM's Thomas Midgley had presented an American Chemical Society paper on the novel dangers and benefits of tetraethyl lead. "He said at the time that the dipping of one's finger into . . . tetraethyl lead brought on insomnia and loss of appetite, and its further seeping into the body produced wild hallucinations of persecution, the nature of which never varied."[13] This was the only time uncovered in this research that newspapers consulted scientific papers during the 3-year controversy.

The next day, Wednesday, October 29, the *Herald Tribune* reported that local authorities were beginning to figure out what had happened even though Standard would not speak with them. The *Herald Tribune* reported ("Ethyl Gas Sale," 1924), "Little by little the Union County (N.J.) officials are picking their way through the maze of heretofore contradictory assertions that followed the disclosures of the wholesale poisoning" (p. 1). Lead poisoning from tetraethyl lead remained the leading suspect in the search for chemical culprits, although the local New Jersey medical examiner told several reporters he had never known lead poisoning to have such a violent impact. Meanwhile, victims had been rushed to Reconstruction Hospital and put under Thompson's care in a closed-off ward.[14]

Standard's official silence can be attributed to its board of directors. Kettering recalled, "They were in a blue funk over the whole thing, and the directors were very much afraid about it. They didn't know what was going to happen to them" (*United States v. du Pont*, 1952). Meanwhile, Kettering was in Europe searching for sources of bromide (needed as an additive to tetraethyl lead). He was also consulting with I. G. Farben officials on less toxic alternatives to leaded gasoline. Because it was impossible for him to return quickly, he insisted that Midgley go to New York City to face the press. On Thursday, October 30, Midgley was introduced to a press conference at Standard's headquarters. One of the first things he did was to pour a thick stream of a clear liquid over his hands and then rubbed the excess off with a handkerchief, according to the *Times* ("Bar Ethyl Gasoline," 1924). Then he held a bottle of liquid under his nose "for more than a minute," the *Herald Tribune* reported, and "insisted that the fumes could have no such effect as was observed in the victims if inhaled only a short time" ("Bar Death Gas," 1924, p. 1). Midgley insisted the injuries were "caused by the heedlessness of workers in failing to follow instructions" rather than by the danger of the poison itself ("Bar Death Gas," 1924, p. 1). If the *Herald Tribune* report of 2 days earlier was accurate, Midgley would have known better than to pour the substance over his hands. Quite possibly he was using pure glycerine or some substance other than undiluted tetraethyl lead.

Reporters asked Midgley whether it was true that other workers had been hospitalized and died in Dayton, Ohio. He acknowledged that two deaths had occurred in April 1924, and that more than 50 GM workers had been "under observation" for the effects of lead poisoning. (He did not say that he had been one of them.) He also acknowl-edged that the du Pont corporation had also had "similar problems." Standard's Thompson was present at the press confer- ence and pointed out that tetraethyl lead was used only in diluted amounts in gasoline and could not have the same effects on motorists as it did on refinery workers. Standard's full formal statement was published in the *World* ("Use of Ethylated Gasoline," 1924; see also the *New York Times,* the *Sun,* and the *Herald Tribune* of the same date; all four carried the statement verbatim):

> Tetraethyl lead is a substance first known to chemists in 1854. Since that time it frequently has been experimented with in chemical laboratories where it was known to be, in concentrated form, poison. It is a compound of metallic lead and one of the alcohol chemical series. Its recently discovered use for greatly promoting the efficiency of gasoline engines has led to its manufacture on a commercial scale through processes still more or less in a stage of development. This has occasioned unforeseen accidents which as processes and appara- tus are further perfected should be avoidable in the future.
>
> One of these has been the sudden escape of fumes from large retorts and the inhalation of such fumes gives rise to acute symp- toms, particularly congestion of the brain, producing a condition not unlike delirium tremens. Although there is lead in the compound,

these acute symptoms are wholly unlike those of chronic lead poisoning such as painters often have.

There is no obscurity whatsoever about the effects of the poison, and characterizing the substance as "mystery gas" or "insanity gas" is grossly misleading. . . . It should be emphasized that the product as destined for final use in gasoline engines has to be greatly diluted, usually with 1,000 parts of gasoline. This extremely diluted product has been for more than a year in public use in over 10,000 filling stations and garages and no ill effects thus far have been reported. (p. 1)

Standard's statement did little to allay suspicion. Much of the mystery surrounding the gas was a result of the company's own failure to communicate not only with the press but also with public health officials, doctors, and state and local New Jersey officials. There were other minor discrepancies; for example, tetraethyl lead was not the subject of previous experiments—it was considered to be a scientific curiosity.[15] More important, there was a strange discrepancy between Midgley inhaling tetraethyl lead fumes and the statement in the press release about "the sudden escape of fumes from large retorts" ("Use of Ethylated Gasoline," 1924, p. 1). If the fumes were not harmful enough to suddenly poison Midgley at the press conference, then there must have been not one but many "sudden escapes" of fumes.[16] Reporters may have wondered at the contradiction, but their skepticism emerged obliquely. For example, the *Herald Tribune* quoted Reconstruction Hospital doctors saying "the violent insanity and nervousness that gripped the sufferers [was] brought on by the gradual infiltration of lead into their systems" ("Cure Found," 1924, p. 1). In fact, workers were consistently exposed to heavy lead fumes throughout their work shifts because of the way Standard's Bayway process was designed. Later, in a 1950s antitrust suit, a General Motors attorney would summarize the roles of Standard Oil and the news media in the Ethyl controversy:

They [Standard] put up a plant that lasted two months and killed five people and practically wiped out the rest of the plant. . . . The furor over it was so great that the newspapers took it up, and they misrepresented it, and instead of realizing that the danger was in the manufacture, they got to thinking that the danger was exposure of the public in the use of it, and the criticism of its use was so great that it was banned in many cities and they had to close down the manufacture and sale of Ethyl.[17]

Although Yale's Henderson initially misunderstood the hazardous nature of the fuel being used by consumers, it is not true that the danger of manufacturing was consistently misrepresented as a danger to the public. Public health advocates were concerned that even diluted lead in gasoline would pose a cumulative threat, and the press reported those concerns. There was very little confusion on the point once Standard began responding to inquiries after October 30, 1924.

Meanwhile, various city and state officials in New Jersey, New York, Pennsylvania, and New England banned leaded gasoline, and the bright future for GM's new invention lay in ruins. The effect was "disaster—sudden, swift and complete," stated a du Pont lawyer (as quoted in Wescott, 1935, p. 22).

As the controversy continued through the fall and into winter, the newspapers continued to take statements by any scientific authority at face value. When controversy arose, the method was to report, without comment or contradiction, one side's claims and the other side's responses. When Standard and GM scientists said that every precaution had been taken to protect workers, journalists reported it. When industry spokesmen finally said that the mystery gas was merely Ethyl, which was nothing new to science; that it was safe for motorists; and that Standard, GM, and du Pont were simply trying to improve the efficiency of automobiles, it was dutifully reported.

By the same token, most New York newspapers provided some space for critics of Standard, GM, and Ethyl. For example, most newspapers carried coverage of a critical speech by Henderson in late April 1925. The issue, Henderson said, was that "breathing day by day of the fine dust from automobiles will produce chronic lead poisoning on a large scale" ("Sees Deadly Gas," 1925, p. 1). Henderson ("Sees Deadly Gas," 1925) stated that the problem was

the greatest single question in the field of public health which has ever faced the American public. Perhaps if leaded gasoline kills enough people soon enough to impress the public, we may get from Congress a much needed law and appropriation for control of harmful substances other than foods. (p. 1)

The question, Henderson said, was whether "commercial interests are to be allowed to subordinate every other consideration to that of profit. It is not a matter of millions or even hundreds of millions of dollars, but literally billions" ("Sees Deadly Gas," 1925, p. 1).

GM's Midgley challenged the idea that only commercial interests were at stake in the fight over leaded gasoline, and the news media reported his comments. Leaded gasoline had been developed after 7 years of scientific work on the problem of engine knock. "Knock is the one important thing which has for a generation past prevented the building of more powerful automotive engines," Midgley stated ("Ethyl Gas," 1925, p. 1). In a speech to chemists a few weeks earlier, reported in the *Times* ("Radium Derivative," 1925), he had insisted that GM's invention was indispensable:

> So far as science knows at the present time, tetraethyl lead is the only material available which can bring about these [antiknock] results, which are of vital importance to the continued economical use by the general public of all automotive equipment. (p. 23)

In an example of the conflict management function of the media, a feature article wrapping up the controversy ran in the *World* on May 3, 1925, under a headline "Will Ethyl Gasoline Poison Us All? Scientists Disagree." The story was based on interviews with Henderson and Midgley. It quoted Henderson as calculating that with cars burning 2 gallons of fuel per hour, the deposit of lead on a New York street would be about a pound per hour per block. The dusty rain of lead on Fifth Avenue alone, Henderson said, would be 300 pounds per day. Midgley did not dispute the assertion, but said the dust would be washed away. The article also gave readers background on the two protagonists—noting, for example, that Midgley was a chemist and that Henderson had reluctantly helped develop poison gas in World War I ("Will Ethyl Gasoline," 1925). It did not give readers, however, any way to seriously consider the technological problem or the alternative high octane fuels.

Whereas the liberal *World* made sure that critics were given ample space for their views, the conservative but comprehensive *Times* kept track of the details of the controversy, printing far more basic details than any other newspaper. The *Times,* however, also made sure that supporters of Ethyl leaded gasoline in the industry had their say and printed more information from industry than any other source. Overall, the *Times* quoted industry sources twice as much as the *World,* whereas the *World* gave university scientists three times more space than did the *Times* and far more than the other newspapers. The *World's* articles were longer and much more likely to provide detailed information on the university public health experts' views of leaded gasoline. Other newspapers, such as the conservative *Sun* and the liberal *Brooklyn Daily Eagle,* attempted to balance industry and university sources; the working-class *Eagle,* in fact, focused more coverage on workers than any other newspaper. The conservative *Herald Tribune* virtually ignored university sources and relied heavily on industry and medical officials.

SCIENCE, WALTER LIPPMANN, AND CARR VAN ANDA

Journalists covering the scientific controversy over leaded gasoline found it difficult to evaluate conflicting claims on a scientific level and turned to the more familiar political paradigm to report the conflict. Liberal editors, such as Walter Lippmann at the *New York World,* supported public health advocates. Conservative editors, such as Carr Van Anda at the *New York Times,* supported industry. This support is seen in both editorial opinion and the amount of news coverage allotted to each side in the debate.

Although the transmutation of science into politics would seem to support the view of a scientifically illiterate news media, such an interpretation would be off the mark. In fact, Lippmann, Van Anda, and other journalists of the era were well aware of the impact of science and technology on society and even on their own profession. Van Anda, managing editor of the *Times* between 1901 and 1925, was one of the early proponents of the "scientific" approach to journalism and accurate science news coverage. Lippmann, editorial page editor of the *World* in the 1920s, was an advocate of "objective" journalism and was deeply concerned with the impact of science on society. Both were impressed with the spirit of disinterested inquiry that motivated science in the 20th century, and both Lippmann and Van Anda believed that journalists should internalize the methods that made scientific progress possible (Schudson, 1978; see also Novick, 1988, p. 42). Journalism was "particularly amenable" to the scientific approach, according to Lippmann (Palen, 1984).

As similar as they were in some respects, the difference between their two approaches represents an important distinction in discussions about public understanding of science and technology. Van Anda understood the nuts and bolts of science and technology like no other journalist of the era. For instance, he once caught a mistake in one of Albert Einstein's equations that had been badly transcribed by an assistant. His interest in the wireless put the *Times* a full day ahead in covering the sinking of the *Titanic*. Van Anda preferred dry facts to interpretation—evident in the Ethyl coverage, to be sure. His approach to writing and editing news about science involved constant study and personal development of expertise in (or "knowledge of") science and technology (Fine, 1968, pp. 44, 89, 100).

On the other hand, Lippmann did not understand all the facts of science and technology and attempted rather to understand their importance in the cauldron of social change. He was more concerned with "knowledge about" science and technology and its effects on society and public policy.[18]

Van Anda, like the *Times* itself, tended to be politically conservative, probusiness, and suspicious of government regulation. Although Van Anda's personal philosophy is not well-known (Fine, 1968, p. 100), as an expert in science, steeped in the ideology of scientific progress in the heroic era of invention, he would be expected to agree with the views of Charles F. Kettering and Thomas Midgley. As the acknowledged science expert on the *Times* staff, Van Anda may very likely have influenced (or written) an unsigned *Times* editorial that saw leaded gasoline as the product of scientific research. The scientific view supported leaded gasoline, and the "sentimental view" of the tragedy at Bayway must not be allowed to stand in the way of progress, the editorial stated ("No Reason," 1924; also see "An Episode," 1924). Although the *Times* provided a generous amount of space for critics of leaded gasoline, *Times* editors clearly deferred to industry, which they saw as having the greater scientific authority.

They did not invest a great deal of credibility in the public health
concerns of university scientists.

Public health authority was seen in a different light at the *World*.
The scientific spirit was also prized at the *World,* but Lippmann
described it as the liberal scientific spirit that tends to resist authority, hates intolerance, and questions dogma. Lippmann saw in the
scientific method the heart of the liberal concern of "remaining
free in mind and action before changing circumstances (p. 162)."
Lippmann's idea of the scientific approach to high octane fuels would
be to openly question the authority of industry scientists. Lippmann
(1931) stated, "Of necessity, the interpretation [of events] must be an
exploration, tentative, sympathetic and without dogmatic precon-
ception. And whoever attempts it, whether as a working newspaperman, as a scholar or as a statesman must find that he is sailing an
uncharted ocean" (pp. 161-162).

Ironically, Lippmann and the *World* behaved as if they were unable to understand the controversy. Very little of the scientific components of the debate were explored, either in the *World* or other
newspapers. Lacking was any understanding of automotive engineering, fuel chemistry, chemical engineering, or public health history and research. In a private letter to Alice Hamilton a few years
after the Ethyl controversy, Lippmann wrote that the news media
were effective "only if we [are] supplied with the necessary technical
information of which we have none, of course, ourselves."[19] Lippmann
(1931), however, would later praise the objective spirit of science and
the "elaborate method for detecting and discounting prejudices"
through peer review and controlled experiments:

> This method provides a body in which the spirit of disinterestedness
> can live and it might be said that modern science—not in its crude
> consequences but in its inward principle, not, that is to say, as mani-
> fested in automobiles, electric refrigerators and rayon silk, but in the
> behavior of the men who invent and perfect these things—is the
> actual realization in a practicable mode of conduct which can be
> learned and practiced, of the insight of high religion. (p. 162)

Lippmann said that scientists were (or should be) completely
disinterested, and automotive inventors (even after the Ethyl

controversy) were his premier exemplars of the scientific spirit. Lippmann (1931, pp. 161-162) railed against those who would "distort the basis of public discussion by the shrewd manipulation of evidence" as having succumbed to the antidemocratic temptations of the era. The scientific spirit he promoted was so powerful, he believed, that it could (in a sense) replace religion. He stated in *A Preface to Morals* (1929), "It is no exaggeration to say that pure science is high religion incarnate" (p. 254).

Lippmann and Van Anda, as the leading journalists of their era, cannot be seen as scientifically illiterate or unconcerned about the impact of science on society. Although their faith in science may seem naive in later light, their differences accurately reflect broad social divisions concerning the goals and ethics of science.

BUREAUCRATIC INTERVENTION

With the tremendous uncertainty surrounding the leaded gasoline issue and in a vacuum of legal authority, the U.S. surgeon general called a conference for May 20, 1925, in Washington, DC, to hear from all parties to the dispute. Alice Hamilton called it the "conference system"—an "informal, extra-legal method" that was effective "given a new and striking danger which lends itself to newspaper publicity" (Hamilton, 1929, p. 587). The conference over leaded gasoline, according to one historian, "tested the limits of academic debate and American politics in resolving such problems" (Young, 1982, p. 158). Reporting on such events is an example of the media relying on institutional sources of news; a system maintenance function may result if the impression left from the reporting is "all is well, scientists (or the government) are on the job."

The conference took place in a federal auditorium several blocks southeast of the capitol. Present were representatives of universities, labor groups, consumer groups, the oil industry, the auto industry, and government agencies. Also crowding into the auditorium were a dozen news reporters. The reporting tended to focus on bureaucratic processes and action, not claims made by individuals or groups. Most articles keyed on the announcement that the surgeon general would form an investigating committee, but other details varied from newspaper to newspaper.

The *Times* attempted to quote from many different points of view, noting an especially dramatic confrontation between Frank Howard of Standard Oil and Grace Burnham of the Workers Health Bureau. As the *Times* reported it, Howard said, "Present day civilization rests on oil and motors. . . . We do not feel justified in giving up what has come to the industry like a gift from heaven on the possibility that a hazard may be involved in it." A few moments later, Grace Burnham stood up and said, "It was no gift of heaven for the 11 who were killed by it and the 149 who were injured" ("Shift Ethyl Inquiry," 1925, p. 7). (Actually, 17 men had been killed and many more had been injured.) The *Times* briefly took notice of Alice Hamilton, who "urged the men connected with the industry to put aside the lead compound entirely and try to find something else to get rid of the knock" ("Shift Ethyl Inquiry," 1925, p. 7).[20]

The *World*'s coverage of the conference described the decision to name a committee and discussed the "attack" on "doped fuel." The story did not include the Howard-Burnham confrontation over the "gift of heaven," and unlike the *Times,* the *World* did not attempt to provide an overview of the conference. It merely piled up facts about one aspect of the event—the "damning" evidence from a Columbia University study that was presented at the conference. In its next story, on May 22 ("U.S. Board," 1925), the *World* emphasized the search for a substitute to tetraethyl lead, quoting Hamilton:

> It would be foolish to talk of the industrial value of tetraethyl lead, when there is a health hazard involved. Men who could discover the fuel value of tetraethyl certainly could invent or discover something equally efficient and in no way dangerous. American chemists can do it if they will. (p. 1)

Hamilton's idea that substitutes could be found flatly contradicted Midgley's assertion that there were no substitutes for tetraethyl lead. By writing about the search for a substitute, the reporter reinforced the idea of a scientific safety valve. Two days after the conference, however, the *World* ("U.S. Board," 1925) reported that something had gone wrong:

The conference itself was to have examined the question of the variety of high octane fuels. Original plans had called for presentation to the Public Health conference of claims of various persons that they have discovered dopes [additives] for fuels which are as efficient as lead but lack the danger. The conference decided at the last minute, however, that such things were not in its province, since it was called to consider only the danger of lead and not the lack of danger of any other chemical or mineral. For this reason, the conference adjourned after only a one day meeting, where it had been thought at first that four or five days might be taken. Many of the delegates to it held informal conferences today, however, at which fuel dopes were discussed. (p. 1)[21]

As expected, news coverage fell off substantially after the conference. An exception was the appointment of a committee to examine tetraethyl lead safety in the summer and fall of 1925. A few articles on alternative fuels surfaced in the summer of 1925, including a curious item out of General Motors's research facility in Dayton, Ohio, describing a new high-octane fuel made from ethyl alcohol, benzene, and gasoline ("Tells of New Type," 1925; see also "New Auto," 1925).

THE PUBLIC HEALTH SERVICE (PHS)
COMMITTEE OF EXPERTS

In June 1925, a month after the Washington conference on leaded gasoline, Surgeon General Cumming announced the appointment of a committee of independent scientists from Johns Hopkins, Harvard, Yale, Vanderbilt, and the universities of Chicago and Minnesota.[22] Hamilton and Henderson were not asked to join the committee, but respected senior colleagues at both of their institutions were. The Ethyl Corporation agreed to stop marketing Ethyl gasoline until the committee report was completed.

This in itself seemed a victory to Hamilton because the problem of regulating industry had apparently been turned over to university scientists without a protracted fight in Congress. This shift in the locus of authority had taken place, Hamilton noted, under the "glare of publicity" and Hamilton felt indebted to the media and particularly the *World* for its role in the Ethyl controversy. Much of the victory Hamilton seemed to celebrate was, however, symbolic. The surgeon general's committee did not conduct the study, but farmed it out, and eventually voiced objections that were not made public.

The committee met June 14 and June 28 to consider the design of the research and corresponded with the PHS on a plan of investigation.[23] In July, J. P. Leake of the PHS Hygiene Laboratory was assigned to conduct the study (National Archives, 1937). Two garages in Dayton, Ohio—one using leaded gasoline and one not using leaded gasoline—were to be selected and the employees tested for blood stippling and fecal lead accumulation. Two garages in Washington, DC, were to have been added to the list "if time and personnel permit," according to the preliminary plan ("Preliminary Plan," 1925). Committee member C. E. A. Winslow wrote back saying that the Washington garages should be included and that it was "most essential that the study cover three garages in which ethyl gas is used and one which it is not used." Winslow also argued for larger test samples but agreed that the test plan seemed "most admirable."[24]

Testing began early in October 1925. Two groups of Dayton and Cincinnati workers (one of drivers and one of mechanics) that had been exposed to leaded gasoline were compared with two similar groups that had not been exposed. A control group of men working in lead industries was also examined. Overall, 252 case histories were taken. Men were given physical exams, and blood and stool specimens were analyzed. Researchers found that drivers exposed to leaded gasoline showed somewhat higher "stippling" damage to red blood cells, whereas garage workers exposed to leaded gasoline showed much more damage to red blood cells, and one quarter of those exposed had more than 1 milligram of lead in fecal samples. In contrast, more than 80% of the heavily exposed industrial workers showed large amounts of lead in fecal samples. Although techniques for measuring lead levels were primitive in contrast with later standards, it is probable that workers with blood damage and high amounts of lead in fecal samples had absorbed amounts of lead that would later be considered dangerous, according to toxicologist Nriagu (Nriagu, personal communication, September 1991).[25] Even then, the lead burdens were considered high. In a 1927 Bureau of Mines final report about the study, the surgeon general's committee experiments are noted as having found blood cell stippling "to a relatively high degree" in garage mechanics whose exposure had been relatively short—as little as 2½ days (Sayers, Fieldner, Yant & Thomas, 1927, p. 12).

One finding that raises questions about the integrity of the study is that leaded gasoline samples from Cincinnati appear to have about half as much lead as expected. In the first draft of the report presented to the committee on December 22, 1925, Leake (as quoted in U.S. Public Health Service, 1925, p. 21) said that "not very far from the plant where we make our studies," four gasoline samples from service stations ranged from 75% to 55% less lead than expected. Thus, in the period before and during the study, lower than usual amounts of lead were being mixed with local gasoline.

In January 1926, the committee reported that it could find "no good grounds for prohibiting the use of Ethyl gasoline." Its most important point was that none of the garage workers and drivers had any of the outright symptoms of lead poisoning that killed 17 refinery workers and poisoned at least several hundred more between 1923 and 1925. Not all the committee members agreed, however. In a meeting on December 22, 1925, committee member David L. Edsall of Harvard objected that "we would be presenting a half-baked report" unless the committee studied "the effects this is going to have on others" (as quoted in U.S. Public Health Service, 1925, p. 21). Reed Hunt of Harvard noted that the "big question" was whether the committee should absolutely prohibit tetraethyl lead. "If we say we shouldn't absolutely prohibit it, then we should say that money should be appropriated to study any further hazard" (as quoted in U.S. Public Health Service, 1925, p. 21). C. E. A. Winslow of Yale insisted on and got the following statement inserted into the report: "A more extensive study was not possible in view of the limited time allowed to the committee" (Winslow notes, Box 101, Folder 1,805, as quoted in Rosner & Markowitz, 1989).

In the end, the report (U.S. Public Health Service, 1926) warned that the uncertain danger and the incomplete data did not lead it to a definite conclusion:

> Owing to the incompleteness of the data, it is not possible to say definitely whether exposure to lead dust increases in garages when tetraethyl lead is used. It is very desirable that these investigations

be continued. . . . It remains possible that if the use of leaded gaso-
lines becomes widespread, conditions may arise very different from
those studied by us which would render its use more of a hazard than
would appear to be the case from this investigation. Longer exposure
may show that even such slight storage of lead as was observed in
these studies may lead eventually in susceptible individuals to rec-
ognizable lead poisoning or chronic degenerative disease of obvious
character . . . . The committee feels this investigation must not be
allowed to lapse. (p. 12)

Winslow also recommended that the "search for and investigation of antiknock compounds be continued intensively with the
object of securing effective agents containing less poisonous metals
(such as iron, nickel, tin, etc.) or no metals at all" (Winslow, 1925).[26]
The recommendation was based on correspondence with Ford Motor
Company that Winslow forwarded to L. R. Thompson of the Public
Health Service asking that a file be established on alternatives. The
letter to Winslow reads as follows:

August 15, 1925
ALCOHOL FOR MOTOR FUEL
Further to my letter of June 19th:

You may probably have observed the production of synthetic alcohol as brought out by the Badische Anilin and Soda Fabrik [BASF
of I. G. Farben], now being produced in Germany at the rate of
60,000 gallons per month. Such alcohol is reported to be produced for between 10 cents and 20 cents per gallon and has much
promise as a mixture with hydrocarbon fuels to eliminate knocking
and carbonization.

(signed) Wm. H. Smith, Ford Motor Co.[27]

The letter is a fragment of more extensive correspondence that
has been lost in the Public Health Service files. Winslow's recommendation about continuing the search was not incorporated in the
final committee report. Although disappointed in the report, Winslow
wrote Henderson, who was in England in the winter of 1925, that
he "did not see how things could have gone differently."

Kettering, too, had his share of disappointments. On April 21,
1925, a month before the surgeon general's hearing, he and Midgley

were fired as president and vice president of Ethyl Corporation at a board of directors meeting in Standard Oil's headquarters at 26 Broadway. GM President Alfred Sloan had written to fellow board member Irenee du Pont just before the board meeting,

> I have felt from the very beginning of the formation of this company, in fact, I felt a year before it was formed, that we would make progress much more rapidly and more constructively if we had more of a business side to the development.[28]

The letter to Sloan described a meeting with the third principal party in the Ethyl triangle, Standard Oil president Walter Teagle. Sloan told du Pont that he and Teagle agreed that Kettering had to go. Sloan warned du Pont that Kettering had been "violently opposed" to losing control of Ethyl Corporation. Sloan said that he had left "the boys" (as he called Kettering and Midgley) in place despite serious misgivings, believing that his point would eventually become so obvious that it would have to be recognized: "We felt that it was a great mistake to leave the management of the property so largely in the hands of Midgley who is entirely inexperienced in organization matters."[29] Kettering's genius lay not in manufacturing but in organizing research (Figure 6.2). No picture of the situation is available from his perspective, and he never mentioned it in his unpublished memoirs. Kettering, however, may have wanted to take the corporation in different research directions. The announcement from GM's Dayton labs of a new synthetic alcohol, "Synthol," fuel in the summer of 1925 is one indication of this. The fuel was said by the United Press to be a mixture of benzene, alcohol, and iron carbonyl or, by the *New York Times* account, benzene, tetraethyl lead, and alcohol. Both methyl and ethyl alcohols may have been involved. Used in combination with a new high-compression engine much smaller than ordinary engines, Synthol would "revolutionize transportation" ("Tells of New Type," 1925; see also "New Auto," 1925) the articles stated, and motorists would get 40 to 50 miles per gallon. Perhaps Kettering would have continued other antiknock research, broadening the field instead of letting it stagnate around one product. Other oil companies, especially Sunoco, made a point of finding substitutes for Ethyl leaded gaso-

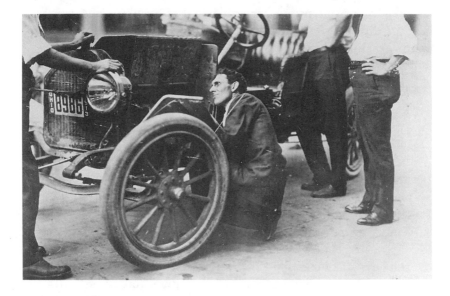

Figure 6.2. Charles F. Kettering.
Inventor of the electric starter motor, Charles Kettering and his protégés at General Motors
discovered in 1921 that leaded gasoline could be used to stop engine knock. The strange deaths
of gasoline refinery workers touched off an environmental controversy about using lead in
gasoline. Reproduced from the Collections of the Library of Congress (No. 56428).

line in the mid- to late 1920s.[30] By October 1925, Kettering noted
that the search for a substitute for petroleum had become problematic: He stated, "Many years of development may be necessary
before the actual development of such a substitute" ("May Take
Years," 1925, Section 9, p. 14; see also "Gas Substitutes," 1925).

Meanwhile, the new Ethyl officials announced that they had been
vindicated, and after agreeing to warning labels on leaded gasoline,
they began to market it again in the spring of 1926. These warning
labels would become familiar to generations of motorists and would
appear in virtually every service station except Sunoco: The warning
labels read, "Contains lead (tetraethyl) and is to be used as a motor
fuel only. Not for cleaning or any other use." Signs began appearing
across the country in Standard, Esso, Amoco, and Gulf stations
stating "Ethyl is back." Competing service stations sometimes put
up humorous responses saying that their fuel "never had to leave."[31]

CONCLUSION

The media covered the story of the leaded gasoline controversy without examining the scientific issues at play. Some papers tended to support industry, whereas liberal papers with a working-class readership extensively quoted public health advocates. In this fashion, the media served to mediate the debate between the two interest groups, although the balance of power was not in the hands of the public health and workers' advocates. The reporting served a conflict management role, and when government hearings and committees "resolved" the matter, the issue disappeared from the pages of the media.

It is interesting that editors at what were then the country's two most powerful newspapers professed such deep interest in scientific issues and yet found no method of weighing facts beyond the simple presentation of conflicting voices, or what would later be called "he said-she said" reporting. Some of the issues were understandably opaque at the time, but others were easily accessible to the media if some research had been attempted. For example, although GM scientists and Standard Oil spokesmen claimed there was no alternative to leaded gasoline, a search of periodical literature, patents, or chemical abstracts would have shown a considerable amount of research activity in antiknock fuels. Even GM scientists had taken out patents on alternatives.

In fact, journalists felt helpless in untangling the complexities of science. When Walter Lippmann said privately that the news media were effective "only if we [are] supplied with the necessary technical information," (see Note 19), he was abdicating responsibility for understanding science. He would never have asked to be "supplied with" the necessary information about politics or the economy. His reporters had the ability and the right to obtain that information for themselves. Although Lippmann associated his ideal of liberalism with scientific research and with criticism of dogma and authority, he found the authority of science difficult to criticize in the 1920s. The leaded gasoline controversy shows how the news media performed a system maintenance function in scientific and environmental arenas at a bureaucratic level and did not broaden public perceptions of the underlying scientific concerns.

EDITOR'S NOTES

1. Quotes fro the Charles-Edward Amory Winslow Papers and from the Walter Lippman Papers are used by permission from Manuscripts and Archives, Yale University Library.

2. All quotes in this chapter from the *New York Times* are used by permission.

NOTES

1. Du Pont owned a 27% share of GM at this time, whereas GM and Standard became equal partners in the Ethyl Gasoline Corporation on August 18, 1924. Standard's entry as a full partner against du Pont's wishes is explained mainly by its independent development of the ethyl chloride process, the cheapest way to produce tetraethyl lead, according to N. P. Wescott (1935).

2. Note that the confrontation is recorded by GM researchers. Following a search of the Hamilton papers at Harvard University's Schlesinger Library, there seems to be no information about her perspective on this confrontation.

3. Even critics, such as *Mother Jones Magazine* (Regush, 1992, p. 24), accepted without question the industry's unsubstantiated claims that the press acted irresponsibly and that leaded gasoline was necessary for the development of the internal combustion engine.

4. Actually, "iso-octane" was the original reference fuel and was pegged at the 100 level, whereas kerosene was set at zero on the scale by Ethyl Corporation scientists in the late 1920s. Simple octane—an eight-carbon liquid distilled from petroleum—does not have a high "octane" rating; branched isomers like iso-octane have the high antiknock properties.

5. Commercial tetraethyl lead also contained a preservative, a dye to color the fuel red, and an ethyl bromide "scavenger" to neutralize burning lead as it passed through the exhaust system.

6. Nriagu also notes that studies of Roman bones show from two to five parts per million of lead, with increasing amounts in bones of people who died at an older age. Pretechnical cultures that did not use lead, such as the Inca of Peru, have a small fraction of this concentration spread across all ages. Also, that some unclassified Roman bones have very high lead content and others very low lead content—which has been used to argue against the theory of lead poisoning as a factor in the fall of the Roman empire—may accurately reflect Roman social structure. The aristocratic group was able to afford plenty of lead-sweetened wine and sapa, and the lower class was unable to afford rich foods. (Quotes from Nriagu, 1983, are used by permission from John Wiley & Sons.)

7. William M. Clark to A. M. Stimson, October 11, 1922; A. M. Stimson to R. N. Dyer, October 13, 1922; Dyer to Surgeon General, October 18, 1922; N. Roberts to Surgeon General, November 13, 1922; H. S. Cumming to Pierre du Pont, December 20, 1922; and Thomas Midgley to Cumming, December 30, 1922, all in U.S. Public Health Service Record Group 90, National Archives, Washington, DC.

8. Midgley to A. W. Browne, December 2, 1922. Unprocessed Midgley files, GMI, Flint, MI.

9. Company advertisements only mentioned Ethyl gasoline, and external correspondence with government agencies deliberately avoided all mention of lead to avoid awakening public fears if documents were leaked to the press.

10. The reporters may not have known that Mann was suffering from lead poisoning. His recovery is mentioned in "Chief Chemist" (1924, p. 1). The article says that Mann had been among those hospitalized but was by then probably out of danger from the most acute stage of lead poisoning.

11. In fact, it was ethyl antiknock compounds being made by a Standard process using chloride, which was Standard's patented improvement over the General Motors bromide process. This improvement was Standard's rationale for entering the manufacturing operation and insisting that General Motors work with it, according to Wescott (1935, pp. 3-6).

12. General Motors abandoned this plan sometime in late 1922 after facing several serious impracticalities, primarily the consumer inconvenience of having two fuel tanks. Henderson had been in touch with GM in 1922 and 1923, before it was decided to use the "ethylizer" at the service station pump. By late 1924, the Ethyl Gasoline Corporation ordered the mixing to be done higher up the fuel stream at bulk distribution plants. That Henderson had heard about ethylizers is noted in a Science Service article "Ethyl Gasoline" in the monthly supplement in *Science* magazine of December 1924.

13. Although the paper that Midgley presented is not found in the archives, this account is consistent with the fact that he had rather freely informed fellow scientists of his case of lead poisoning. He turned down at least three speaking engagements to take time off in Florida to recuperate from lead poisoning in February 1923. Midgley to H. N. Gilbert, January 19, 1923, unprocessed Midgley papers, GMI, Flint, MI; see also Midgley to G. A. Round, Vacuum Oil Co. (later Mobil), February 14, 1923, unprocessed Midgley papers, GMI, Flint, MI; Leslie (1983, p. 165).

14. Contrary to assertions by industry historians, only official statements about treatments being attempted to clean the lead out of the workers' blood was printed. There were no "lurid details" of life on the wards in any of the news accounts. Nor was there any follow-up, then or in months to come, on the condition of the 44 Bayway men who survived but who may have endured lifelong brain damage. Their fate, to this day, is unknown.

15. Boyd (1957) notes that "no such compound was in existence" (p. 145) when Midgley first decided to try tetraethyl lead in Dayton in November 1921, and it took 3 weeks to produce it in the Dayton laboratory.

16. Kettering later insisted that the Bayway refinery had experienced an "explosion" (*U.S. v. du Pont,* Transcript No. 3578).

17. Ferris Hurd, attorney for General Motors (closing statement, *U.S. v du Pont,* Transcript No. 7986).

18. The distinction between "knowledge of " and "knowledge about" is usually attributed to John Dewey (1938).

19. W. Lippmann to A. Hamilton, June 25, 1928, Box 12, Folder 496, Lippmann collection, Yale University Library, New Haven, CT.

20. It is interesting that the *New York Times* account does not correspond with the Public Health Service stenographic record. Howard and Burnham referred to a "Gift of God" according to the PHS, instead of (as the *Times* reported) a "gift from heaven."

21. No record of these "informal conferences" on safe fuel dopes is found in the news media or in the PHS archives, and the *World* never followed up. That the formal conference was originally scheduled for more than 1 day is consistent with Secretary of the Interior Hubert Work's welcoming address, in which he said, "The purpose of this conference is very important, and your deliberations will take, I assume, some days." On Tuesday, May 19, a *Times* correspondent noted that the conference "will be opened tomorrow and probably will consume all of that day and Thursday" ("Scientists to Pass," 1925, p. 1), whereas the *New York Journal* noted on May 20 that the conference "will continue through tomorrow" ("Lead Gasoline," 1925, p. 1). Another angle to the conference question was noted by Joseph A. Pratt (1980, p. 40). Pratt notes that Henderson wanted to return to classes and could not stay at the conference.

22. These were David L. Edsall, Dean of the Harvard Medical School; W. H. Howell, Johns Hopkins; A. J. Chesley, State of Minnesota; W. S. Leathers, Vanderbilt; Julius Stieglitz, University of Chicago; and C. E. A. Winslow, Yale Medical School.

23. Cumming to C. E. A. Winslow, June 12 and August 24, Box 101, Folder 1800, Winslow papers, Yale University.

24. Winslow to Cumming, September 9, 1925, Box 101, Folder 1800, Winslow papers, Yale University.

25. An international expert in toxicological studies of heavy metals, Nriagu reviewed the original PHS report at the authors' request and roughly estimated that blood lead levels would have exceeded 50 to 100 micrograms per milliliter in the group of highly affected garage workers. The currently acknowledged threshold of contamination for lead is 10 micrograms per milliliter, but some studies suggest that this standard is not stringent enough to protect public health.

26. It is interesting to note that Winslow must have been well briefed on available alternatives because the three metals he mentions—iron, nickel, and tin—had undergone extensive testing along with lead.

27. W. H. Smith to C. E. A. Winslow, Box 101, Folder 1800, Winslow papers, Yale University. Forwarded to surgeon general in September 1925. Winslow also attempted to have alternatives mentioned in the report but was voted down by others on the committee.

28. C. E. A. Winslow to Y. Henderson, Box 101, Folder 1800, C. E. A. Winslow papers, Yale University, New Haven, CT.

29. Sloan to du Pont, March 28, 1925, *U.S. v. du Pont,* Government Trial Exhibit No. 678.

30. For example, Ludlow Clayden, Chief Engineer of Sun Oil Co., predicted 75- to 100-mile per gallon fuel in 20 years—without Ethyl gasoline. He stated, "The cost of fuel shouldn't exceed present prices, as it is possible to improve the quality of natural gasoline without resorting to use of Ethyl—a more expensive product" ("Predicts Double," 1926). Clayden was referring to Sunoco's development of catalytic reforming at its Marcus Hook, New Jersey, refinery that boosted octane by 15 to 20 points—twice as much as Ethyl and at a much lower cost. See "Predicts Double" (1926).

31. Transcript of a memoir by Charles Kettering for "The Story of Ethyl Gasoline," early 1945, GMI. Ethyl was a typical woman's name, and this phrase may be a play on the practice whereby an unwed mother would "have to leave" town so her baby could be delivered and adopted apart from local communities.

7

THE IMPORTANCE OF DRAMATIC EVENTS

The Donora Killer Smog and Smoke Abatement Campaigns

ews coverage of dramatic events may accelerate social change when other factors are resisting it. This was the case with the most dramatic event in U.S. air pollution history—a "killer smog" that smothered the town of Donora, Pennsylvania, in 1948. The smog killed 22 people and affected almost 5,000. Previously, campaigns for clean air had been successful in some cities but stalled without achieving national momentum. After the Donora incident, groups fighting against air pollution were mobilized and energized. The system reacted when the Public Health Service called the first national conference on clean air and elected representatives introduced bills to fund research. News coverage of subsequent air pollution incidents—including a lethal industrial accident in Mexico in 1950, the "killer fogs" of London of 1952 and 1956, and the air pollution incidents in Los Angeles in 1954 and 1956—became part of the media's normal routine.

The impact of dramatic events on social change has been noted since Machiavelli, and social scientists have attempted to explain the process by which dramatic events move issues from one public arena to another public arena (Hilgartner & Bosk, 1988). Of course, public awareness of the event has always been a major factor in such transitions. Donora marked a shift in the battle for smoke abatement, and it came to be seen as a defining moment in the green crusade against air pollution. As such, it has also been seen as the launching point of hysterical and "antiscientific" reactions to environmental problems. The conflict made scientists not so much victims as beneficiaries of the national attention, which furthered their research agenda and helped them illuminate the need for funding to investigate the social problem of air pollution.

THE DISASTER AT DONORA

Dr. William Rongaus chewed an unlit cigar and cursed the greasy black smog that settled over Donora, Pennsylvania, on a Friday night in October 1948. Behind him, the lights of an ambulance moving at walking speed illuminated a grim scene. Donora residents stumbled from their homes, choking, vomiting, coughing up blood, and gasping for breath. Some were barely conscious. Some who could not stop choking were rushed to the hospital or a temporary emergency center in the downtown community hall.

Other doctors in town also abandoned their cars to make rounds on foot that night. They found it was quicker to walk than to drive through the impossibly thick smog. Block by block, they encountered dozens of people with identical symptoms. Most were elderly, but

Figure 7.1. Donora, Pennsylvania.
Smoke from the steel and wire mill obscures much of the town of Donora, seen here in 1949 from the other side of the river. A killer smog on the evenings of October 29 and 30, 1948, left 22 dead and thousands ill. The smog disaster attracted national media attention after a Walter Winchell radio broadcast and wire services picked up the story. Reproduced from the National Archives, U.S. Public Health Service.

many healthy younger people were also affected in the town of 14,100. Between late Friday night, October 29, and Sunday morning, 20 people died, 400 were treated, and about 3,000 had been seriously ill in what became known as America's first air pollution disaster (Figure 7.1).

The dramatic event unfolded as air pollution built up from a cluster of steel, wire, and zinc plating mills during a period of unusual weather. The complex stretched more than 5 miles along the Monongahela River below the hilly town of Donora. Several dozen smokestacks belched out dense clouds of black smoke at levels below the surrounding hillsides. Usually, the smoke drifted down the valley, leaving only soot and a scorched landscape in its wake. That weekend in October, however, as a stationary weather front created an inversion of warm air covering cold air in the river valley, the smoke was trapped and people breathed in the fumes. The first media coverage came from an institutional source on Friday, when the newspaper in the small neighboring town of Monessen ran an article about overcrowding of area hospitals from patients with breathing problems ("Fog Crowds Hospitals," 1948).

As Donora's doctors took to the streets to make door-to-door calls, Donora's mayor and fire chief called other fire departments for aid and supplies. The town lacked enough drugs to fight asphyxiation, and more fresh oxygen tanks were needed to assist stricken people. This keyed another wave of press reports. As Pittsburgh and other towns rushed medical supplies to Donora and Monessen, the regional news media became alerted to the story ("Donora Smog," 1948; "Fog in Fifth Day," 1948).

Most physicians and rescue workers barely stopped to rest between Friday afternoon and Saturday night. Finally, the calls of desperate citizens began to taper off. Sunday morning, the exhausted mayor, city council, and board of health met in an emergency session and ordered the wire and steel mills closed. The superintendents of the mills told the council they had already shut down a few hours before "as a precautionary measure" on the advice of a company attorney. At the same time, however, they claimed there was only a "small chance" that the mills had anything to do with the disaster because they had been running since 1917 without these effects ("20 Dead," 1948, p. 1). Later, the mills would deny all responsibility.

As sometimes happens in a dramatic event, at first few people in Donora realized that they were in the midst of a major disaster, and the media reflected the relatively low level of concern on the first day or two. The Sunday *Pittsburgh Press* did not highlight the story; only doctors and emergency workers knew the extent of the problem until Sunday night, when nationally syndicated news announcer Walter Winchell first spoke of the 20 deaths and the hundreds of illnesses in the town (Snyder, 1994). Historian Lynn Page Snyder uncovered testimony from public hearings that revealed many residents learned of the extent of the disaster through radio reports such as Winchell's.

Winchell's broadcast may or may not have tipped off other media to the story. The next morning, newspapers in the region and across the nation carried an Associated Press report on the disaster, and the *New York Times* ("20 Dead," 1948) ran a front-page story about Donora quoting an angry Doctor Rongaus, who said, "It's murder. . . . There's nothing else you can call it. There was smog in Monessen too, but it didn't kill people there the way this did. There's something in the air here that isn't found anywhere else" (p. 1). The *Times* story said Donora was suffering from a "mysterious air-borne plague" ("20 Dead," 1948, p. 1). Donora residents, however, were not mystified. Donora physician Edwin Roth later stated, "It was no mystery. . . . It was obvious—all the symptoms pointed to it—that the fog and smoke were to blame" (as quoted in Rouche, 1953, p. 201).

In an editorial appraisal on November 1, the *Pittsburgh Post-Dispatch* called the disaster a "grim warning" that "smoke control meets only one part of the urgent problem of air pollution" ("Air Poisoning," 1948). Although expressing confidence that science could help solve the problem, the editorial cautioned, "The catastrophe at Donora should destroy the last opposition here to a strong city and county smoke law" ("Air Poisoning," 1948). The *Post-Dispatch, Times,* and other papers also printed an accompanying Associated Press story recalling a similar Belgian disaster in 1930 in which an industrial smog incident killed 70 people ("Belgian Disaster," 1948).[1] Public officials and the press assumed that Donora was only the second incident of its kind.[2]

In fact, incidents far more deadly than the one in Donora had already occurred in Britain many times in the previous decades, and smoke had been a problem in American and European industrial cities for generations. Pittsburgh, just 25 miles northwest, was often called the "smoky city" or, less politely, "hell with the lid on." City officials in Pittsburgh, St. Louis, Chicago, New York, and London had struggled with "smoke abatement" for almost a century beforehand and rarely managed to attract media interest, much less controversy. Of course, people usually died slowly from the effects of urban smoke, rather than the dramatic deaths of the western Pennsylvania incident. Donora's smog, which killed 20 people quickly and incapacitated thousands, riveted the attention of the nation and dramatized the consequences of unregulated industrial growth.

A prevailing view of the Donora incident is that the coverage it received helped start the national fight against air pollution. "Many people, including [Dr. William] Rongaus, figure the national attention given to their 1948 tragedy started a national drive to clean up air pollution," wrote *Pittsburgh Post-Gazette* reporter David Warner (1978) in a 30th anniversary article. Historian John Burnham said that the role of the media in reporting Donora and other dramatic environmental incidents was to derail the scientific worldview and "popularize science into impotence." Burnham (1992) said of the overall environmental movement: "What started out as an unimportant story of an accident at Donora has, in journalists' hands, been safely derailed from the . . . world view . . . in which the scientific method determines validity" (p. 41).

Burnham's (1992) argument deals with what he sees as the long-term trivialization of science, and he makes many convincing points. He may have picked a debatable starting point for the environmental movement and an even worse example of how dramatic events spur the media to ignore scientists. Scientists and public health service officials repeatedly invoked the memory of the Donora disaster during the 1950s to justify new funding for scientific work in air pollution, especially after funding requests for air pollution research were turned down in the late 1940s and early 1950s (*New York Times,* 1949; see also Bernstein, 1984, pp. 151-152).

At the time of the disaster, the primary sources in articles by the *New York Times,* the *Pittsburgh Post-Dispatch,* and other news organizations were area doctors and scientists. The press then carefully followed the scientific investigations in Donora over the next 2 years, quoting from scientific sources at federal and state levels. Far from trivializing science, the press put scientists on a pedestal as among the only legitimate sources in the story.

The drama of Donora was magnified by a scientific mystery, and some of the confusion was reflected in the news coverage. The experts did not understand why people had been safe in nearby towns that also had smoke-producing industries. Was there something in Donora that was not present anywhere else, as Rongaus charged? Was the steel complex, with its blast furnaces, wire mill, and zinc works, to blame? How was the problem scientifically studied?

INVESTIGATING THE DISASTER

Following an emergency meeting on Sunday, 2 days after the disaster, the Donora board of health began a series of hearings. Historian Snyder (1994, p. 121) stated, "Accusations were fired squarely at the zinc works," by Rongaus and others on the board. Zinc workers testified about what they saw as an excessive use of reprocessed materials. They also said that the numbers of Donora residents who had been sick that week had been under-reported because of fear of reprisals by the company. When the managers at American Steel and Wire insisted that the works had operated without incident since 1915, board of health members replied angrily that after three decades without modernization, the zinc works deserved to go out of business (Snyder, 1994).

Although board of health members were outraged at the deaths and suffering, the town's borough council did not believe it was realistic to demand that the zinc works be shut down. Donora was still a company town. The council also disliked the idea of passing local smoke control laws to regulate the mill, although such laws had been used for almost a century to regulate the worst forms of industrial air pollution in other areas. The laws were making dramatic differences in the post-World War II appearance of Pittsburgh and St. Louis, but they depended on a large-scale cooperative effort between many local industries and governments backed by civic improvement groups, business groups, and an often enthusiastic news media. In 1939, a St. Louis newspaper even proposed its own smoke control plan.

Donora was in a different situation. American Steel and Wire was the only major employer, and six of seven borough council members belonged to the United Steelworkers union. They feared the town would lose jobs if they passed the smoke control laws demanded by board of health members. In a classic case of bureaucratic conflict management, the council asked for an investigation. Board of health members believed that any state-level investigation would be a "whitewash," so the board decided to ask the federal Public Health Service (PHS) to assist. At first, the PHS declined, but it eventually sent an engineer to talk with the borough council. The engineer endorsed a state plan to monitor pollution in the Donora valley and order the mills to shut down if pollution levels became dangerous. Based on that plan, the PHS engineer felt there was no reason to prohibit the mills from restarting a week after the incident.

American Steel and Wire, meanwhile, contracted with the University of Cincinnati's Kettering Laboratory of Applied Physiology to perform a study. The laboratory's founder, Robert Kehoe, had longstanding ties to the auto and oil industries and had helped defend leaded gasoline from regulation in the 1920s and 1930s (Rosner & Markowitz, 1987, pp. 121-139). Both the Cincinnati study and the state study focused on the weather (rather than the industry) as the chief culprit in the disaster. Many local residents refused to cooperate with both the state and Kettering Laboratory researchers.

The local board of health decided to conduct its own research. By mid-November 1948, its study found that thousands of Donora residents had been sick, rather than the hundreds first suspected. One board of health consultant, coincidentally also from the University of Cincinnati, Clarence A. Mills, became involved in an environmental organization that mobilized across the river from Donora in the small town of Webster. The group called itself the Webster Society for Better Living and adopted the motto "Clean Air and Green Grass!" (Snyder, 1994, p. 127).[3] The group's main goal was the adoption of smoke control ordinances by the borough council.

Amid the controversy, the Public Health Service announced in late November that it would begin a survey of Donora as a "scientific test tube" for studying the effects of air pollution on humans. From the beginning, the survey focused on health impacts rather than air pollution sources. Thousands of hours were spent on interviews and physical examinations of randomly selected city residents. As a result, very little was done to estimate the amounts and sources of various pollutants present at the time of the disaster. One exception was that the state health department made a few measurements early Sunday' morning, October 31, showing sulfur dioxide at 0.75 parts per million (ppm). That level met or exceeded even the very loose scientific guidelines for ground-level concentrations of sulfur dioxide at the time (0.50-0.75 ppm), and the health department observed that considerably higher concentrations would have been found October 29 and 30 (Shilan, 1949). Critics, such as Mills and

Rongaus, saw the attempts at monitoring and modeling the pollution at the time of the disaster as weak at best.

As the PHS study got under way, charitable relief poured into Donora. One group chartered a plane and flew the sickest citizens to a coastal vacation on the Outer Banks of North Carolina. Forty-one Donorans took the trip, but two died a week after returning home, bringing the final death toll to 22. In the aftermath of the Donora smog disaster, 128 Donora residents sued American Steel and Wire Co. and U.S. Steel, eventually reaching settlements of about $1,500 each (Knezevich, 1973).

The PHS report, issued in November 1949, concluded, "The episode was not due to an accidental occurrence but rather resulted from the accumulation of atmospheric pollutants during an unusually intense and prolonged stable air condition" (Schrenk, Heimann, Clayton, Gafafer, & Wexler, 1949, p. 161). The report also stated that similar conditions had occurred in Donora in 1923 and 1938, and that both of these previous incidents had been associated with a rise in deaths from heart and lung disease, although not on the scale of the 1948 disaster. The report recommended reductions in pollutants from the major operating centers at the steel complex and a system of weather forecasts that could alert the community to possible air pollution problems (Schrenk et al., 1949).

"The whole nation was shocked," said PHS Administrator Oscar Ewing in a preface to the Donora report. Although the PHS was concerned with smoke abatement, Ewing wrote, "We have regarded [air pollution] as a nuisance and annoyance rather than a serious health problem" (Schrenk et al., 1949, p. 161). Not everyone was satisfied with the report. Clarence Mills said the report blamed household chimneys "as much as the zinc smelter and sulfuric acid plant, which almost certainly supplied the killing fumes" (Schrenk et al., 1949, p. 161). In a talk at a Citizens Committee for Smoke Control meeting in New York in 1950, Mills also took aim at another problem with the Donora report—the idea that long-term exposure to pollution caused no change in the death rate. Pneumonia and tuberculosis death rates, his evidence showed, could be 2 to 10 times higher among men living in industrial districts than those living in the suburbs ("Death Held Hidden," 1950). This kind of argument had been made dozens of times before in many other locations, but with the added drama of the Donora controversy, it began to have an effect. The salience of the single dramatic incident transferred legitimacy to the deeper yet less tangible problem.

Few argued with the bottom-line conclusion of the Donora disaster, and scientists who had previously had difficulty proving the danger of low concentrations of pollutants could now simply point to Donora as a concrete example of the menace of air pollution. Thus, throughout the 1950s, the Donora disaster stood out as a grim wake-up call, a symbol of unregulated industry and the need for new science on air pollution. After a century of small, local controversies, the Donora disaster registered on the national political scale.

The impact of the Donora incident was reinforced by three more events in the next few years. In 1950, in the small Mexican refinery town of Poza Rica on the gulf coast, 22 people suffocated to death and more than 250 were hospitalized after a gas line ruptured in the refinery. Mexican oil officials compared the accident to the Donora disaster ("Night Smog," 1950; see also "Mexican Gas Toll," 1950; " 'Poison Fog,' " 1950). Another major incident involved an estimated 6,000 deaths in a series of London smogs in December 1952. "Massacre" was the glaring headline of one sensational London tabloid, and newspapers, members of Parliament, and many thousands demanded government action ("Alarmed Londoners," 1953). London's smog came from households burning coal in small furnaces, unlike the industrial air pollution in Donora or Poza Rica.[4] Racked by two world wars and a depression, Britain had not been able to invest in new fuel systems, and the famous London fogs of the 1950s were simply the same phenomenon that had plagued the city for centuries magnified by a growing population.

Now that air pollution had a dramatic focus, it became a household word and a regular beat for news coverage. The mass media began to see it as an important front-page news story, and "air pollution" replaced the "smoke abatement" civic improvement concerns that were sometimes dismissed as women's issues. Taking advantage of the new visibility, the 1948 Donora disaster sparked a coordinated green crusade among public health officials to study and regulate air pollution in the 1950s and early 1960s, and this crusade created its own publicity machine. Thus, Donora was really a transitional moment between the modern air pollution controversies and the previous smoke abatement campaigns. Because most of these previous campaigns were forgotten, however, Donora is often seen as the beginning of the air pollution crusade. Like a bookmark protruding from a long-neglected text, Donora symbolized green crusades that had been known for centuries.

AIR POLLUTION IN
ANCIENT AND MEDIEVAL CITIES

"The smoke, the wealth, the noise of Rome" held no charms for the Roman poet Horace and many of his contemporaries. As residents of what had become the largest city in the world, ancient Romans were well aware of the problem of air pollution. They called it *gravioris caeli* (heavy heaven) or *infamis aer* (infamous air) (Hughes, 1994, p. 150). The Roman architect Vitruvius gave detailed instructions for ventilation of buildings and encouraged the planting of trees in the city to provide shade and more wholesome air (Leake, 1959, p. 20). Sources of air pollution included wood smoke, dust, and odors from sewage and industries such as leather tanneries (Halliday, 1961, p. 9).

Historian J. Donald Hughes (1994) wrote about Rome and other cities, "Many people are surprised to discover these ancient references to air pollution . . . but it should be remembered that [even today] in . . . large nonindustrial cities with few cars, fires and the dust of human activities [also] produce a heavy pall" (p. 165).

The elites worried about air pollution in preindustrial England: "Unendurable" air pollution from wood smoke, for example, led Henry II's wife Eleanor of Aquitaine to flee Tutbury Castle in Nottingham in 1157. Along with the growing pall of wood smoke in European cities, use of a new fuel—coal—created some of the early air pollution controversies. Coal was unknown in most of Europe until Marco Polo wrote about the burning black stone in China. Even in England, with large coal deposits on the northeastern coast, coal was rarely used for fuel until the early 13th century, when residents of Newcastle received royal permission to open coal mines. Ships loaded with coal sailed the coast to London where traders sold it as an alternative to wood for cooking fires, which had become scarce as the city of London grew larger. "Sea coal" from Newcastle, however, was much dirtier than wood, and during the reign of Edward I (1272-1307), the English nobility protested its use. Edward obliged the nobles and decreed a death penalty for anyone caught burning coal. The penalty was probably never imposed, but during the succeeding reign of his son, Edward II, at least one Londoner was tortured for filling the air with coal's "pestilential odor" (Carr, 1965, p. 35). A similar royal decree was issued in 1607 ("Commons Cheers," 1955, citing a speech by a member of Parliament).

Over the centuries, London became notorious for its air pollution, and many inhabitants of the city came to detest it. Typical was a 1631 lament that the people "are constrained to make their fires of sea-coal or pit coal, even in the chambers of honourable personages" (Armytage, 1961, p. 61). One of the first green crusaders, English scientist John Evelyn, wrote a book proposing an air pollution reduction program in 1661. He suggested moving the factories to the outskirts of the city and starting a campaign of tree planting for wood fuel in the suburbs of London. If the factories refused to move, he suggested that sweet-smelling gardens should be planted to mask the stench. In his book *Fumifugium* (as quoted in Wall, 1994), he wrote,

> The immoderate use of, and indulgence to, sea-coale in the city of London exposes it to one of the fowlest inconveniences and reproaches that can possibly befall so noble and otherwise incomparable City. . . . Whilst they are belching it forth their sooty jaws, the City of London resembles the face rather of Mount Aetna, the Court of Vulcan . . . or the suburbs of Hell [rather] than an assembly of rational creatures. (p. 45)

Londoners may have sympathized with Evelyn's views, but a firewood shortage and the growing demands of industry led to a greatly expanded coal trade. Whereas only two ships sailed the coal route between Newcastle and London in 1650, as many as 600 ships sailed hauling coal 50 years later. Around the same time, the French, Germans, and Americans also began mining coal on a smaller scale for industry and heating.

Air pollution and other environmental problems associated with coal mining and other industries were noticed as early as the 14th century. In *De Re Metalica,* Georgius Agricola (as quoted in Wall, 1994) wrote that Italian city-states passed laws against mining because of its effects on woodlands, fields, vineyards, and olive groves: "The critics say further that mining is a perilous occupation to persue [*sic*] because the miners are sometimes killed by the pestilential air which they breathe; sometimes their lungs rot away" (p. 55). Agricola discounted these and other environmental concerns: "Things like this rarely happen, and only insofar as workmen are careless" (p. 55). The idea that workmen were to blame for occupational disease would be repeated with surprising frequency into the mid-20th century.

Pestilential air was the strongest reason for sanitation for many centuries. Most of the very early concern about air pollution had to do with the idea that poor-quality air, especially from swamps and sewers, could generate disease-creating "miasmas." In the decades before the germ theory of disease was accepted, public health crusaders and "sanitarians" believed that bad air did not simply harbor disease, it created it. One example is in the word "malaria"—literally meaning bad air. Historian Henry E. Sigerist (1945) wrote,

> Experience taught that malaria occurred in the vicinity of swamps. . . . The theory was that in the summer and autumn swamps developed pernicious exhalations. The theory was wrong, yet it was helpful. On the basis of it, the popes from the 16th to 18th centuries drained portions of the Pontine marshes, with good results. (p. 165)

Odors arising from sewage concerned the sanitarians of the mid- to late 19th century, who used the same theory. "Filth is the deadliest of present removable causes of disease," said John Simon, one of Britain's leading public health crusaders, because it "may breed and convey the poison" of cholera and typhoid through pollution of the air (as quoted in Hodgkinson, 1973, p. 46).

The germ theory of disease and the development of the science of bacteriology in the late 19th century increased concern about water pollution because it helped explain the spread of disease. The germ theory may have helped set aside unfounded fears about malaria, typhoid, and cholera carried by bad odors and, with them, some of the concerns about the impact of air pollution.

SANITARY REFORM
AND SMOKE ABATEMENT

If London's atmosphere resembled a suburb of hell in 1661, two more centuries of sea coal created a nightmare landscape. Novelist Charles Dickens (1853/1951) began his novel *Bleak House* with an image of London as a twisted, twilight world of shadows and wraiths. He described "Smoke lowering down from chimney-pots, making a soft black drizzle, with flakes of soot in it as big as full-grown snow flakes—gone into mourning, one might imagine, for the death of the sun" (p. 1). Another Londoner wrote of "a fog so thick that one might have spread it on bread; in order to write I had to light a candle as early as eleven o'clock" (Leff, 1957, p. 130). The smoky fogs of London and many other industrial cities were thick enough in the 19th century that children walked to school with lamps in what should have been broad daylight.

What could be done? In 1819, a Parliamentary committee found that steam engines and furnaces "could work in a manner less prejudicial to public health" (Stern, 1984, p. 6). Nothing was done to follow up on these observations because the British government gave itself little authority to intervene in questions of public health at the time. London, however, was not the only island city with industrial problems. In Glasgow, Scotland, the Saint Rollox soda works became one of the biggest chemical factories in the world by the 1820s. The works produced enormous clouds of hydrochloric acid gas, and "the resulting uproar from outraged citizens and landowners led [the owner] to build a chimney 455 feet high to disperse the poisonous smoke in the atmosphere" (Johnson, 1991, p. 280). The chimney destroyed the view of the skyline, but at least the clouds of poison gas were kept away from the ground. Continued cries for regulation led, 40 years later, to the Alkali Act of 1863. This impotent law did regulate the amount of hydrochloric acid that could be released, but it also allowed government agents only to question industrialists and suggest improvements in their operations, not to penalize them.

Parliament passed no serious air pollution regulations until 1906 (Johnson, 1917).

Smoke problems affected not only industrial cities in Europe but frontier towns in the United States. In 1804, Pittsburgh official Presley Neville (Mellon Institute of Industrial Research and School of Specific Industries, 1914) wrote about "the general dissatisfaction which prevails and the frequent complaints which are exhibited, in consequence of the Coal Smoke from many buildings in the Borough, particularly from smithies and blacksmith shops" (p. 11). The smoke affected the "comfort, health and . . . peace and harmony" (p. 11) of the new city. As in Glasgow, the remedy was to build higher chimneys.

The accelerating pace of the industrial revolution in America led to enormous increases in coal consumption, matching the pace of a national population that doubled between 1850 and 1890 and then doubled again by 1920. Smoke problems were compounded when hard anthracite coal was replaced by soft bituminous coal, which was more volatile, more sulfur-laden, and far dirtier.

Thick black smoke from bituminous coal poured from chimneys, smokestacks, and railroad engines across the nation, particularly in the northeastern and midwestern cities. To a certain extent, it was celebrated as evidence of progress and industrial growth. City councils or health departments sometimes raised objections locally, when dense smoke directly affected populations, and frequently a spirit of cooperation was evident. In Newark, New Jersey, the completion of a 350-foot smokestack in 1905 was pleasing "not only because it promised to remove objectionable odors" but also because it was built in a civic spirit without "legal interference or threats from the local board of health" ("The Photography," 1905, p. 436). Efficiency was also a concern. One engineer who raised questions about smoke control in 1881 estimated that the inefficient combustion that resulted in smoke represented an annual loss to Allegheny County, Pennsylvania, of about a million dollars (Mellon Institute of Industrial Research and School of Specific Industries, 1914, p. 13).

The spirit of civic improvement that animated the Progressive era touched on smoke abatement in many cities. In April 1881, Chicago became the first American city to create a local ordinance regulating smoke discharges, followed that same year by Cincinnati. Pittsburgh's first smoke ordinance passed in 1892, and St. Louis created a smoke ordinance in 1893 (Cooper, 1959, p. 416). The ordinances were extremely feeble, and as late as 1906, the *Chicago Record-Herald* noted sarcastically that a judge who normally handled smoke cases thought it to be "cruel and unusual punishment" if fines of $100 were handed out more than once or twice a year (*Chicago Record-Herald,* July 13, 1906, as cited in Grinder, 1980, p. 86).

A sudden shock sparked action in Pittsburgh in 1892. After the city had been known for its pall of coal smoke for many decades, two thirds of the homes and industries switched to a new fuel source, natural gas, in the late 1880s. The city's air became noticeably cleaner, but after 5 years, the natural gas supply ran down and prices went up. Economic reality set citizens to burning coal. One observer lamented, "We are going back to smoke. . . . We had four or five years of wonderful cleanliness in Pittsburgh, and we have all had a taste of knowing what it is to be clean" (Mellon Institute of Industrial Research and School of Specific Industries, 1914, p. 13). In 1892, the Women's Health Protective Association proposed a city ordinance encouraging smokeless fuels, abatement of smoke from stationary furnaces, and better flue designs for new buildings. Pittsburgh's city council, in a symbolic gesture that had no effect whatsoever, made thick smoke illegal in the city except in the industrial district.

The problem was so annoying, steel tycoon Andrew Carnegie told a Chamber of Commerce meeting in 1898 that it was driving people "to leave Pittsburgh and reside under skies less clouded than ours." Although Carnegie was not sure what to do, he acknowledged, "The man who abolishes the Smoke Nuisance in Pittsburgh . . . [will earn] our deepest gratitude" (as quoted in Mellon Institute of Industrial Research and School of Specific Industries, 1914, p. 16). A committee on smoke abatement was appointed by the chamber, but the Engineer's Society of Allegheny County refused to cooperate with it, saying legislation was needed, not engineering. By 1906, Pittsburgh got its ordinances, and a "Smoke Inspector" went to work. Gross emissions noticeably decreased. The city lost a legal challenge in 1911 when the Pennsylvania Supreme Court said that only the state legislature, and not city governments, had the authority to create smoke abatement laws. Within months, the Pennsylvania legislature specifically gave city governments that authority.

Similar smoke abatement movements began with civic groups in Cincinnati, St. Louis, Chicago, Milwaukee, and Kansas City. Their origins varied, but most were started with the backing of business groups or community elites. The civic conscience of a former American Medical Association president, Charles A. L. Reed, was the driving force behind the smoke abatement movement in Cincinnati around the turn of the century. "Smoke must be reckoned among the demonstrated causes of consumption," he said (as quoted in Grinder, 1980, p. 85). Preparations for the Louisiana Exposition of 1903 sparked the St. Louis smoke abatement movement. Civic boosters who wanted Chicago to stay ahead of St. Louis added fuel to the movement there (Grinder, 1980, p. 86). The idea, according to a New York City health commissioner, was to keep one's city out of the "notorious circle" of cities with a smoky reputation that might decrease a city's appeal to business. Blue skies were almost as important a matter of civic pride (and business climate) as the public's health (Walker, 1928).

Strengthening regulations against polluters proved difficult, even with a strong smoke abatement movement, because clear relationships between health effects and common causes were hard to establish. In terms of health effects, risks from air pollution were scientifically much harder to support than those from water pollution, in which poor sewage systems were known to cause typhoid and other diseases. As late as the 1950s, some scientists could claim that there were no provable dangers from air pollution. Others saw a link to tuberculosis and chronic lung problems, and still others believed that the lack of sunlight robbed the body of vital forces. Partly in reaction to this latter concern, and partly to test a new monitoring technique, the U.S. Public Health Service devised a solar monitoring device that would measure how much sunlight was being blocked by atmospheric haze and smoke (Figure 7.2). In 1927, for example, the PHS found that New Yorkers were being deprived of an average of 37% of their sunlight (Walker, 1928).

Proving common causes was difficult as well. The link between the problem of air pollution and the many small homes and businesses that heated with coal was not apparent to many people. E. C. Halliday (1961), in a 1960 review of air pollution for the World Health Organization, stated,

Figure 7.2. Solar pollution meter.
Created by the U.S. Public Health Service, this device measures the strength of solar radiation as a way to gauge the amount of smoke and haze in the air. Seen here during tests in 1927 in Arlington, Virginia, the solar pollution meter would give scientists a measurement of overall particulate pollution. Reproduced from the National Archives, U.S. Public Health Service.

> The history of smoke control in American cities . . . shows that even when a very large volume of public opinion was convinced of the need for smoke reduction, that same public was militantly unwilling to take the technical steps necessary for the reduction, the mental attitude being that the responsibility for cure must surely lie at someone else's door. (p. 9)

In studies of St. Louis in 1907, Chicago in 1910, and Pittsburgh in 1912, investigators found most homes and small factories heated with dirty bituminous coal instead of cleaner but more expensive anthracite. Although scientific research had focused on inefficient combustion and, increasingly after 1890, on pollution control (Halliday, 1961),[5] and although laws got increasingly tougher on industry, individual home heating systems proved impossible to regulate.

In 1912, a Bureau of Mines study found that all 28 U.S. cities with more than 200,000 people had some form of smoke control regulation, whereas only 10% of cities the bureau surveyed under 200,000 had any regulations. The regulations varied tremendously. Some were aimed at all smoke, whereas others defined categories. Some allowed dense smoke for certain periods of time to allow furnaces and locomotives to "stoke up," whereas others did not take the problem into consideration (Flagg, 1912). In a follow-up study in 1939, the bureau found that 80 major cities had some smoke ordinances and that 25 of them based their rules on a model ordinance provided by a group of engineering societies. Also, cities were getting cleaner after the new regulations kicked in. For example, Pittsburgh in 1917 sustained more than 900 tons of ash settling per square mile per year, whereas 10 years later, 300 tons settled per square mile per year ("Find More Soot," 1928).

Technological developments and economic forces had a great deal to do with the decrease in city smoke between the Progressive era and World War II. Engineers developed new stokers for the mechanical firing of coal. Industries introduced smoke "scrubbers" for removing acid gasses. Dust collectors, in the form of cyclone and bag house models, came to be in widespread use. In addition, overall, engineering concepts of physical and chemical principles in smoke controls were far better understood. Also in this period, electric motors replaced stationary steam engines at factories, diesel locomotives replaced coal-fired steam locomotives, and long-distance oil and gas pipelines made it possible for consumers to switch to cleaner home heating fuels (Stern, 1984).

The news media in the Progressive era smoke abatement campaigns were consistent in their support for civic virtues, such as clean air, and frequently lent support and editorial advice to green crusaders. The lack of drama, however, proved to be a problem in promoting public health concerns on a sustained basis. For instance, the New York City health commissioner said,

> If we could dramatize typhoid germs, diphtheria bacilli and the streptococcus germs, as they [the media] dramatize gangsters and hold-up men, there would be an outcry from the public that would not be settled until more health inspectors were added. ("New York Starts War," 1927, Section II, p. 10)

Regular stories on clean air problems were found in the media but usually on the women's pages or in the context of the women's movements. In 1926, for example, the *New York Times* ran a story titled "Women Open Drive to Clean the Air" (1926, p. 41).

Although news coverage was not spectacular, or even high on the agenda, it was locally pervasive, as is evident from the many citations found under the heading of smoke control in the *Reader's Guide to Periodical Literature* and the *New York Times* index during this period. One scholarly paper on the smoke abatement campaigns also reflects this influence: R. Dale Grinder, writing about the smoke problem, cited newspapers in 29 of 47 references (Grinder, 1980).

SMOKE ABATEMENT IN ST. LOUIS

Although smoke could be seen as indicating a booming local economy, it could also be a source of civic embarrassment, as officials with the city of St. Louis found while they waited in vain at the city's airport for a world-famous aviator. Art Goebel, on his way back from a record-breaking nonstop flight to Hawaii in October 1927, circled St. Louis for an hour, searching for a runway in a dense smog. Eventually, he had to land at a small airport 25 miles away and be driven into town ("Aviator Can't Find Field," 1927).

More than embarrassing was a dangerous smog incident in November 1939, which upset any notion of long-term progress for residents of St. Louis. Some called it "the dirtiest city in the United States." According to the *New York Times,* its "smoke was the blackest and the most villainous of any to be found in America, or in Europe for that matter" ("St. Louis," 1982, Section 2, p. 1). For 4 days in November 1939, street lights alone illuminated the darkened city because the sun could not penetrate the smoke. In a photo taken to record the darkness at noon, the glow from a match reflects from a man's hand and face as he lights a cigarette (Figure 7.3).

Unlike Donora 9 years later, there was no immediate death toll in the St. Louis smog incident, but the resulting outcry was the beginning of a new round of serious smoke prevention laws. Leading the outcry was the *St. Louis Post-Dispatch,* and over the next 2 years, the *Dispatch* printed dozens of articles about smoke abatement, about what other cities had done, and about what could be done in St. Louis. In one instance, the newspaper proposed a buying co-operative for less smoky fuels such as anthracite coal or desulfurized bituminous coal. The idea was praised but quickly pushed aside by city officials.

On April 8, 1940, a new city ordinance prohibited inherently smoky fuels if they were fired in a regular furnace or required automatic fuel-burning equipment when smoky fuels were to be used. It also required coal washing to remove dirt and sulfur, and the use of less smoky fuels wherever possible. The aggressive campaign apparently paid off, and Washington University professor Raymond R. Tucker, who became smoke commissioner, reported in 1941 that city smoke had decreased substantially thanks to fuel substitution in regular furnaces and new diesel locomotives ("Moderate Smoke," 1941).[6] From 1937 to 1950, sulfur dioxide had been reduced by an average of 78% (McCabe, 1959, p. 49). Tucker stated in 1958 from his vantage point as mayor of St. Louis, "It can be truthfully said that the battle against the city smoke palls has been won. . . . The control agencies can congratulate themselves on this. It's a battle they fought, almost alone, for many years" (Tucker, 1959, p. 49). Citizens' groups sometimes felt otherwise; in 1957, a group marched on city hall with pickets protesting air pollution grievances. Newspapers and television programs covered the protest, which was organized in part by local Teamsters unions to draw attention to the staff shortages in the regulatory office (Wetzel, 1959, p. 447; Figure 7.4).

SMOKE ABATEMENT IN PITTSBURGH

Pittsburgh suffered air pollution problems as difficult as St. Louis. After World War II, Pittsburgh civic leaders were determined to overcome the long-standing prejudice against the community as a grimy place to live. Journalist Ernie Pyle wrote in 1937, "Pittsburgh is a dirty city. . . . But Pittsburgh people, like people everywhere, love prosperity. And a dirty shirt collar here means prosperity, so people don't seem to mind" (Pyle, 1943).

Figure 7.3. St. Louis, before and after.
On the left, a scene before pollution control regulations in St. Louis, Missouri, at 11:00 a.m., November 28, 1939. A match illuminates a man's hand and face as he lights a cigarette. Notice the street lights are also on. The same spot, at right, is shown a year later on a clear day after new regulations were put in place. Much of the dramatic difference was due to weather, but the smoke control ordinances were far reaching and tough, and by the mid-1950s, St. Louis was a cleaner town. Reproduced from the National Archives.

Pittsburgh's reputation would be difficult to repair, let alone improve, after assaults by journalist H. L. Mencken. "I am not speaking of mere filth—One expects steel towns to be ugly. What I allude to is the unbroken and agonizing ugliness, the sheer revolting

Figure 7.3. St. Louis, before and after (continued).

monstrousness, of every house in sight," Mencken (1927, pp. 187-
193) stated in what one historian called his "celebrated environmental piece" of 1926 (Muller, 1991, pp. 50-62).

Mencken (1927) continued,

> Here was the very heart of industrial America, the center of its most
> lucrative and characteristic activity, the boast and pride of the richest

Figure 7.4. Air pollution protest, 1958.

In a time-honored protest tactic assured to gather media attention, the Community Stewards of St. Louis complain about a lack of enforcement of smoke abatement regulations in the 16th ward in a July 1958 march on city hall. The physician referred to in the sign was connected to the board of health. Reproduced from the National Archives by permission of the *St. Louis Post Dispatch*.

and grandest nation ever seen on earth—and here was a scene so dreadfully hideous, so intolerably bleak and forlorn that it reduced the whole aspiration of man to a macabre and depressing joke. Here was wealth beyond computation, almost beyond imagination—and here were human habitations so abominable that they would have disgraced a race of alley cats. (pp. 187-193)

After World War II, a dirty shirt collar no longer meant prosperity. Pittsburgh was losing businesses rapidly, just as Carnegie had predicted in 1898. Real estate values in the "Golden Triangle" downtown area were dropping by $10 million per year. Even the steel companies were talking about relocating ("Pittsburgh Rebuilds," 1952). Editorials in the *Pittsburgh Press* called the community to action. Proposals for an antismoke campaign, a campaign for road improvements, and a cleanup of urban blight all caught the imagination of a host of organizations, including the chamber of commerce, the women's clubs, the convention bureau, the Better Business Bureau, and other civic groups. Many of these groups joined the Allegheny Conference on Community Development, and smoke abatement was the first priority in its initial legislative report (Report of the Allegheny Conference on Community Development, 1946).

The enthusiasm might have gone nowhere without the backing of financier Richard K. Mellon. According to a Newspaper Enterprise Association reporter, Mellon forced coal and railroad companies to cooperate with the smoke abatement campaign, "dragging them into the program by the heels" (Heath, n.d.).

Between 1945 and 1950, Pittsburgh reduced its smoke by 77% and reduced ash fall from 60 tons per square mile in 1938 to 50 tons by 1950 (McCabe, 1959; see also Ely, 1951). In 1950, more than 100 new companies moved to Pittsburgh, and a civic opera, a state park, and an airport were under construction (Patterson, 1950). The cost was high. By 1952, Pittsburgh spent $200 million on the fight against air pollution, most of it switching from coal to diesel locomotives and cleaning up smoke from factories and power plants ("Pittsburg Keeps Trying," 1952). Despite the cost, the *Pittsburgh Post-Gazette* could claim in a gush of civic pride that "we have made tremendous strides" ("Air Poisoning," 1948).

SMOKE ABATEMENT IN NEW YORK

New York City also encouraged its smoke abatement committees, although the *Times* frequently reported them, along with other air pollution news, on the women's pages next to articles about fashion and recipes. In one 1948 editorial ("An Anti-Smoke Rally," 1948) promoting an antismoke rally, the paper recognized the role of women's groups in the clean air movement:

This is a critical time in the movement to control air pollution because legislation reorganizing the city government's machinery to abate the nuisance is now being written. We urge housewives and others to take this opportunity to become better informed and, by their presence at the rally, demonstrate their determination to keep fighting until effective action is taken. (p. 26)

The women's groups followed a course set by Ellen Swallow Richards and other leaders of the home economics movement, which highlighted environmental concerns around house and home (Gottlieb, 1993, pp. 207-234). It was a short step for these groups from sanitary reform to clean air.

The smoke abatement movements of New York, Pittsburgh, St. Louis, and other cities in the late 1940s and 1950s reflect a broad concern with civic improvement, a continuation of the "municipal housekeeping" role for women, and a generally cooperative approach in the face of mutual interests involving cities and their industries. Gradual progress resulted from civic organizations, businesses, bureaucrats, and the news media highlighting the problem to an often-receptive city or state legislature, with industry being forced to reduce or alter emissions at the smokestack and consumers switching to cleaner and more expensive alternative fuels. One way the problem received media coverage was when bureaucratic organizations, such as the Air Pollution Engineering Program (in the surgeon general's office), issued a news release ranking cities by levels of pollution. The news stories had a multiplier effect; cities complained about their ratings, whereas others boasted of their progress, all in newspaper and television stories (Bernstein, 1984).

Until the 1950s, air pollution control meant keeping track of factory smoke and sulfur dioxide from coal. No one could anticipate how rapidly the air pollution problem would be compounded by the rapidly growing use of automobiles in the 1950s or how uncooperative automakers could be in dealing with pollution control efforts.

TAILPIPES AND SMOG:
THE CHALLENGE FROM LOS ANGELES

Although automobiles were first seen as a remedy for the tons of horse manure that plopped on city streets each day, as early as the 1920s health officials began to worry about the growing presence of carbon monoxide from auto exhausts in the urban air. New York health commissioner Louis Harris found some parts of Manhattan to have 284 ppm carbon monoxide in the air. "The tests have shown conclusively that the poison is here in a much more marked concentration than anyone has suspected," the *Times* quoted Harris saying. Harris "sounded a city-wide call to arms against fuel smoke and the dangerous carbon monoxide gas left in the wake of gasoline burning automobiles" (Walker, 1928, p. 16).

Local smoke abatement movements, however, were not equipped to deal with auto manufacturers, which operated on a national level. Little research on automotive air pollution was conducted until the late 1940s and early 1950s. In any event, automotive air pollution was not seen as a significant social problem, outside the confines of Manhattan, until around 1943, when smoke from industry and automobiles began to darken the skies of the Los Angeles area. One day became known as Black Monday because of its thick air pollution. In 1947, the California legislature authorized the Los Angeles Air Pollution Control District, the first large-scale air pollution control bureau in the nation.

For its first 10 years, the district focused almost exclusively on industrial sources of smog even though scientists said more than half of the Los Angeles pollution problem stemmed from automobiles (Chass, 1959, p. 354). By the mid-1950s, several thousand industrial air pollution control devices were in place on Los Angeles factories, including bag houses, electrostatic precipitators, fume burners, cyclone separators, scrubbers, vapor collection equipment, and absorbers. These technological interventions did not address a core issue, and as the city became the prototypical automobile commuter's residence, the air pollution problem grew worse; in September of 1955, a "first alert" smog condition was declared when a weather inversion held pollution in. *New York Times* science writer Gladwin Hill (1955) wrote,

> People everywhere have always been warned against staying as long as a minute in a closed garage with a car engine running. . . . When the atmospheric lid is on, the Los Angeles basin is in effect a closed garage with 2,500,000 auto engines running. (p. 12)

Between 1950 and 1959, the number of cars on the road in the United States jumped from 49 million to 71 million, more than twice the rate of population growth, and the average engine horsepower increased from 100 in 1946 to 240 in 1958, resulting in more fuel being burned. Perhaps no city depended on the automobile as did Los Angeles; with government-subsidized roads, cheap gasoline, and available land, the region grew as fast as the asphalt and concrete could be poured. The key to the equation was the automobile; the car culture of California was born.

With industry regulated and automobiles deified, one remaining course of political and legal action was to stop the incineration of garbage. This "obvious solution" was not employed right away because the waste collection business was run by "a syndicate of rubbish collectors and dump owners operating a multi-million dollar monopoly" ("Racket Charged," 1955, p. 66). Mayors of two Los Angeles suburbs, Maywood and Long Beach, told a grand jury that when they contracted with outside firms to handle the garbage, the operators were harassed and threatened ("Racket Charged," 1955, p. 66).

With more than half of the Los Angeles smog problem blamed on automobiles by scientists, research into internal combustion air pollution control was uneven. Industry sponsored its own research and challenged other findings. Auto manufacturers insisted that air pollution was not their problem. To the carmakers, air pollution was a question of how the consumer uses or misuses the product long after the sale. In 1958, the president of the Automobile Manufacturers Association (AMA) blamed the consumer: "In eliminating smoke from vehicle exhaust, much progress has been made. True, there is still room for improvement, but mostly this must come from the owners, who alone are responsible for the maintenance of their vehicles" (Williams, 1959, p. 57). After all, the AMA president said, air pollution in the modern era is nothing compared to the malodorous stables, pigsties, and dirt streets of previous generations (Williams, 1959, p. 57).

One industry organization, the Air Pollution Foundation (APF), spent hundreds of thousands of dollars annually researching the problem. Funded by philanthropists and the auto industry, the APF channeled thinking about automotive engineering problems into nonthreatening areas and rejected challenges to the status quo. When asked to look into cleaner alternative fuels, the APF said, according to the *New York Times* ("Adjustments Key," 1955), "An extensive research program on alternative automotive fuels has just been reported as fruitless by the Air Pollution Foundation." Released in the middle of a smog episode, the study found that "proposals that motor vehicles be required to use alternative fuels to reduce smog are impractical, according to a scientific research report" (Air Pollution Foundation, press release, September 14, 1955; see Kovarik, 1993). The report said that alcohol or alcohol gasoline blends would cost one third more than gasoline and would not markedly reduce hydrocarbon emissions, and that unleaded gasoline for use in catalytic converters was also "shown to be economically unfeasible" (Air Pollution Foundation, press release, September 14, 1955). Just how this conclusion was reached was not made clear to the news media.

Meanwhile, other efforts to clean up automotive technology were not only misguided but, according to a Justice Department antitrust suit, deliberately sidetracked by the automakers. The allegations included that positive crankcase ventilation and carburetor improvements could have been made in the 1950s but were deliberately delayed when the automakers claimed the devices needed more research. In a 1969 consent decree, the automakers did not admit wrongdoing but agreed not to conspire to block implementation of pollution control equipment in the future (Graham, 1969, p. 1; see also *United States v. Motor Vehicles Manufacturers of the United States, Inc.*, 1969).

CONCLUSION

Although smoke abatement won the backing of civic reformers and the news media at the local level, it took a dramatic incident to inspire national interest in air pollution control. The Donora catastrophe, the call for help to surrounding communities, and the publicity surrounding it thrust air pollution into the national media arena. Some historians have seen Donora as the starting point of the green crusades and of a perceived deterioration of respect for science. Donora was a symbol used by scientists to justify funding air pollution research, however, and the news coverage of the Donora focused on scientists and their investigations.

Cleaner alternative fuels, such as anthracite and desulfurized coal, proved one answer to the smog episodes of the early and mid-

20th century, but proposals to use alternative fuels in automobiles were dismissed by organizations with scientific credentials but industrial connections. The long battle for cleaner air was dramatized by the Donora incident, but the St. Louis experience was probably more characteristic. Just as St. Louis Mayor Raymond R. Tucker declared the war won in the late 1950s, it entered a different and more complex phase far beyond the resources of local and state governments. Automobiles, rather than coal-fired industrial boilers, had become the major source of pollution. Although Tucker and other mayors could order fuel substitution for stationary power plants in their jurisdictions, they had little influence on automakers or the oil industry in distant cities. As ever more complex issues began to emerge, such as acid rain, ozone depletion, and global warming, the limitations of even national efforts became apparent.

Donora awakened the conscience of the nation and paved the way for serious debate. This could be seen at the second National Conference on Air Pollution in Washington, DC, in 1962 when biologist and science writer Rachel Carson took the stage. Her new book on chemicals and nature was already beginning to create controversy, but no one knew at the time that *Silent Spring* (Carson, 1962), like Donora, would come to be seen as a starting point rather than a transitional event in America's green crusades. The point she made, which was not reported in the news media, was reproduced in the conference proceedings (as quoted in U.S. Public Health Service, 1963):

> It seems to me that air pollution should be viewed in the larger context to which it belongs. It is part of one of the most vital problems that confronts mankind today: how to control the spreading contamination from many sources that is rapidly causing the deterioration of our environment. In biological history, no organism has survived long if its environment became in some way unfit for it. But no organism before man has deliberately polluted its own environment.

EDITOR'S NOTE

1. All quotes in this chapter from the *New York Times* are used by permission.

NOTES

1. This incident involved a toxic fog that settled over an industrial region in southeastern Belgium in December of 1930, killing 60 people and hospitalizing 6,000.

2. As a Pennsylvania health department report put it, Donora was "the second time in recorded history" (after the Belgian incident of 1930), that "a persistent fog has resulted in the death of many persons" (Shilan, 1949, p. 1). Many people at this time were unaware of the extent to which London was subject to killer smogs from 1871 on.

3. Although the call for "green grass" may seem prosaic, it was in fact as scarce as clean air in Webster and Donora at the time.

4. In fact, 95% of all energy in London was derived from coal at this time, according to Carey (1959, p. 207).

5. A U.S. Bureau of Mines (Davenport & Morgis, 1955) bibliography of air pollution research shows 30 articles on air pollution between 1860 and 1890, another 121 in the 1890 to 1900 period, of which 88 are on methods of control, and more than 250 in the next decade, of which more than 100 concern control. The main peaks of research publications are in the years 1908 and 1912 (about 20 per year) and 1940 (about 40 that year) and 1950 (about 150 papers).

6. Reprinted with permission of the *St. Louis Post-Dispatch,* © 1958.

8

CONCLUSION

he ideational model suggested by Max Weber (1968) was created to analyze politics, which he defined as the conflict over who shall control the state. In a simplified version of Weber's notions, politics is made up of three components: groups fighting for power, organizations through which power is sought and exercised, and ideas (see Collins & Makowsky, 1978). In this book, we have looked at how ideas are communicated through the mass media and the media's relationship with other social components. The role of ideas cannot be underplayed. When an influential, media-minded citizen who represented powerful business interests attempted to organize an environmental crusade with a radical idea, the results could be disappointing. Such was the case with Benjamin Franklin in Philadelphia.

In May 1739, Franklin and his Philadelphia neighbors endorsed a petition to the Pennsylvania Assembly to stop water pollution in the city's commercial district. Leather tanneries and slaughterhouses dumped their wastes into a small tributary of the Delaware River called Dock Creek that ran through the city. Describing the problem, Franklin noted that "many offensive and unwholesome smells do arise from the Tan-Yards, much to the great Annoyance of the Neighborhood." In an article in his newspaper, the *Pennsylvania Gazette,* Franklin stated that the Tanners "choaked the Dock—which was formerly navigable as high as Third Street—with the Tan, Horns, &c." (Franklin, 1739, p. 1). The petition was delivered to the assembly on May 15, 1739. Franklin probably signed it, but even if he did not, it is clear from his reporting in the *Gazette* that he was in favor of cleaning up the creek. The petition asked the assembly to declare the tanneries a nuisance and asked that they be "removed in such Time as might be tho't reasonable" (Franklin, 1739, p. 1). Franklin was no disinterested protester, wrote historian A. Michael McMahon (1992), "His residences and business properties in the area involved him personally, and as an affluent citizen desiring to protect his investments. . . . Perhaps more than his fellow citizens, [he] saw the problems as inherent in unchecked growth" (p. 157).

McMahon (1992) took notice of how Franklin and the petitioners said that the smells affected property values and that the waste choking the creek limited its use in fighting fires. They also said if the creek were not polluted, it would be "of great use" for delivering supplies to the city. The Dock had been created "for publick Service." Franklin's argument was for "public rights," and the restraints on the liberty of the tanners would be "but a trifle" compared to the "damage done to others, and the city, by remaining where they are." Franklin also noted a compromise position: "If the tanners could be so regulated to become inoffensive, the Petitioners declar'd that they should be therewith satisfied" (Franklin, 1739, p. 1).

The tanners responded with their own petition, proposing to wash the pavement once a day, build a fence around the tan yards, and release the waste into Dock Creek only at high tide. They also found a champion in Franklin's rival, Andrew Bradford, publisher of the *American Mercury,* who defended their liberty and property rights (McMahon, 1992).

On August 27, 1739, a committee of the assembly heard the petition. Sometime before the hearing, perhaps that day, the tanners staged a parade through town, carrying their grievances to the people and insisting on their rights. Apparently, Bradford's *Mercury* carried an article falsely stating that the Franklin-inspired petition had been rejected. Its headline read, "A Daring Attempt on the Liberties of the Tradesmen of Philadelphia." Franklin's temper boiled at this story, and he printed the full text of the assembly resolution, which supported a clean creek. The resolution declared that the water pollution was indeed a nuisance and that regulations should be drawn up. Franklin wrote, "It is hard to imagine what could induce the tanners to publish a relation [account] so partial and so false. . . . In Prudence they ought not to have triumphed before the victory" (Franklin, 1739, p. 1). It was not a question of the liberties of the tradesmen but rather "only a modest Attempt to deliver a great Number of Tradesmen from being poisoned by a few, and restore to them the Liberty of Breathing freely in their own Houses" (Franklin, 1739, p. 1). Whether the tanneries were subsequently cleaned up is unclear, but they were not moved, to Franklin's chagrin. Two years later, an epidemic of yellow fever that killed 500 Philadelphia residents was blamed on the polluted Dock Creek. Philadelphia's leading physician, Thomas Bond, said in a 1741 article that the creek was linked to malaria and other diseases and that not so much "bark" or quinine would be needed if the waterway would be filled in (as cited in McMahon, 1992, p. 170). The epidemic led to a new round of concern about Dock Creek, and by 1747, Franklin was appointed to a committee to consider what to do about restoring it. The committee recommended an extensive sewer system and a rebuilt dock that could accommodate various sizes of boats. The proposal, however, was defeated due to its high costs, and the effort failed.

Franklin's argument fell on deaf ears because the ideas of the regulation of business and limits to human waste were not accepted views in the 1730s. Although Franklin represented both the business elites and the mass media in his community, his efforts at pollution reduction were not enough for any meaningful social change to take place. The individual rights of the tanners carried the day.

Franklin was writing about ideas. Max Weber saw the mass media as the vehicle for the dissemination of ideas. Ideas include both knowledge and beliefs, just as the ideational culture of a particular society may be both a bridge and a dam.[1] Weber used the analogy of the railroad switchmen: "Not ideas, but material and ideal interests directly govern man's conduct. Yet very frequently 'world-images' that have been created by 'ideas' have, like switchmen, determined the tracks along with action has been pushed by the dynamic of interest" (as quoted in Schroeder, 1992, pp. 6-7). In Franklin's day and in the years to follow in America, there existed an ideational barrier to the development of environmental protection. The dominant values were those derived from individual freedom, capitalism, material growth, and its exploitation of resources, both natural and human. As an ideology of environmental thought developed in the United States, the basis for social change was established. An ideology of the wilderness was an important mobilizing force for John Muir and his friends when the fight to stop the Hetch Hetchy dam became something of a moral crusade. The idea of justice—a powerful notion in a democracy—was a legitimating force for the Radium Girls and their courtroom conflicts. Ideational factors concerning the excesses of corporate monopolies and the use of public lands highlighted conflicts and promoted change in the Alaskan coal affair. Weber also realized that, in describing social change, ideational factors alone are not sufficient causes. Material conditions—such as the dramatic, deadly event at Donora or the near-extinction of the buffalo—also play an important role in environmental conflict.[2]

Weber also viewed the press as part of an element of social control, while acknowledging the need of a particular movement to use a mass communication outlet in its struggle for power (Hardt, 1979, p. 169). No movement, including the environmentalists, has been successful at producing change all of the time. In this book, we have attempted to show how the mass media have functioned in the realm of environmental conflict as a force for both social control and social change. In certain circumstances, when the ideational culture and the powerful interest groups in society (including the media and environmentalists) were in alignment, social change occurred. The creation of a system of national parks, the protection of various species of animals and birds, and the reduction in smog and airborne pollutants from some cities represents real change.

External forces, including dramatic events, sometimes pushed groups into coadvocacy positions or drove them into conflict. Reporting of conflict is part of the process of conflict management, which may serve the goals of groups involved but often favors the status quo. Other times, groups created their own media vehicles to communicate their messages, promote their interests, and keep members together and active.

By the late 1960s, the environmental movement had followed the Weberian pattern of routinization, and the belief system about the value of the natural world and humans' effects on our surroundings became well established and integrated into society. As our views about environmental conflict shifted, the mass media reflected and participated in the changes, helping to control their direction and speed. In this way, the interdependency of mass media and society is not unlike the interdependency between humans and the natural environment.

NOTES

1. For example, in Weber's work on world religions, he argued that ideational barriers to capitalism existed in China and India in the dominant religious values of those countries.

2. Charles Harper (1989, p. 62) notes that, because material and ideational factors are both causes of change, one difference between Marxists and Weberians is that Marxists place more emphasis on material factors and Weberians focus on ideas, although both recognize the other factor as causal.

APPENDIX

Timeline of Environmental
Conflict in History

- 2,500 B.C. — Mohenjo Darro civilization in India had universal sewer system. Some cities, especially in Babylonia and Israel, have strict rules about sanitation. Others, such as Greek and Roman classical cities, use streets for sewers and occasionally build sewer mains.

- 80 A.D. — Roman Senate passes law to protect water stored during dry periods for street and sewer cleaning. Aqueducts built because springs and pools polluted.

  Dust and wood smoke create a visible pall over large preindustrial towns and cities. Thermal inversions and dry, windless weather often create what Romans called "heavy heaven." Odors from fetid garbage, sewage, and industries such as smelting or tanning also foul air.

  Hillsides in China and Peru are terraced to prevent soil erosion in agricultural areas.

- 1306 — Edward I forbids coal burning when English Parliament is in session.

- 1300s — First English game laws written.

- 1656 — Izaak Walton writes *The Complete Angler.*

- 1661 — John Evelyn writes *Fumifugium, or the Inconvenience of the Aer and Smoake of London Dissipated* to propose remedies for London's air pollution problem.

- 1663 — Storm water drains built in Paris.

- 1681 — William Penn requires Pennsylvania settlers to preserve 1 acre of trees for every 5 acres cleared.

- 1739 — Benjamin Franklin and neighbors petition Pennsylvania Assembly to stop waste dumping in Delaware River and remove tanneries from Philadelphia's commercial district. Foul smell, lower property values, disease, and interference with fire fighting are cited.

- 1741 — Foundling Hospital of London is established. Other children's hospitals in Germany and France are built, showing concern for infant mortality. By 1800, infant mortality in one London hospital dropped from 66 per 1,000 to 13 per 1,000.

- 1748-1762 — Jared Eliot, clergyman and physician, writes *Essays Upon Field Husbandry in New England* (originally published 1760) and other papers promoting soil conservation.

- 1750s — *Gin Lane* (originally published 1750) and other engravings by William Hogarth depicting slum scenes serve as a spur to social reform in England. Others in the media make strong efforts to help reformers.

- 1751 — Gin Acts give magistrates control over licensing pubs in Britain.

- 1762-1769 — Philadelphia committee led by Benjamin Franklin attempts to regulate waste disposal and water pollution.

- 1767 — English physician George Baker (with help from Benjamin Franklin) traces notorious "Devonshire colic" to lead poisoning from cider mills built with lead linings.

- 1775 — English scientist Percival Pott finds that coal is causing an unusually high incidence of cancer among chimney sweeps.

- 1777 — John Howard, sheriff of Bedfordshire, writes *State of the Prisons,* an early example of "An aroused public opinion [that] could be employed as a lever to compel reform."

- 1779 — Johann Peter Frank (1745-1821) writes *A Complete System of Medical Policy* in Germany advocating governmental responsibility for clean water, sewage systems, garbage disposal, food inspection, and other health measures under an authoritative "medical police."

- 1789 — Benjamin Franklin leaves money in a widely publicized codicil to his will to build freshwater pipeline to Philadelphia due to the link between bad water and disease. Within a few years, one quarter of the population of the town dies in a yellow fever epidemic.

- 1791 — The New York state assembly closes the hunting season on the heath hen. The species is extinct by the early 1900s.

- 1799 — Manhattan Company formed to build water line. Company survives as Chase Manhattan Bank.

- 1800s — First modern municipal sewers built in London, but water supply still frequently contaminated.

- 1803 — Louisiana Purchase.

- 1804 — First health inspector in United States appointed in New York.

- 1817 — U.S. secretary of navy authorized to reserve lands producing hardwoods for constructing naval ships.

- 1818 — Massachusetts bans the hunting of robins, a popular food, and horned larks.

- 1819 — British parliamentary committee concerned that steam engines and furnaces "could work in a manner less prejudicial to public health." Although alternatives were found, nothing was done.

- 1820 — Reformer and Parliamentarian Jeremy Bentham writes *The Constitutional Code* (originally published 1830), including proposals for reforming the London medical assistance system and water, sewer, and public works districts.

- 1823 — James Fenimore Cooper writes *The Pioneers,* in which he writes of the idea that humans should "govern the resources of nature by certain principles in order to conserve them." He continues the theme in several books.

- 1827 — French scientist J. B. Fourier outlines the atmospheric process by which Earth's temperature is altered, using a hothouse analogy.

- 1832 — Arkansas Hot Springs established as a national reservation.

- 1834 — New York bans the use of batteries in duck hunting; ban is repealed the following year.

- 1835 — Ralph Waldo Emerson writes the essay *Nature.*

- 1837 — Benjamin McCready writes pioneering essay on occupational medicine and conditions of New York City slums.

- 1842 — Edwin Chadwick writes *The Sanitary Condition of the Labouring Population of Great Britain.* Report is a scientific inquiry about infectious disease, child mortality, and the link to polluted water supplies and lack of sanitation.

- 1842 — English engineers lay out sewer system in Hamburg, Germany, and English system of house-by-house sewer lines adopted elsewhere in Europe.

- 1843 — Royal Commission inquiries begin; dreadful working conditions, child labor, and public health problems exposed.

- 1845 — Massachusetts Sanitary Commission formed; survey of Boston slums shows high infant and maternal mortality rates as well as many communicable diseases. A second report in 1850 confirms findings. Finally, in 1869, a state board of health is established.

- 1847 — American Medical Association founded.

- 1847 — Johnny Appleseed, who planted apple trees across Ohio and Indiana for nearly 50 years, dies.

- 1848 — Public Health Act is passed by a reluctant Parliament fearful of spread of cholera. National Board of Health and local boards to regulate water supply, sewerage, and offensive trades. Smoke abatement becomes a political responsibility of the health department.

- 1850 — U.S. Steamboat Inspection Service founded; it is among the first attempts to regulate technology on behalf of public safety.

- 1852 — Mother of the Forest giant sequoia tree is chopped down in Calaveras Grove of Big Trees.

- 1854 — Henry David Thoreau writes *Walden.*

- 1854 — John Snow, London doctor, maps spread of cholera in Broad Street neighborhood and traces cases to a contaminated drinking water pump. Snow's epidemiological studies support "contagionist" views, partly supplanting "sanitarian" views about public health.

- 1855 — First comprehensive city sewer plan in United States built in Chicago. By 1905, almost all U.S. towns with populations over 4,000 have city sewers. Baltimore, whose sewer system was begun in 1915, is the last city to build a comprehensive system.

- 1857 — State of Vermont commissions study on depleted fish populations in Connecticut River. George Perkins Marsh gets the job.

- 1858 — The "Great Stink" of sewage in the Thames spurs work of British Royal Commission on Sewage Disposal.

- 1861 — Civil War expenses lead to tax on alcohol-based camphene lamp fuel, vastly increasing demand for new fuel from petroleum called "sun fuel" or "kerosene."

- 1863 — George Perkins Marsh writes *Man and Nature: The Earth as Modified by Human Action* (originally published 1864), with emphasis on forest preservation and soil and water conservation.

- 1863 — Air pollution from British chemical industry spurs feeble Alkali Act, allowing government agents to question industry and suggest improvements; there are no actual regulations over air pollution until act is revised in 1906.

- 1864 — Federal government grants State of California land for Yosemite Valley Park.

- 1866 — Founding of the American Society for the Prevention of Cruelty to Animals.

- 1867 — Pennsylvania legislature rejects bill to regulate water pollution despite heavy industrial pollution in Delaware River.

- 1869 — Massachusetts State Board of Health formed. Ellen Swallow Richards, public health crusader, takes thousands of water and food samples for the board of health.

- 1860s-1880s — French scientist Louis Pasteur's germ theory of disease revolutionizes concepts of public health, making it possible to isolate and treat specific diseases.

- 1870 — First coal mine safety laws passed in Pennsylvania following a fire that suffocated 179 men.

- 1871 — U.S. Fish Commission formed to study decline of coastal fisheries.

- 1872 — American Public Health Association is formed.

- 1872 — President Grant signs Yellowstone National Park bill.

- 1873 — London fog kills 1,150. Similar incidents occur in 1880, 1882, 1891, and 1892.

- 1873 — Henry Winchester perfects the repeating rifle.

- 1874 — German graduate student Othmar Zeider discovers chemical formula for DDT.

- 1875 — British Public Health Act consolidates authority to deal with pollution, occupational disease, and other problems.

- 1876 — American Forestry Association campaigns to cut timber on government reserves, and American Association for the Advancement of Science calls for federal legislation to protect timberlands.

- 1876 — British River Pollution Control Act makes it illegal to dump sewage into a stream.

- 1877 — Massachusetts passes the first factory inspection law, with 22 states following over the next 20 years.

- 1878 — Iowa enacts first state bag limit law, limiting hunters to 25 prairie chickens and other game birds per day.

- 1880s — First U.S. municipal smoke abatement laws aimed at reducing black smoke and ash from factories, railroads, and ships; Regulation under local boards of health.

- 1882 — Massachusetts passes first pure food laws, inspired by investigations of Ellen Swallow Richards.

- 1885 — U.S. Biological Survey created, partly out of concern over depletion of buffalo and passenger pigeon.

- 1885 — Bureau of Labor Statistics is established in Department of Labor.

- 1886 — First Audubon societies are formed by George Bird Grinnell.

- 1886 — Major water rights court ruling in the case of Lux and Miller holdings in California.

- 1890 — General Federation of Women's Clubs is founded; conservation and "ecology" are among top priorities.

- 1890 — Yosemite National Park is formed; it surrounds small California state park. Two other California national parks are created.

- 1891 — Forest protection bill passes Congress. Thirteen million acres are set aside by 1893.

- 1892 — Sierra Club is founded.

- 1899 — Refuse Act prevents certain discharge into streams and places Corps of Engineers in charge of permits and regulation.

- 1900 — Lacey Act regulates interstate traffic in wild game and brings importation of birds and mammals under federal control.

- 1900 — Wild buffalo population drops to fewer than 40 animals.

- 1900 — The automobile is welcomed as bringing relief from pollution. New York City, with 120,000 horses, scrapes up 2.4 million pounds of manure every day.

- 1903 — President Theodore Roosevelt creates first national wildlife refuge on Pelican Island, Florida. In all, by 1909, the Roosevelt administration creates 42 million acres of national forests, 51 national wildlife refuges, and 18 areas of "special interest," including the Grand Canyon.

- 1905 — National Audubon Society is organized.

- 1905 — U.S. Forest Service is created.

- 1906 — Food and Drug Administration is founded.

- 1906 — Yosemite Valley comes under federal control after 42 years as a state park.

- 1906 — 100,000 acres of Alaskan coal land are withdrawn from public use and sold by USGS.

- 1907 — USDA Animal Health and Plant Health Inspection Service is founded.

- 1907 — Smoke Prevention Association of America is founded in Chicago.

- 1908 — White House conference of governors on conservation policy is held.

- 1908 — Swedish chemist Svante Arrhenius argues that the greenhouse effect is warming the globe.

- 1909 — In Glasgow, Scotland, winter inversions and smoke accumulations kill more than 1,000. While preparing a report about the incidents, Dr. Harold Antoine Des Voeux coins the term "smog" as a contraction for smoke-fog.

- 1909 — National Conservation Commission suggests "broad plans . . . be adopted providing for a system of waterway improvement."

- 1909 — Charles Van Hise writes *The Conservation of Natural Resources* (originally published 1910).

- 1909 — United States-Canada boundary pollution commission is established.

- 1909 — Louis Glavis blows whistle on Alaskan coal deal.

- 1910 — Bureau of Mines is founded to promote safety and welfare of miners. Bureau of Mines and Public Health Service begin studies of lung diseases.

- 1912 — Bureau of Mines begins first smoke control study.

- 1912 — Federal Water and Sanitation Investigation Station is established in Cincinnati.

- 1912 — National Waterways Commission report recommends waterway improvements.

- 1912 — National Audubon Society begins campaign to boycott hatmakers using endangered tropical bird feathers.

- 1913 — Migratory Bird Act to regulate hunting runs into controversy; spring hunting and marketing of hunted birds are prohibited; treaty with Canada in 1918 solidifies regulations. Act also prohibits importation of wild bird feathers for women's fashion into the United States.

- 1913 — William T. Hornaday, head of New York Zoological Society, writes *Our Vanishing Wildlife, Its Extermination and Preservation.* By 1914, he establishes Permanent Wildlife Protection Fund with grants from Andrew Carnegie, Henry Ford, and George Eastman.

- 1913 — Hetch Hetchy dam in Yosemite National Park is approved by Congress.

- 1913 — Weeks-McLean Act gives secretary of agriculture power to regulate waterfowl seasons.

- 1914 — Corps of Engineers, Bureau of Mines, and Public Health Service begin pollution surveys of streams and harbors. Reports filed by early 1920s show an accumulation of heavy damage from oil dumping, mine runoff, untreated sewage, and industrial waste.

- 1916 — National Park Service is created by Congress.

- 1917 — Corps of Engineers removed lock gates in old canal in Virginia's Dismal Swamp, allowing salt water into North Carolina's Currituck Sound, a major waterfowl estuary. Fight finally ends with an act of Congress in 1930 to preserve the Sound.

- 1920 — Mineral Leasing Act opens up rich deposits on federal lands for token rental fees; Water Power Act authorizes federal hydroelectric projects.

- 1921 — General Motors researchers discover tetraethyl lead as an antiknock gasoline additive. Despite warnings about its danger, the new gasoline goes on sale without safety tests within 14 months.

- 1922 — National Coast Anti Pollution League is formed in New Jersey to stop oil dumping.

- 1922 — Amelia Maggia, first "Radium Girl" victim of U.S. Radium Corporation, dies of radiation poisoning.

- 1922 — Izaak Walton League is founded; it fights Mississippi valley dredging project with Washington, DC, lobbying effort.

- 1924 — Oil Pollution Act is passed prohibiting discharge from any vessel within the 3-mile limit, except by accident.

- 1924 — Five refinery workers die "violently insane" at Standard Oil refinery making tetraethyl lead gasoline additive in grossly unsafe conditions. News that seven others previously died surfaces.

- 1925 — Five more workers die making tetraethyl lead in du Pont plant. In May, the surgeon general conference on leaded gasoline is held; investigation of alternatives is sidetracked; and a hasty report recommends further study. Ethyl gas goes back on the market.

- 1926 — First large-scale survey of air pollution in United States is performed in Salt Lake City.

- 1926 — Surgeon general's committee of experts reluctantly permit tetraethyl lead back on the fuel market. Recommended further research is never funded.

- 1927 — Rivers and Harbors Act gives Corps of Engineers task of surveying and planning a navigation system for inland waters.

- 1927 — Five New Jersey women, dying from radium poisoning, file first lawsuits against U.S. Radium Corp.

- 1928 — Radium lawsuits are settled out of court.

- 1928 — PHS begins checking air pollution in eastern U.S. cities.

- 1929 — More than 100 wildlife sanctuaries are consolidated under federal protection by Norbeck-Anderson Act.

- 1930 — Meuse River Valley killer smog incident occurs in Belgium; 3-day inversion kills 63, with 6,000 made ill.

- 1933 — Civilian Conservation Corps is formed; 2,000 camps are opened, trees are planted, and roads, fire towers, buildings, and bridges are constructed. More than 2.5 million people serve until the program ends in 1942. Other federal programs, including the Tennessee Valley Authority and the Soil Conservation Service, begin during FDR presidency.

- 1935 — Wilderness Society is cofounded by Aldo Leopold and Arthur Carhardt.

- 1936 — National Wildlife Federation is formed.

- 1937 — Survey of air pollution in New York is performed.

- 1937 — Pittman-Robertson Act passes Congress; it provides excise tax on sporting arms and ammunition for wildlife projects.

- 1939 — St. Louis smog episode spurs serious smoke abatement campaign.

- 1940 — St. Louis adopts the first strict smoke control ordinance in the United States.

- 1941 — "Action Club" is formed to combat pollution from paper mills near Augusta, Maine.

- 1942 — Controversy over dam that would inundate Cook Forest, a state park with the last of Pennsylvania's virgin forests.

- 1945 — Corps of Engineers abandons Potomac River Project dam after a storm of controversy and protests from Izaak Walton League, National Parks Association, garden clubs, and others.

- 1945 — Truman Proclamation on the Continental Shelf clears the way for oil drilling offshore.

- 1947 — Los Angeles Air Pollution Control District is formed; it is the first air pollution control bureau in the nation.

- 1947 — Defenders of Wildlife is founded.

- 1948 — The Federal Water Pollution Control Act is passed; it is the beginning of active House and Senate Public Works Committee interest in water pollution.

- 1948 — Twenty-two dead and 600 hospitalized in Donora, Pennsylvania, smog attack.

- 1948 — Six hundred deaths occur in London due to killer fog.

- 1948 — Aldo Leopold writes *A Sand County Almanac* (originally published 1949).

- 1949 — Canadian complaints about Detroit pollution launch PHS study of Detroit-Windsor area under 1909 boundary treaty.

- 1949 — First national conference on air pollution sponsored by PHS.

- 1949 — Izaak Walton League writes *Crisis Spots in Conservation*, identifying specific water projects to be opposed.

- 1950 — Poza Rica killer smog incident leaves 22 dead and hundreds hospitalized in Mexico.

- 1950 — Truman says government and industry should join forces in a battle against death-dealing smog.

- 1951 — The Nature Conservancy is formed.

- 1952 — Three thousand to 4,000 untimely deaths are attributed to London "killer fogs."

- 1952 — Dingell-Johnson Act, an excise tax on fishing tackle, is implemented.

- 1953 — New York smog incident kills between 170 and 260 in November.

- 1954 — Heavy smog conditions shut down industry and schools in Los Angeles for most of October.

- 1955 — Congress passes Air Pollution Research Act.

- 1955 — International Air Pollution Congress is held in New York City.

- 1956 — Congress passes Water Pollution Control Act.

- 1956 — Another killer smog in London; 1,000 die.

- 1956 — Echo Park dam proposal is defeated in Congress.

- 1956 — Protesters picket Fermi nuclear power plant near Detroit.

- 1958 — First PHS National Conference on Air Pollution is held.

- 1959 — California becomes first state to impose automotive emissions standards, requiring "blow-by" valve to recycle crankcase emissions. Automakers combine to fight mandatory use of $7 device, a fight which leads to an antitrust suit by the U.S. Justice Department.

- 1960 — Schenk Act funds 2-year PHS study on air pollution from cars.

- 1960 — Clean Water Act passes Congress.

- 1961 — International Clean Air Congress is held in London.

- 1961 — World Wildlife Fund is founded.

- 1962 — Another London smog; 750 die.

- 1962 — Rachel Carson writes *Silent Spring*.

REFERENCES

Achilles and his rage. (1909, December 4). *Collier's*, p. 16.

Adjustments key to smog solution. (1955, September 27). *New York Times*, p. 39.

Advertise in Forest and Stream. (1876, January 16). *Forest and Stream*, p. 345.

Agricola, G. (1994). De re metallica. In D. Wall (Ed.), *Green history: A reader in environmental literature, philosophy and politics* (pp. 55-58). London: Routledge.

Air poisoning in Donora. (1948, November 1). *Pittsburgh Post-Gazette*. Pittsburgh: Historical Society of Western Pennsylvania, Pittsburgh Post Library and Archives Division.

Air Pollution Foundation. (1955, September 14). *Different auto fuels to reduce smog impractical* (press release). Los Angeles: Author.

Alarmed Londoners ask anti-smog steps. (1953, January 25). *New York Times*, p. 33.

Altschull, J. H. (1994). *Agents of power: The media and public policy* (2nd ed.). White Plains, NY: Longman.

Amateur management of Yosemite scenery. (1890, September). *Century*, p. 798.

American Opinion Research, Inc. (1993). *The press and the environment: How journalists evaluate environmental reporting*. Princeton, NJ: Author.

American Sportsman. (1874). Vol. 3, p. 100.

An anti-smoke rally. (1948, November 18). *New York Times*, p. 26.

An episode without precedent. (1924, October 31). *New York Times*, p. 18.

An immense tree. (1853, October 1). *Gleason's Pictorial Drawing Room Companion*, p. 217.

Announcement. (1873, August 14). *Forest and Stream*, pp. 8-9.

Another man dies from insanity gas. (1924, October 28). *New York Times*, p. 1

Armytage, W. H. G. (1961). *A social history of engineering*. Cambridge: MIT Press.

Associated Press. (1991, May 22). *Attorneys General issue final report on green advertising*. New York: Author.

Association for the protection of game. (1874, November 10). *New York Times*, p. 5.

Avery, R. K., & Eason, D. (Eds.). (1991). *Critical perspectives on media and society*. New York: Guilford.

Aviator can't find field. (1927, October 30). *New York Times,* Section III, p. 1.

Badash, L. (1979). *Radioactivity in America: Growth and decay of a science.* Baltimore, MD: Johns Hopkins University Press.

Baker, C. E. (1994, September). *Ownership of newspapers: The view from positivist social science.* Cambridge, MA: The Joan Shorenstein Center at Harvard University.

Baldwin, D. (1972). *The quiet revolution: Grass roots of today's wilderness preservation movement.* Boulder, CO: Pruett.

Bar death gas in city as 5th victim dies. (1924, October 31). *New York Herald Tribune,* p. 1.

Bar ethyl gasoline as 5th victim dies. (1924, October 31). *New York Times,* p. 22.

Bean, W. (1952). *Boss Ruef's San Francisco: The story of the union labor party, big business, and the graft prosecution.* Berkeley: University of California Press.

Bedford, E. (1928, May 17). Radium victims too ill to attend court tomorrow. *Newark Ledger,* p. 1.

Belgian disaster of 1930. (1948, November 1). *New York Times,* p. 12.

Bent, S. (1925, June 22). Tetraethyl lead fatal to makers. *New York Times,* p. 3.

Bentham, J. (1830). *Constitutional code: For the use of all nations and all governments professing liberal opinions.* London: Heward.

Berger, P. L., & Luckmann, T. (1967). *The social construction of reality.* New York: Doubleday.

Bergonie is latest of 140 martyrs to X-ray and radium. (1924, November 16). *New York World,* Section II, p. 1.

Bernstein, S. (1984). *The rise of air pollution as a national political issue: A study of issue development.* Unpublished doctoral dissertation, Auburn University, Auburn, AL.

Betts, J. R. (1953). Sporting journalism in nineteenth-century America. *American Quarterly, 5,* 39-56.

The big trees of California. (1858, June 5). *Harper's Weekly,* p. 357.

Blame odd deaths on mesothorium. (1925, June 21). *New York World,* p. 3.

Blum, T. (1924, September). Osteomyelitis of the mandibula and maxilla. *Journal of the American Dental Association, 11,* 802-805.

Borland, H. (1975). *The history of wildlife in America.* Washington, DC: National Wildlife Federation.

Bowles, S. (1865). *Across the continent.* New York: Hurd & Houghton.

Boyd, T. A. (1943, June 8). *The early history of ethyl gasoline* (unpublished Report No. OC-83, Project No. 11-3). Detroit, MI: Research Laboratory Division, G.M. Corp.; Flint, MI: GMI.

Boyd, T. A. (1957). *Professional amateur.* New York: E. P. Dutton.

Bramwell, A. (1989). *Ecology in the 20th century: A history.* New Haven, CT: Yale University Press.

Brasch, W. (1990). *Forerunners of revolution: Muckrakers and the American social conscience.* Lanham, MD: University Press of America.

Bunnell, L. H. (1890, September). The date of the discovery of Yosemite. *Century,* p. 796.

Burnham, J. (1992). Of science and superstition, In C. L. LaMay & E. E. Dennis (Eds.) *Media and the environment.* Washington, DC: Island Press.

Can this be whitewashed also? (1909, December 18). *Collier's,* pp. 8-9.

Carey, G. C. (1959). Exposure to low concentrations. In *Proceedings of the National Conference on Air Pollution, November 18-20, 1958*. Washington, DC: Government Printing Office.

Carey, J. (1974). The problem of journalism history. *Journalism History, 1*, 3-5, 27.

Carr, D. E. (1965). *The breath of life*. New York: Norton.

Carson, R. (1962). *Silent spring*. New York: Houghton Mifflin.

The case of the five women. (1928, May 19). *New York World*, p. 23.

Castle, W. B., Drinker, K. R., & Drinker, C. K. (1925, August). Necrosis of the jaw in radium workers. *Journal of Industrial Hygiene, 7*, 373-378.

Chadwick, E. (1965). *Report on the sanitary condition of the labouring population of Gt. Britain*. Edinburgh, UK: Edinburgh University Press. (Original work published 1842)

Chapman, J. (Ed.). (1982). *Wild mammals of North America: Biology and economics*. Baltimore, MD: Johns Hopkins University Press.

Chase, A. (1987). *Playing God in Yellowstone: The destruction of America's first national park*. New York: Harcourt, Brace.

Chass, R. L. (1959). Extent to which available control techniques have been utilized by communities—Los Angeles County. In *Proceedings of the National Conference on Air Pollution, November 18-20, 1958*. Washington, DC: Government Printing Office.

Chief chemist escapes as "loony gas" victim. (1924, November 2). *Brooklyn Daily Eagle*, p. 1.

Chomsky, N., & Herman, E. (1988). *Manufacturing consent: The political economy of the mass media*. New York: Pantheon.

Clark, X. (1885, May). The Hetch Hetchy Valley: A new Yosemite. *Outing*, p. 151.

Clements, K. A. (1979). Politics and the park: San Francisco's fight for Hetch Hetchy, 1908-1913. *Pacific Historical Review, 48*, 184-215.

Cohen, M. (1988). *History of the Sierra Club*. San Francisco: Sierra Club Books.

Cohen, M. P. (1984). *The pathless way: John Muir and American wilderness*. Madison: University of Wisconsin Press.

Collins, R., & Makowsky, M. (1978). *The discovery of society* (2nd ed.). New York: Random House.

Commons cheers plan to rid Britain of smog. (1955, February 5). *New York Times*, p. 15.

Company denies negligence led to gas deaths. (1924, October 27). *New York Sun*, p. 1.

Cong. Rec., 38th Cong., 1st Sess., Stat. 13 (1864, May 17).

Connolly, C. P. (1910a, January 8). Raiding the people's land. *Collier's*, pp. 18-19.

Connolly, C. P. (1910b, April 2). Ballinger-Shyster. *Collier's*, pp. 16-17.

Cooper, J. F. (1838). *The pioneers, or, The sources of the Susquehanna: A descriptive tale*. Philadelphia: Carey, Lea, & Blanchard.

Cooper, W. S. (1959). Solving interstate air pollution problems. In *Proceedings of the National Conference on Air Pollution, November 18-20, 1958*. Washington, DC: Government Printing Office.

Co-operative game laws. (1874, March 12). *Forest and Stream*, p. 74.

Coser, L. (1956). *The functions of social conflict*. Glencoe, IL: Free Press.

Coser, L. (1971). *Masters of sociological thought: ideas in historical and social context*. New York: Harcourt Brace Jovanovich.

The cost of gridlock. (1996, January 15). *Newsweek*, p. 4.

The Country Gentleman. (1856, October 8). p. 43.

Cracknell, J. (1993). Issue arenas, pressure groups and environmental agendas. In A. Hansen (Ed.), *The mass media and environmental issues* (pp. 3-21). New York: Leicester University Press.

Cronon, W. (1983). *Changes in the land: Indians, colonists, and the ecology of New England.* New York: Hill & Wang.

Cronon, W. (1992, March). A place for stories: Nature, history and narrative. *Journal of American History, 78*(4), 1347-1376.

Crosby, A. W. (1986). *Ecological imperialism: The biological expansion of Europe, 900-1900.* New York: Cambridge University Press.

Cumbler, J. T. (1991). The early making of an environmental consciousness: Fish, fisheries commissions and the Connecticut River. *Environmental History Review, 15*(4), 73-91.

Cure found for mystery gas as 4th victim dies. (1924, October 30). *New York Herald Tribune,* p. 1.

Curran, J., Gurevitch, M., & Woollacott, J. (Eds.). (1977). *Mass communication and society.* Beverly Hills, CA: Sage.

Davenport, S. J., & Morgis, G. G. (1955). *U.S. Bureau of Mines Bulletin No. 537.* Washington, DC: Government Printing Office.

Death held hidden in cities' sooty air. (1950, November 17). *New York Times,* p. 18.

Dennis, E. E., & Rivers, W. L. (1974). *Other voices: The new journalism in America.* San Francisco: Canfield.

Dewey, J. (1927). *The public and its problems.* Chicago: Swallow Press.

Dewey, J. (1938). *Logic: The theory of inquiry.* New York: Holt, Rinehart & Winston.

Dicken-Garcia, H., & Stevens, J. (1980). *Communication history.* Beverly Hills, CA: Sage.

Dickens, C. (1951). *Bleak house.* New York: Dodd, Mead. (Original work published 1853)

Diettert, G. A. (1992). *Grinnell's glacier.* Missoula, MT: Mountain Press.

Dilsaver, L. M., & Tweed, W. C. (1990). *Challenge of the big trees.* Three Rivers, CA: Sequoia Natural History Association.

Dr. G. B. Grinnell, naturalist, dead. (1938, April 12). *New York Times,* p. 23.

Donohue, G. A., Tichenor, P. J., & Olien, C. L. (1973). Mass media functions, knowledge and social control. *Journalism Quarterly, 50,* 652-659.

Donora smog deaths rise to 20. (1948, November 1). *Pittsburgh Post-Gazette,* p. 1.

Doomed to die, they tell how they'd spend fortune. (1928, May 13). *Newark Sunday Call,* p. 1.

Dow, C. M. (1921). *Anthology and bibliography of Niagara Falls.* Albany: State of New York.

Downing, J., Mohammadi, A., & Sreberny-Mohammadi, A. (1990). *Questioning the media: A critical introduction.* Newbury Park, CA: Sage.

Dunlap, T. R. (1988). *Saving America's wildlife.* Princeton, NJ: Princeton University Press.

Editorial. (1909, October 2). *Collier's,* p. 9.

Efron, E. (1984). *The apocalyptics.* New York: Simon & Schuster.

Eliot, J. (1934). *Essays upon field husbandry in New England, and other papers, 1748-1762.* New York: Columbia University Press. (Original work published 1760)

Ely, S. B. (1951, January). Air pollution in Pittsburgh. *AMA Archives of Industrial Hygiene and Occupational Medicine, 3,* 44-47.

Emerson, R. W. (1883). *Nature, addresses and lectures: The works of Ralph Waldo Emerson.* Boston: Standard Library edition.

Emerson, R. W. (1905). *Nature.* East Aurora, NY: The Roycrofters. (Original work published 1836)

Estes, D. C. (1985). The rival sporting weeklies of William T. Porter and Thomas Bangs Thorpe. *American Journalism, 2,* 135-143.

Estrada, H. M. (1996, January 14). Carbon monoxide strikes again. *Star Tribune,* pp. 1B-2B.

Ethyl gas official denies monopoly. (1925, April 23). *New York Times,* p. 1.

Ethyl gas sale stopped today by Standard Oil. (1924, October 28). *New York Herald Tribune,* p. 1.

Evelyn, J. (1994). Fumifugium, or the inconvenience of air and smoke of London dissipated; Together with some remedies humbly proposed. In D. Wall (Ed.), *Green history: A reader in environmental literature, philosophy and politics* (pp. 45-48). London: Routledge.

Ewin, S. (1976). *Captains of consciousness: Advertising and the social roots of the consumer culture.* New York: McGraw-Hill.

Exume girls body to find death cause. (1927, October 16). *Newark Sunday Call,* p. 1.

Fausold, M. L. (1961). *Gifford Pinchot: Bull moose progressive.* Syracuse, NY: Syracuse University Press.

Ferguson, D. (1989, April 15). Groups "adopt" highways and vie to keep them clean. *Associated Press.*

Filler, L. (1976). *The muckrakers.* University Park: Pennsylvania State University Press.

Find more soot here than in Pittsburgh. (1928, April 1). *New York Times,* Section II, p. 1.

Findley, R. W., & Farber, D. (1988). *Environmental law* (2nd ed.). St. Paul, MN: West.

Fine, B. (1968). *A giant of the press: Carr Van Anda.* Oakland, CA: Acme.

5 Radium victims may live, he finds. (1928, May 18). *New York World,* p. 1.

Five women doomed to die. (1928, May 10). *New York World,* p. 28.

5 Women smile, fearing death, in radium case. (1928, January 12). *Newark Ledger,* p. 1.

Flader, S. L. (1974). *Thinking like a mountain: Aldo Leopold and the evolution of an ecological attitude toward deer, wolves and forests.* Columbia: University of Missouri Press.

Flagg, S. B. (1912). *City smoke ordinances and smoke abatement* (U.S. Bureau of Mines Bulletin No. 49). Washington, DC: Government Printing Office.

Fog crowds hospitals. (1948, October 29). *Monessen Daily Independent,* p. 1.

Fog in fifth day. (1948, October 30). *Pittsburgh Post-Gazette.* Pittsburgh, PA: Historical Society of Western Pennsylvania, Library and Archives Division.

Foss, F. O. (Ed.). (1971). *Conservation in the United States: A documentary history-recreation.* New York: Chelsea House.

Fox, S. (1981). *John Muir and his legacy: The American conservation movement.* Boston: Little, Brown.

Frank, J. P. (1793-1794). *System einer vollstandigen medicinischen polizey.* Frankenthal, Germany: Gegel.

Franklin, B. (1739, August 23-30). *Pennsylvania Gazette,* p. 1.

Fryer et al. v. U.S. Radium Corp. (1927, July 6), *aff'd.,* Records of the National Consumers League, Raymond H. Berry files, Manuscript Division, Library of Congress, Washington, DC.

Fryer et al. v. U.S. Radium Corp. (1927, July 18). New Jersey State Chancery Court, unpublished original complaint. Raymond H. Berry files, Reel 3, Manuscript Division, Library of Congress, Washington, DC.

Fryer et al. v. U.S. Radium Corp. (1928, January 11). Records of the National Consumers League, Raymond H. Berry files, Manuscript Division, Library of Congress, Washington, DC.

Galbraith, J. K. (1978). *The new industrial state* (3rd ed.). Boston: Houghton Mifflin.

Game in season for October. (1873, October 23). *Forest and Stream,* p. 170.

Game in season for September. (1873, September 21). *Forest and Stream,* p. 24.

Game protection. (1875, December 27). *Forest and Stream,* pp. 312-313.

Game protection. (1887, April 28). *Forest and Stream,* pp. 300-301.

Game protection. (1897, April 7). *Forest and Stream,* p. 268.

Gans, H. J. (1979). *Deciding what's news.* New York: Vintage.

Garfield, J. (1909, February 20). Review of Roosevelt's administration. *Outlook,* p. 391.

Gas substitutes held uneconomical. (1925, October 2). *Detroit Free Press.* Flint, MI: General Motors Institute Alumni Foundation's Collection of Industrial History.

Gerth, H. H., & Mills, C. W. (Eds.). (1946). *From Max Weber: Essays in sociology.* New York: Oxford University Press.

Gitlin, T. (1980). *The whole world is watching.* Berkeley: University of California Press.

Glavis, L. (1909, November 13). The whitewashing of Ballinger. *Collier's,* pp. 15-17, 27.

Goldmark, J. (1953). *Impatient crusader: Florence Kelly's life story.* Westport, CT: Greenwood.

Gottlieb, R. (1993). *Forcing the spring: The transformation of the American environmental movement.* Washington, DC: Island Press.

Graham, F., Jr. (1971). *Man's dominion.* New York: J. B. Lippincott.

Graham, F. P. (1969, September 12). US settles suit on smog devices. *New York Times,* p. 1.

Grainger, D. (1978). *Animals in peril.* Toronto: E. P. Dutton.

Grinder, R. D. (1980). The battle for clean air: The smoke problem in post-Civil War America. In M. V. Melosi (Ed.), *Pollution and reform in American cities: 1870-1930* (pp. 83-103). Austin: University of Texas Press.

Greeley, H. (1964). *An overland journey.* New York: Knopf. (Original work published 1860)

Grove, R. H. (1995). *Green imperialism: Colonial expansion, tropical island Edens and the origins of environmentalism, 1600-1860.* Cambridge, UK: Cambridge University Press.

Habusch, E. (1980). *Fair game: A history of hunting, shooting, and animal conservation.* New York: Arco.

Haines, A. L. (1977). *The Yellowstone story* (Vols. I and II). Yellowstone National Park, WY: Yellowstone Library and Museum Association.

Halliday, E. C. (1961). An historical review of atmospheric pollution. In *Air pollution*. New York: World Health Organization-Columbia University Press.

Hallock, C. (1913). *An angler's reminiscences*. Cincinnati, OH: Sportsmen's Review.

Hamilton, A. (1929, October). Nineteen years in the dangerous trades. *Harper's Magazine*, pp. 580-591.

Hamilton, A., Reznikoff, P., & Burnham, G. (1925, May 16). Tetra ethyl lead. *Journal of the American Medical Association, 84,* 1481-1486.

Hampton, H. D. (1971). *How the U.S. cavalry saved our national parks*. Bloomington: Indiana University Press.

Hapgood, N. (1930). *The changing years*. New York: Holt, Rinehart & Winston.

Hardt, H. (1979). *Social theories of the press*. Beverly Hills, CA: Sage.

Hardt, H. (1992). *Critical communication studies: Communication, history and theory in America*. London: Routledge.

Harper, C. (1989). *Exploring social change*. Englewood Cliffs, NJ: Prentice Hall.

Hayden, F. V. (1872, February). The wonders of the west II: More about the Yellowstone. *Scribner's Monthly,* Vol. 3, p. 390.

Hayes, A. A., Jr. (1880, March). Vacation aspects of Colorado. *Harper's Monthly,* pp. 542-557.

Hays, S. (1959). *Conservation and the gospel of efficiency*. Cambridge, MA: Harvard University Press.

Heath, S. B. (n.d.). *Smoky city gets its face cleaned up*. Pittsburgh: Historical Society of Western Pennsylvania, Library and Archives Division.

Heroes and martyrs of medicine. (1928, May 13). *New York World Magazine,* p. 2.

The Hetch Hetchy bill. (1913, November 27). *The Independent,* p. 381.

Hiebert, R. (1966). *Courtier to the crowd: The story of Ivy Lee and the development of public relations*. Ames: Iowa State University Press.

Hilgartner, S., & Bosk, C. L. (1988). The rise and fall of social problems: A public arenas model. *American Journal of Sociology, 94,* 53-78.

Hill, G. (1955, September 26). Los Angeles smog tied up in politics. *New York Times,* p. 12.

Hodgkinson, R. (1973). *Science and public health*. London: The Open University Press.

Hoffman, F. (1925, September 26). Radium (mesothorium) necrosis. *Journal of the American Medical Association, 85,* 963-965.

Hofstadter, R. (1925). *The age of reform*. New York: Knopf.

Hogarth, W. (1947). Ten reproductions of original engravings, including *Beer street, Gin lane, The bench,* and *The analysis of beauty*. New York: Touchstone Press. (Original work published 1750)

Hornaday, W. T. (1970). *Our vanishing wildlife: Its extermination and preservation*. New York: Arno. (Original work published 1913)

Hough, G. A., III. (1995). *News writing* (5th ed.). Boston: Houghton Mifflin.

Howard, J. (1777). *The state of the prisons in England and Wales: With preliminary observations and an account of some foreign prisons*. London: T. Cadell, N. Conant, and W. Eyers.

Hughes, J. D. (1975). *Ecology in ancient civilizations*. Albuquerque: University of New Mexico Press.

Hughes, J. D. (1994). *Pan's travail: Environmental problems in Ancient Greeks and Romans.* Baltimore, MD: Johns Hopkins University Press.

Huth, H. (1948). *Yosemite: The story of an idea.* Yosemite National Park, WY: Yosemite Natural History Association.

Huth, H. (1957). *Nature and the American.* Berkeley: University of California Press.

Ise, J. (1961). *Our national park policy: A critical history.* Baltimore, MD: Johns Hopkins University Press.

Izaak Walton League of America. (1949). *Crisis spots in conservation.* Chicago: Author.

Johnson, A., & Malone, D. (Eds.). (1946). *Dictionary of American biography* (Vol. 3). New York: Charles Scribner's Sons.

Johnson, L. (1917, February 15). The history and legal phases of the smoke problem. *Metallurgical and Chemical Engineering,* pp. 199-204.

Johnson, P. (1991). *The birth of the modern.* New York: HarperCollins.

Johnson, R. U. (1890). The care of Yosemite valley. *Century,* p. 474.

Johnson, R. U. (1923). *Remembered yesterdays.* Boston: Little, Brown.

Jones, H. R. (1965). *John Muir and the Sierra Club: The battle for Yosemite.* San Francisco: Sierra Club Books.

Kates, J. (1995). The conservationist as journalist: P.S. Lovejoy and the fight for the cutover. *American Journalism, 12*(2), 123-141.

Kellner, D. (1990). *Television and the crisis of democracy.* Boulder, CO: Westview.

Kessler, L. (1984). *The dissident press: Alternative journalism in American history.* Beverly Hills, CA: Sage.

Kielbowicz, R. B., & Scherer, C. (1986). *The role of the press in the dynamics of social movements: Research in social movements, conflicts and change* (Vol. 9, pp. 71-96). Greenwich, CT: JAI.

Kimball, D., & Kimball, J. (1969). *The market hunter.* Minneapolis, MN: Dillon Press.

King, E., & Schudson, M. (1995). The press and the illusion of public opinion: The strange case of Ronald Reagan's popularity. In T. Glasser & C. Salmon (Eds.), *Public opinion and the communication of consent* (pp. 132-155). New York: Guilford.

Knezevich, N. (1973, October 28). 25 years after killer smog, Donora is breathing easier. *Pittsburgh Press,* p. A2.

Kolodny, A. (1984). *The land before her: Fantasy and experience of the American frontiers, 1630-1860.* Chapel Hill: University of North Carolina Press.

Koppes, C. R. (1988). Efficiency, equity, esthetics: Shifting themes in American conservation. In D. Worster (Ed.), *The ends of the earth: Perspectives on modern environmental history* (pp. 230-251). New York: Cambridge University Press.

Kovarik, W. (1993). *The ethyl controversy: How the news media and health advocates set the agenda for a 1920s environmental debate over leaded gasoline and the alternatives.* Unpublished doctoral dissertation, University of Maryland, College Park.

Kovarik, W. (1994a, October 24). Charles F. Kettering and the development of tetraethyl lead in the context of alternative technologies. In *Proceedings of the Society of Automotive Engineers* (Paper No. 943924). Baltimore, MD.

Kovarik, W. (1994b, April). *Agenda setting in the 1924-1926 public health controversy over ethyl (leaded) gasoline.* Paper presented at the meeting of the Association for Education in Journalism and Mass Communication, Reno, NV.

LaBastille, A. (1980). *Women and wilderness.* San Francisco: Sierra Club Books.

Langford, N. P. (1871a, May). The wonders of Yellowstone. *Scribner's Monthly, 2,* 10.

Langford, N. P. (1871b, June). The wonders of Yellowstone [part 2]. *Scribner's Monthly, 2,* 128.

Lathrop, J. E., & Turner, G. K. (1910, January). Billions of Treasure. *McClure's,* pp. 339-354.

Laut, A. (1909, October 16). The fight for water in the West. *Collier's,* pp. 17-19, 24, 26.

Lead gasoline peril taken up today. (1925, May 20). *New York Journal,* p. 1.

Leake, C. B. (1959). Social aspects of air pollution. In *Proceedings of the National Conference on Air Pollution, November 18-20, 1958.* Washington, DC: Government Printing Office.

Leff, S. (1957). *From witchcraft to world health.* New York: Macmillan.

Lendt, D. L. (1979). *Ding: The life of Jay Norwood Darling.* Ames: Iowa State University Press.

Leonard, T. (1986). *The power of the press: The birth of American political reporting.* New York: Oxford University Press.

Leopold, A. (1966). *A Sand County almanac. With other essays on conservation from Round River.* New York: Oxford University Press. (Original work published 1949)

Leslie, S. (1983). *Boss Kettering.* New York: Columbia University Press.

Lippmann, W. (1929). *A preface to morals.* New York: Macmillan.

Lippmann, W. (1931, June). The press and public opinion. *Political Science Quarterly, 46,* 161-162.

Lowell, J. R. (1857, March). Humanity to trees. *The Crayon,* p. 96.

Lund, T. A. (1980). *American wildlife law.* Berkeley: University of California Press.

Mme. Curie urges safety from radium. (1928, June 4). *Newark Evening News,* p. 1.

Marsh, G. P. (1864). *Man and nature; or, physical geography as modified by human condition.* New York: Scribner.

Martland, H. S., Conlon, P., & Knef, J. P. (1925, December 5). Some unrecognized dangers in the use and handling of radioactive substances. *Journal of the American Medical Association, 85,* 769-776.

Marx, L. (1970, November 27). American institutions and ecological ideals. *Science, 170,* 945-952.

Mason, A. T. (1941). *Bureaucracy convicts itself.* New York: Viking.

Masthead. (1928, May 19). *New York World,* p. 30.

Mathews, J. L. (1909, November). The Pinchot-Ballinger controversy. *Hampton's,* pp. 659-674.

May take years to find good gasoline substitute. (1925, October 25). *New York Times,* Section 9, p. 14.

McCabe, L. C. (1959). Technical aspects—The 1950 assessment. In *Proceedings of the National Conference on Air Pollution, November 18-20, 1958.* Washington, DC: Government Printing Office.

McKerns, J. P. (1977). The limits of progressive journalism history. *Journalism History, 4,* 88-92.

McKerns, J. P. (Ed.). (1989). *Biographical dictionary of American journalism.* New York: Greenwood.

McMahon, A. M. (1992). "Small matters": Benjamin Franklin, Philadelphia and the "progress of cities." *The Pennsylvania Magazine of History and Biography, 66*(2), 157-182.

McManus, J. H. (1994). *Market-driven journalism: Let the citizen beware?* Thousand Oaks, CA: Sage.

McQuail, D. (1994). *Mass communication theory* (3rd ed.). Thousand Oaks, CA: Sage.

Mellon Institute of Industrial Research and School of Specific Industries. (1914). *Some engineering phases of Pittsburgh's smoke problem* (Bulletin No. 8). Pittsburgh: Historical Society of Western Pennsylvania, Library and Archives Division.

Melosi, M. V. (1979). Urban pollution: Historical perspective needed. *Environmental Review, 3,* 37-45.

Melosi, M. V. (Ed.). (1980). *Pollution and reform in American cities, 1870-1930.* Austin: University of Texas Press.

Melosi, M. V. (1981). *Garbage in American cities: Refuse, reform, and environment, 1880-1980.* College Station: Texas A&M University Press.

Mencken, H. L. (1927). *Prejudices, sixth series.* New York: Knopf.

Merchant, C. (1980). *The death of nature: Women, ecology and the scientific revolution.* San Francisco: Harper & Row.

Merchant, C. (Ed.). (1984). Women and environmental history. *Environmental Review, 8.*

Merton, R. & Nisbet, R. (Eds.). (1961). *Contemporary social problems.* New York. Harcourt, Brace.

Mexican gas toll mounts to 20. (1950, November 26). *New York Times,* p. 39.

Moderate smoke pall, 9th of season, record better than that of 1940. (1941, November 26). *St. Louis Post-Dispatch,* p. 1.

Morison, E. (Ed.). (1951). *The letters of Theodore Roosevelt* (Vo. 5). Cambridge, MA: Harvard University Press.

A most valuable accident. (1959, May 2). *The New Yorker,* p. 49.

Mott, F. L. (1938a). *A history of American magazines* (Vol. 3). Cambridge, MA: Harvard University Press.

Mott, F. L. (1938b). *A history of American magazines* (Vol. 4). Cambridge, MA: Harvard University Press.

Mowry, G. E. (1958). *The era of Theodore Roosevelt, 1900-1912.* New York: Harper.

Muir, J. (1890a, August). The treasures of Yosemite. *Century,* p. 484.

Muir, J. (1890b, September). Features of the proposed Yosemite National Park. *Century,* p. 667.

Muir, J. (1907, November 2). The Tuolumne Yosemite in danger. *Outlook,* p. 489.

Muir, J. (1909). *Let everyone help to save the famous Hetch Hetchy valley and stop the commercial destruction which threatens our national parks.* San Francisco: Author.

Muir, J. (1991). *Our national parks.* San Francisco: Sierra Club Books.

Muller, E. K. (1991). Ash pile or steel city: H. L. Mencken helps mold an image. *Pittsburgh History, 74*(2), 50-62.

Munsche, P. B. (1981). *Gentlemen and poachers: The English game laws 1671-1831.* Cambridge, UK: Cambridge University Press.

Myers, G. (1939). *The ending of hereditary American fortunes.* New York: Messner.

Nash, R. (1974). *The American conservation movement.* St. Charles, MO: Forum.

Nash, R. (1982). *Wilderness and the American mind* (3rd ed.). New Haven, CT: Yale University Press.

Nash, R. (1989). *The rights of nature.* Madison: University of Wisconsin Press.

National Archives. (1937, April 17). *Memorandum for the files, Ethyl Gasoline Corp.* (U.S. Department of Justice Records Division No. 60-57-107). Washington, DC: Author.

Neuzil, M. (1991). *On the front burner: How the greenhouse effect entered the public arena of the mass media* (No. 91-1). Master's thesis, University of Minnesota, Minneapolis.

New auto, fuel to save costs are announced. (1925, August 6). United Press. Flint, MI: General Motors Institute Alumni Foundation's Collection of Industrial History.

Newark pathologist shows part of Miss Maggia's jaw. (1927, October 18). *Star Eagle,* p. 1.

New York starts war on its smoke nuisance. (1927, December 4). *New York Times,* Section II, p. 10.

New York Times, October 13, 1949: 26.

Nicholson, M. (1970). *The environmental revolution.* London: Hodder & Stoughton.

Night smog fatal to 15 in Mexican oil town. (1950, November 25). *New York Times,* p. 5.

No reason for abandonment. (1924, November 28). *New York Times,* p. 20.

Nord, D. P. (1986). Tocqueville, Garrison and the perfection of journalism. *Journalism History, 13,* 56-63.

Novick, P. (1988). *That noble dream: The objectivity question and the historical profession.* New York: Cambridge University Press.

Nriagu, J. (1983). *Lead and lead poisoning in antiquity.* New York: Wiley Interscience.

Odd gas kills one, makes four insane. (1924, October 27). *New York Times,* p. 1.

Orsi, J. (1994). From Horicon to hamburgers and back again: Ecology, ideology, and wildfowl management, 1917-1935. *Environmental History Review, 18*(4), 19-40.

Our candid advice. (1883, November 8). *Forest and Stream,* p. 281.

Palen, J. (1984). *Science and Walter Lippmann.* Unpublished master's thesis, University of Michigan, Ann Arbor.

Park, R. (1941). News and the power of the press. *American Journal of Sociology, 47*(1), 1-11.

Patterson, C. C., Boutron, C., & Flegal, R. (1985). Present status and future of lead studies in polar snow. In C. C. Langway, Jr., H. Oeschger, & W. Dansgaard (Eds.), *Greenland ice core: Geophysics, geochemistry and the environment* (pp. 101-104). Washington, DC: American Geophysical Union.

Patterson, J. (1950, January 22). Story of Pittsburgh's boom. *Pittsburgh Press,* Sunday magazine, p. 4.

Penick, J., Jr. (1968). *Progressive politics and conservation.* Chicago: University of Chicago Press.

Pepper, D. (1984). *The roots of modern environmentalism.* London: Croom Helm.

Pfalzgray, F. L. (1928, April 30). Radium victim battles death with courage. *Daily Courier,* p. 1.

The photography of a chimney. (1905, December 2). *Scientific American,* p. 436.

Pigeon matches. (1879, February 27). *Forest and Stream,* pp. 145, 171.

Pinchot, G. (1947). *Breaking new ground.* New York: Harcourt, Brace.

Pinchot: A millionaire with a mission. (1909, October). *Current Literature,* p. 388.

Pittsburgh keeps trying. (1952, April 21). *New York Times,* p. 29.

Pittsburgh rebuilds. (1952, June). *Fortune Magazine,* p. 88.

"Poison fog" deaths reach 22. (1950, November 27). *New York Times,* p. 27.

Ponder, S. (1986). Federal news management in the progressive era: Gifford Pinchot and the conservation crusade. *Journalism History, 13*(2), 42-48.

Ponder, S. (1986b). Conservation, community economics and newspapering: The Seattle press and the forest reserve controversy of 1897. *American Journalism, 1,* 50-60.

Ponder, S. (1994). "Nonpublicity" and the unmaking of a president: William Howard Taft and the Ballinger-Pinchot controversy of 1909-1910. *Journalism History, 19*(4), 111-120.

Pratt, J. A. (1980). Letting the grandchildren do it: Environmental plan- ning during the ascent of oil as the major energy source. *The Public Historian, 2*(4), 28-61.

Predicts double gasoline mileage. (1926, January 20). *New York Sun.* Flint, MI: General Motors Institute Alumni Foundation's Collection of Industrial History.

Preliminary plan for ethyl gas investigation. (1925, August 24). Box 101, Folder 1800, Winslow papers, Yale University, New Haven, CT.

The property in game. (1883, August 2). *Forest and Stream,* p. 1.

Protess, D. L., Cook, F. L., Doppelt, J. C., Ettema, J. S., Gordon, M. T., Leff, D. R., & Miller, P. (1991). *The journalism of outrage: Investigative reporting and agenda building in America.* New York: Guilford.

Pyle, E. (1943, October 2). Roving reporter (reprint of a 1937 column). *Pittsburgh Post.* Pittsburgh: Historical Society of Western Pennsylvania, Library of Archives Division.

Racket charged in smog trouble. (1955, October 2). *New York Times,* p. 66.

Radium derivative $5,000,000 an ounce; Ethyl gasoline defended. (1925, April 7). *New York Times,* p. 23.

Radium poison hopeless. (1926, May 26). *New York Journal,* p. 1.

The real facts about Hetch Hetchy. (1913, December 2). *San Francisco Examiner,* p. 1.

Regush, N. (1992, May-June). MMT. *Mother Jones,* p. 24.

Reiger, J. F. (1972). *The passing of the great west: Selected papers of George Bird Grinnell.* New York: Winchester.

Reiger, J. F. (1975). *American sportsmen and the history of conservation.* New York: Winchester.

Report of the Allegheny Conference on Community Development. (1946, September 17). *Recommended legislative program.* Pittsburgh: Historical Society of Western Pennsylvania, Library and Archives Division.

A review of the world. (1910, February). *Current Literature,* p. 119.

Richardson, E. R. (1959). The struggle for the valley: California's Hetch Hetchy controversy, 1905-1913. *California Historical Quarterly, 38,* 249-258.

Robert, J. C. (1983). *Ethyl, a history of the corporation and the people who made it.* Charlottesville: University Press of Virginia.

Rosner, D., & Markowitz, G. (1987). *Dying for work: Workers' safety and health in twentieth century America.* Bloomington: Indiana University Press.

Roth, D. (1988). *The wilderness movement and the national forests.* College Station, TX: Intaglio.

Rothman, S., & Lichter, R. (1986, August). *The media, elite conflict and risk perception in nuclear energy policy.* Paper presented at the meeting of the American Political Science Association, Washington, DC.

Rouche, R. (1953). *Eleven blue men.* New York: Little, Brown.

Runte, A. (1979). *National parks: The American experience.* Lincoln: University of Nebraska Press.

Runte, A. (1984). *Trains of discovery: Western railroads and the national parks.* Flagstaff, AZ: Northland.

Runte, A. (1990). *Yosemite: The embattled wilderness.* Lincoln: University of Nebraska Press.

The sacrifice of song birds. (1884, August 7). *Forest and Stream,* p. 19.

St. Louis will push its flood plans. (1928, October 30). *New York Times,* Section 2, p. 1.

Sale, K. (1993). *The green revolution: The American environmental movement, 1962-1992.* New York: Hill & Wang.

The sale of game. (1885, January 22). *Forest and Stream,* p. 345.

Save Hetch Hetchy. (1913a, October 2). *The Independent,* p. 8.

Save Hetch Hetchy. (1913b, October 30). *The Independent,* p. 204.

Sayers, R. R., Fieldner, A. C., Yant, W. P., & Thomas, B. G. H. (1927). *Experimental studies on the effect of ethyl gasoline and its combustion products* (U.S. Bureau of Mines, p. 12). Washington, DC: Government Printing Office.

Schiller, D. (1981). *Objectivity and the news: The public and the rise of commercial journalism.* Philadelphia: University of Pennsylvania Press.

Schnaiberg, A. (1980). *The environment: From surplus to scarcity.* New York: Oxford University Press.

Schrenk, H. H., Heimann, H., Clayton, G. D., Gafafer, W. M., & Wexler, H. (1949). *Air pollution in Donora, Pa.: Epidemiology of the unusual smog episode of October, 1948* (Bulletin No. 306). Washington, DC: U.S. Public Health Service.

Schrepfer, S. R. (1989, February). Establishing administrative "standing": The Sierra Club and the Forest Service, 1897-1956. *Pacific Historical Review, 58,* 55-81.

Schroeder, R. (1992). *Max Weber and the sociology of culture.* Newbury Park, CA: Sage.

Schudson, M. (1978). *Discovering the news.* New York: Basic Books.

Schudson, M. (1995). *The power of news.* Cambridge, MA: Harvard University Press.

Scientists to pass on tetraethyl gas. (1925, May 20). *New York Times,* p. 1.

Sees deadly gas a peril in streets/Dr. Henderson warns public against auto exhaust of tetraethyl lead/worse than tuberculosis. (1925, April 22). *New York Times,* p. 1.

S. Res. 203, 38th Cong., 1st Sess., Cong. Rec. 1310 (1864, March 28).

Shabecoff, P. (1993). *A fierce green fire: The American environmental movement.* New York: Hill & Wang.

Shift ethyl inquiry to Surgeon General. (1925, May 21). *New York Times,* p. 7.

Shilan, J. (1949, November 18). *The Donora smog disaster.* Pittsburgh: Commonwealth of Pennsylvania, Bureau of Industrial Hygiene, Department of Health.

Sicherman, B. (1984). *Alice Hamilton: A life in letters.* Cambridge, MA: Harvard University Press.

Sigerist, H. E. (1945). *Civilization and disease.* Ithaca, NY: Cornell University Press.

Sign this. (1905, January 20). *San Francisco Examiner,* p. 4.

Smelser, N. (1963). *Theory of collective behavior.* Chicago: Free Press.

Smith, A. (1977). *The wealth of nations.* New York: Dutton.

Smith, H. N. (1950). *Virgin land: The American west as symbol and myth.* Cambridge, MA: Harvard University Press.

Smith, M. (1986). Lead in history. In R. Lansdown & W. Yule (Eds.), *Lead toxicity: History and environmental impact* (p. 20). Baltimore, MD: Johns Hopkins University Press.

Smith, N., & Theberge, L. J. (1983). *Energy coverage media panic.* New York: Longman.

Snyder, L. P. (1994, Spring). The death-dealing smog over Donora, Pennsylvania: Industrial air pollution, public health policy and the politics of expertise, 1948-1949. *Environmental History Review,* pp. 117-138.

Some lighter aspects of Ballinger. (1910, March 12). *Collier's,* pp. 22-23.

Stern, A. C. (1984). *Fundamentals of air pollution* (2nd ed.). Orlando, FL: Academic Press.

Stewart, D. (1978). *From the edge of extinction.* New York: Methuen.

Strodthoff, G. G., Hawkins, R. P., & Schoenfeld, A. C. (1985). Media roles in a social movement: A model of ideology diffusion. *Journal of Communication, 35*(2), 135-153.

Sugar of lead. (1957, August 29). *Scientific American,* p. 403.

Susman, W. (1984). *Culture as history: The transformation of American society in the twentieth century* (rev. ed.). New York: Pantheon.

Swain, D. C. (1970). *Wilderness defender: Horace M. Albright and conservation.* Chicago: University of Chicago Press.

Taylor, R. W. (1926). *Hetch Hetchy: The story of San Francisco's struggle to provide a water supply for her future needs.* San Francisco: R. J. Orozco.

Tebbel, J., & Zuckerman, M. E. (1991). *The magazine in America, 1741-1990.* New York: Oxford University Press.

Tells of new type of auto and fuel. (1925, August 7). *New York Times,* p. 4.

Thoreau, H. D. (1950). In B. Atkinson (Ed.), *Walden and other writings.* New York: Random House.

Tichenor, P. J., Donohue, G. A., & Olien, C. (1980). *Community conflict and the press.* Beverly Hills, CA: Sage.

Tober, J. A. (1981). *Who owns the wildlife?* Westport, CT: Greenwood.

Tocqueville, A. (1969). In J. P. Mayer (Ed.), *Democracy in America.* Garden City, NY: Doubleday.

Tucker, R. R. (1959). Accomplishments in air pollution control by the control agencies. In *Proceedings of the National Conference on Air Pollution, November 18-20, 1958.* Washington, DC: Government Printing Office.

Turner, R. H., & Killian, L. M. (1957). *Collective behavior.* Englewood Cliffs, NJ: Prentice Hall.

Twain, M. (1913). *Roughing it.* New York: Harper.

20 dead in smog; Rain clearing air as many quit area. (1948, November 1). *New York Times,* p. 1.

Udall, S. (1988). *The quiet crisis and the next generation.* Salt Lake City, UT: Gibbs-Smith.

United States v. du Pont, trial testimony, No. 2169, 126 F. Supp. 235 (November 18, 1952, U.S. District Court, Chicago, IL).

United States v. Motor Vehicles Manufacturers of the United States, Inc. (C.D. Cal 1969), No. 69-75-JWC.

U.S. board asks scientists to find new "doped gas." (1925, May 22). *New York World,* p. 1.

U.S. Census Office. (1902). *Twelfth Census of the United States, Agriculture, Part 1* (pp. 692-693). Washington, DC: Author.

U.S. Public Health Service. (1925, December 22). *Minutes of the Surgeon General's committee of experts on tetraethyl lead* (File No. 1340, Record Group No. 90). Washington, DC: U.S. National Archives.

U.S. Public Health Service. (1963). *Proceedings of the Second National Conference on Air Pollution, December 10-12, 1962.* Washington, DC: Government Printing Office.

U.S. Public Health Service, Treasury Department. (1926). *The use of tetraethyl lead gasoline in its relation to public health* (Public Health Bulletin No. 163). Washington, DC: Government Printing Office.

Use of ethylated gasoline barred pending inquiry. (1924, October 31). *The World,* p. 1.

Van Hise, C. (1910). *The conservation of natural resources.* New York: Macmillan.

Walker, W. (1928, January 8). Motor exhaust gas now stirs health fears. *New York Times,* p. 1.

Wall, D. (1994). *Green history: A reader in environmental literature, philosophy and politics.* London: Routledge.

Walton, I. (1996). *The complete angler, or, the contemplative man's recreation.* New York: The Modern Library. (Original work published 1653)

Wanners, W. (1969). *TR & Will: A friendship that split the Republican Party.* New York: Harcourt, Brace.

Warner, D. (1978, October 23). Donora recalls smog that turned killer 30 years ago. *Pittsburgh Post-Gazette.* Pittsburgh: Library and Archives Division, Historical Society of Western Pennsylvania.

Weart, S. R. (1988). *Nuclear fear: A history of images.* Cambridge, MA: Harvard University Press.

Weaver, D. H., & Wilhoit, G. C. (1986). *The American journalist: A portrait of U.S. news people and their work.* Bloomington: Indiana University Press.

Weber, D. B. (1964). *John Muir: The function of wilderness in an industrial society.* Unpublished doctoral dissertation, University of Minnesota, Minneapolis.

Weber, M. (1947). *The theory of social and economic organization.* New York: Free Press.

Weber, M. (1958). *The Protestant ethic and the spirit of capitalism.* New York: Scribner.

Weber, M. (1968). *Economy and society* (3 Vols.). New York: Bedminster.

Weisskopf, M. (1990, April 19). From fringe to political mainstream: Environmentalists set policy agenda. *Washington Post,* p. 1.

Wescott, N. P. (1935). *Origins and early history of the tetraethyl lead business* (unpublished du Pont Corp. Report No. 1936, Longwood MS group 10, Series A 418-26). Wilmington, DE: General Motors Anti-Trust Suit documents, Hagley Library. (Used by courtesy of Hagley Museum and Library.)

Wetzel, R. E. (1959). Cooperation in the administration of air pollution control. In *Proceedings of the National Conference on Air Pollution, November 18-20, 1958.* Washington, DC: Government Printing Office.

What the investigation has proved. (1910, April 2). *Collier's,* pp. 18-19.

Wheeler, O. D. (1915). Nathaniel Pitt Langford: The vigilante, the explorer, the expounder and first superintendent of the Yellowstone Park. *Minnesota Historical Society Collections,* pp. 630-668.

White, R. (1985). American environmental history: The development of a new historical field. *Pacific Historical Review, 54,* 297-335.

Will ethyl gasoline poison us all? Scientists disagree. (1925, May 3). *The World* (U.S. Public Health Service No. RG 90). Washington, DC: U.S. National Archives.

Williams, H. A. (1959). Accomplishments in the air pollution control by the automobile industry. In *Proceedings of the National Conference on Air Pollution, November 18-20, 1958.* Washington, DC: Government Printing Office.

Winslow, C. E. A. (1925, December 31). *Recommendations for the drawing up of a report on the use of lead tetra-ethyl gasoline by the public* (memo to Public Health Service committee members, Box 101, Folder 1801, Winslow papers). New Haven, CT: Yale University Library.

Wolfe, L. M. (Ed.). (1938). *John of the Mountains: The unpublished journals of John Muir.* New York: Houghton Mifflin.

Wolfe, L. M. (1945). *Son of the wilderness.* New York: Knopf.

Woman awaiting death tells how radium poison slowly, painfully kills. (1928, May 13). *New York Telegram,* p. 1.

Women open drive to clean the air. (1926, April 21). *New York Times,* p. 14.

A word in season. (1873, September 18). *Forest and Stream,* p. 88.

Worster, D. (1977). *Nature's economy: The roots of ecology.* San Francisco: Sierra Club Books.

Worster, D. (1990, March). Transformation of the earth: Toward a agroecological perspective in history. *Journal of American History,* pp. 1087-1106.

Worster, D. (1993). *The wealth of nature.* New York: Oxford University Press.

Would you die for science? Some would. (1928, April 28). *New York Journal.*

The Yellowstone National Park. (1872, May). *Scribner's Monthly 4,* 120.

Young, A. N. (1982). *Exploring the dangerous trades: Workers' health in America and the career of Alice Hamilton, 1910-1935.* Unpublished doctoral dissertation, Brown University, Providence, RI.

Young, A. N. (1983). Organizing trade unions to combat disease: The Workers Health Bureau, 1921-1928. *Labor History,* 424-446.

Young, R. (1961). *Boss Ket: A life of Charles Kettering.* New York: Longman.

NAME INDEX

SUBJECT INDEX

ABOUT THE AUTHORS

Mark Neuzil is Assistant Professor of Journalism and Mass Communications and a member of the environmental studies committee at the University of St. Thomas in St. Paul, Minnesota. He earned his PhD in mass communication from the University of Minnesota. He has worked for the Associated Press and several daily newspapers. His freelance writing has appeared in *Field & Stream, Better Homes & Gardens,* the *Christian Science Monitor,* and many other publications. He is the author of several journal articles and book chapters.

William Kovarik is author of *Fuel Alcohol: Energy and Environment in a Hungry World* and coauthor of *The Forbidden Fuel: Power Alcohol in the 20th Century.* He is Associate Professor of Media Studies at Radford University in Radford, Virginia. He earned his PhD in public communication at the University of Maryland. He has worked for the *Baltimore Sun,* the Charleston, South Carolina, *Courier,* the Associated Press, and Washington columnist Jack Anderson. His freelance writing has appeared in the *New York Times, Time* magazine, Time-Life Books, and many other publications. (E-mail address: http://www.runet.edu/~wkovarik)